WORLD POPULATION

WORLD
POPULATION

PAST GROWTH AND PRESENT TRENDS

BY

A. M. CARR-SAUNDERS

NEW YORK

BARNES & NOBLE, INC.

Publishers · Booksellers · Since 1873

Originally published by the Oxford University Press (1936) under the auspices of the Royal Institute of International Affairs, by whose permission the present edition is published.

The Royal Institute of International Affairs is an unofficial and non-political body, founded in 1920 to encourage and facilitate the scientific study of international questions.
The Institute, as such, is precluded by its rules from expressing an opinion of any aspect of international affairs; opinions expressed in this book are, therefore, not those of the Institute.

This edition published by Frank Cass & Co. Ltd.
10 Woburn Walk, London, W.C.1 in 1964.

First edition   *1936*
Second impression   *1964*

Published in the United States in 1965
by Barnes & Noble, Inc.
105 Fifth Avenue, New York, N.Y. 10003.

Printed in Great Britain

PREFACE TO FIRST EDITION

TOWARDS the end of last year I was invited by the Royal Institute of International Affairs to assist with the preparations for an international conference on peaceful change. When I learnt that the Institute were contemplating a study of the problems of population and migration as part of their contribution to the conference, I informed them that I had almost completed a book on these subjects and described its scope. The Council of the Institute considered that it was the kind of study which they had in mind and suggested that the book should be published under their auspices. To this I gladly agreed. It seems desirable, however, that the responsibility for the book should be made plain. It was not commissioned by the Institute, nor are its scope or contents in any way different from what they would have been if it had not appeared under their auspices. The book was designed to fill a gap in population literature. Many valuable studies of population problems have recently appeared, but there is no general survey of the world situation. Such a survey might take the form of an abstract of the position in the various continents and countries, or it might treat the different problems of population one by one. But the danger of surveys planned in such ways is that the trees might hide the wood. In order to avoid this danger and to give the study coherence, an historical approach to the problems of the day has been made in this book. Beginning with such knowledge as we have of world population three hundred years ago, the book attempts to discuss the causes and consequences of the immense expansion in numbers which has taken place since that time and to indicate the problems which arise from the position as it is now. It hardly needs to be said that only the most important matters can be mentioned in a work of this length. The book is merely a brief introduction to a subject of enormous scope and complexity.

I desire to express my indebtedness to Mr. R. R. Kuczynski, who has been kind enough to read through a large part of the manuscript and to give me much valuable advice. To Mr. D. V. Glass I am also indebted. He has prepared most of the tables, graphs, and diagrams which the book contains; furthermore, Chapter XVI is no more than an abstract of his interesting work, *The Struggle for Population*, which has just been published. Lastly, I must thank the staff of the Information Department of the Royal Institute of International Affairs for supplying me with certain information.   A. M. C.-S.

1936

CONTENTS

LIST OF FIGURES

REFERENCES TO FIGURES

THE data which have been used in the tables, graphs, and diagrams are mostly derived from obvious and easily available official sources. It is necessary therefore only to indicate the origin of those data that are taken from unofficial publications.

Figure 2. The data for various European countries before 1770 and for Europe as a whole in 1770 are taken from Mr. R. R. KUCZYNSKI's article *Population* in the *Encyclopaedia of the Social Sciences*. The data for Europe from 1800 to 1900 are from G. SUNDBÄRG's *Aperçu statistiques internationaux* (1906), Table 11. The data for Europe from 1910 to 1930 are from an unpublished thesis by Dr. G. G. LEYBOURNE.

Figure 7. Professor WILLCOX's figures are given on p. 78 of *International Migrations*, vol. ii (1931), and occur in his chapter on 'The Increase of the Population of the Earth and of the Continents since 1650'.

Figure 9. The data up to 1924 are taken from *International Migrations*, vol. i (1929). The data from 1924 to 1932 are from various publications of the International Labour Office.

Figure 10. This diagram is based on Table 1, *International Migrations*, vol. i (1929), so far as it relates to the period 1846 to 1924. Later figures are from publications of the International Labour Office.

Figures 11 and 12. These diagrams are based on diagrams 8 and 3 respectively of *International Migrations*, vol. i, for the periods up to 1924. Later figures are from publications of the International Labour Office.

Figure 13. The earlier data for Sweden are from SUNDBÄRG, op. cit., Table 36. The earlier data for England and Wales are from J. BROWNLEE's article in *Public Health*, vol. xxix, June and July 1916.

Figure 14. The data up to 1900 for births are from Table 28 and for deaths from Table 29 in SUNDBÄRG, op. cit. From 1910 they are from Dr. LEYBOURNE's unpublished thesis mentioned above (her figures do not include war deaths).

Figure 15. The birth-rate for the white population of the United States is based on Table 74 in *Population Trends in the United States* (1933), by WARREN S. THOMPSON and P. K. WHELPTON.

Figure 17. The birth-rate of the Catholic population of Quebec is based on data given by Mr. R. R. KUCZYNSKI in his *Birth Registration and Birth Statistics* in Canada (1930), p. 198.

Figure 18. The graphs are based on data given by Mr. R. R. KUCZYNSKI in his *Measurement of Population Growth* (1935), Table 50.

Figure 25. The rate for England and Wales in 1921 is from Mr. R. R.

KUCZYNSKI's *Balance of Births and Deaths* (1928), vol. i, p. 50; the rate for England and Wales in 1931 has been calculated by Mr. D. V. GLASS; the rate for England and Wales in 1933 is from Mr. R. R. KUCZYNSKI's *Measurement of Population Growth*, Table 57; the rate for Scotland in 1934 is from Dr. ENID CHARLES's paper in the *Proceedings of the Royal Society of Edinburgh*, 1936, p. 7; the rates for the white population of the United States in 1920 and 1930 are from *Dynamics of Population*, by F. LORIMER and F. OSBORN (1934), p. 358; and the remaining rates are from Mr. R. R. KUCZYNSKI's article *The Decline in Fertility* in *Economica*, 1935, Table 5.

Figure 26. The papers or books in which the estimates mentioned will be found are as follows: G. LEYBOURNE, *An Estimate of the Future Population of Great Britain*, Sociological Review, April 1934. E. CHARLES, *The Effect of Present Trends in Fertility and Mortality upon the Future Population of England and Wales and upon its Age Composition*. London and Cambridge Economic Service, Special Memorandum, No. 40, August 1935. E. CHARLES, *The Effect of Present Trends in Fertility and Mortality upon the Future Population of Scotland and upon its Age Composition*, Proceedings of the Royal Society of Edinburgh, vol. lvi, part 1, no. 2, March 1936. E. KAHN, *Der internationale Geburtenstreik*, 1930. F. BURGDÖRFER, *Ausblick auf die zukünftige Bevölkerungsentwicklung*, Statistik des Deutschen Reich, Band 401, part 2, 1930. C. GINI and B. DE FINETTI, *Calcoli sullo sviluppo futuro della popolazione italiana*, Istituto Centrale di Statistica, Serie 6, vol. x, 1931. A. JENSEN, *Horoscope of the Population of Denmark*, Bulletin de l'Institut International de Statistique, vol. xxxv, part 3, 1931. A. SAUVY, *Prévisions sur l'avenir de la population française*, Société de Statistique de Paris, May 1932. F. BAUDHUIN, *L'Avenir de la population belge*, Bulletin d'information de la Banque Nationale de Belgique, June 10, 1931. W. S. THOMPSON and P. K. WHELPTON, *Population Trends in the United States*, 1933.

Figure 31. The data are quoted by G. MAUCO in *Les Étrangers en France* (1932), p. 267.

Figure 32. The data are from THOMPSON and WHELPTON, op. cit., Table 85.

Figure 39. The data are quoted in *The Peopling of Australia*, edited by P. D. PHILLIPS and G. L. WOOD (1928), Table 6.

BIBLIOGRAPHY

MOST of the recent contributions of importance to the rapidly growing literature of population are in the shape of papers communicated to scientific periodicals. This note is intended only to indicate some of the more valuable books which are of general interest. Mention may first be made of the studies of population history and of the population situation in various countries and regions. Unfortunately there is no such study for this country. The best study for any country is *Population Trends in the United States* (1933) by WARREN S. THOMPSON and P. K. WHELPTON. Attention may be drawn to the following either on account of their intrinsic merits or on account of the importance of the countries to which they refer: J. BERTILLON, *La Dépopulation de la France* (1911); T. OBERLÄNDER, *Die agrarische Überbevölkerung Polens* (1935); *The Peopling of Australia*, edited by P. D. PHILLIPS and G. L. WOOD (1928); R. R. KUCZYNSKI, *Birth Registration and Birth Statistics in Canada* (1930); W. R. CROCKER, *The Japanese Population Problem* (1931); M. REQUIEU, *Le Problème de la population au Japon* (1934); P. K. WATTAL, *The Population Problem in India* (1934); S. H. ROBERTS, *Population Problems of the Pacific* (1927); E. DENNERY, *Foules d'Asie* (1930); L. KRYWICKI, *Primitive Society and its Vital Statistics* (1934). With these books may be mentioned F. BURGDÖRFER, *Sterben die weissen Völker?* (1934), a brief survey of the position as between Europeans and non-Europeans, and WARREN S. THOMPSON, *Danger Spots in World Population* (1934), a survey of over- and under-populated countries in which, however, the conclusions differ from those reached in this book.

The facts relating to migration have been exhaustively examined in *International Migrations* (National Bureau of Economic Research, vol. i, 1929, and vol. ii, 1931). *Migration and Business Cycles* (1926), by H. JEROME, is a very careful study of the relation between the volume of immigration into the United States and the growth of opportunities for employment. An interesting account of immigration into France is to be found in *Les Étrangers en France* by G. MAUCO (1932). *The Menace of Colour* (1925) and *Human Migration and the Future* (1928), by J. W. GREGORY, are popular treatments of this subject.

The causes of the decline in the birth-rate have been examined by F. LORIMER and F. OSBORN in a very valuable work *Dynamics of Population* (1934). *The Twilight of Parenthood* (1934), by ENID CHARLES, is an able, stimulating, and provocative book on the same subject. A. LANDRY, *La Révolution Démographique* (1934), and R. von UNGERN-STERNBERG, *The Causes of the Decline in the Birth-Rate within the Sphere of European Civilization* (1932), are also useful.

The attempts to raise the birth-rate have been examined by D. V. GLASS in *The Struggle for Population* (1936). Reference may also be made to F. BURGDÖRFER, *Bevölkerungsentwicklung im Dritten Reich* (1935), and to H. SEELER, *Die Bevölkerungspolitik in Frankreich nach dem Weltkriege* (1930).

The modern methods of measuring population trends and also the results of applying such methods to various countries are described in Mr. R. R. KUCZYNSKI's very important books, especially *The Balance of Births and Deaths* (vol. i, 1928, and vol. ii, 1931) and *The Measurement of Population Growth* (1935).

For the theory of population HAROLD WRIGHT'S *Population* may be recommended. The rule of mentioning only books may be broken to permit reference to *The Optimum Theory of Population*, by L. ROBBINS, in *London Essays in Economics* (1927) and to *The Theory of Population* by H. DALTON in *Economica*, vol. vii, 1928. *Population Theories and their Application*, by E. F. PENROSE (1934), is an interesting attempt to carry the analysis farther.

CHAPTER I

SOURCES OF INFORMATION

No one has yet written an adequate account of the efforts made by men to count themselves. It would be an interesting story; for it would throw light upon the attitude of men to the world around them and upon their knowledge of it. In relation to the problems with which this book deals the matter has considerable importance. This book attempts, though very briefly, to reconstruct population history and to describe the present population situation. Figures will therefore be frequently employed, and figures convey an impression of clarity and exactitude. But there is a world of difference between a figure which is the result of careful counting and subsequent verification, and a figure which is the mean of a number of guesses. If the purpose of this book is to be achieved, it is impossible not to use many figures of the latter kind. But however careful we may be to describe such figures as rough or approximate, it is difficult to appreciate the significance which attaches to them unless the sources whence they are derived have been sketched. This is one reason for devoting the first chapter to this topic. Another reason is that such a sketch indicates why statistical information is lacking even at the present day for many important areas, and why it is fragmentary and otherwise unsatisfactory even for some countries which are not generally regarded as backward.

The proper application of modern methods should give us in the first place an accurate count, repeated at regular intervals, of all the people in a certain area. That is what we call a census. The census should do more than give a bare total; it should also provide information about the age, sex, and marital status of the population. A series of periodical countings would tell us whether the population was increasing or decreasing and, if so, at what rate. But

B

upon the basis of such information alone we should not be able to explain the changes observed as having taken place between one census and another. For this purpose we require a record of births and deaths; this record should include certain particulars such as the age and sex of each person who dies, and the sex of the child and age of the mother when each baby is born. But this does not suffice to explain all the changes between two dates if there has been movement into or out of the area in question during the period. Therefore we require in addition a record of immigrants and of emigrants. It is not proposed to attempt in this chapter even to outline either the story of the invention of methods intended to achieve these three objects, or the story of their application in different parts of the world up to the present day. There is space only to illustrate by means of a few examples what has happened, and we may begin with some reference to the collection of data which bear upon the size of populations.

We may omit any reference to the enumerations which were carried out in the ancient world; the fact that they were conducted is of great interest because it illustrates the mechanism of government in those days. We are concerned only with enumerations of which the results survive, and the results of all these ancient enumerations have perished. We may first note that contemporary countings of things as well as of men sometimes survive from early dates whence tentative deductions may be made concerning the total population. For England in 1086 we have Domesday which was a kind of inventory of the country intended to discover the fiscal rights of the king; it did more than record things, for it recorded a certain number of men as well. Upon the basis of all this information it is possible to make a rough estimate of the population of the country at that time. There are also records such as those made in connexion with hearth taxes; these taxes were levied in many countries for long periods, and if we make a guess at the average size of a family, and suppose that all hearths were counted and that each family had one hearth, we can arrive at a total for the population. This is obviously a very precarious basis for an estimate. The doubtful nature even of the figure which at first sight seems best authenticated, namely the number of hearths, can be illustrated from the case of Ireland. The hearth tax was instituted in that country in 1662. In 1788 Bushe, one of the commissioners of the Irish revenue, made a close investigation and found that, owing to the laxity of the tax-collectors, no less than 200,000 hearths had been omitted from the latest returns. The validity of the earlier returns remains doubtful; they may all be equally defective, or they may have gradually deteriorated in accuracy. We may also note that it is sometimes possible to count things which existed at some former date, and to obtain in this way a very rough idea of the population at that time; thus for this purpose Professor Collingwood has used evidence of sites in use during the Roman occupation of Britain, and Mr. Fitzgerald has employed evidence derived from the foundation of cities in China.

In the absence of direct information data of this kind yield results which are better than nothing; but it is not until we have direct evidence that estimates of population are much more than informed guesses. The earliest direct evidence is provided by data relating to taxation; thus for England we have the subsidy rolls of the thirteenth and fourteenth centuries and the poll-tax returns of 1379 and 1381; that is to say, we have the number of those who paid certain taxes. In order to obtain a figure for the whole population the proportion which taxpayers formed of all persons must be estimated; this in turn involves an inquiry into the class of persons subject to taxation and into the proportion of those subject who evaded payment. Partial enumerations provide evidence of much the same nature as taxation returns, since their object was to ascertain the number of persons belonging to a special class or category. Thus in 1662 a count was made in Norway for military purposes of all males over the age of 12. If the count was fairly accurate it is possible to estimate the total population; for the proportion which males over 12 then formed of the whole can be assumed with some confidence. The most remarkable series of such partial enumerations comes from Japan. There had long been in existence a system of registration by families. In 1721 an edict was issued which ordered that the numbers registered should be reported; the Samurai and their dependents, however, were excepted. In 1726 another edict commanded that the number should be reported every six years. Until 1804 the reports were made regularly; thereafter they were made at longer and irregular intervals. But we possess the results of eighteen estimates made between 1721 and 1846. The figures exclude the court nobles, the Samurai and their dependants, and also apparently the depressed classes known as the Eta and the Henin. Furthermore, it would seem that in some districts those under 15, in others those under 2 or 1 years of age, were omitted. The island of Hokkaido was generally left out of account. Perhaps in all 10 per cent. of the population was omitted; if this is a proper measure of the degree of defectiveness, and if the persons recorded were enumerated with fair accuracy as seems to have been the case, this lengthy series of figures has considerable importance and interest.

Partial enumerations are unsatisfactory, not only because they are partial, but also because the intention is in almost all cases to ascertain the number of persons subject to some onerous duty, fiscal or military; in consequence there is reason why persons, due to be enumerated, should attempt to evade enumeration. When the object of the enumeration is merely to ascertain the facts, there is no reason why any one should wish to evade the counting. When Mr. Smith is asked on census day to state his sex, age, and marital status, he may think it a nuisance, but there is no reason why he should not correctly state that he is a male, aged 30, and married. He does not suppose that his liability to taxation, military duty, or any other onerous service will be affected by his reply; and he is right because the census authorities are not interested in Mr. Smith, but only in the number of married men aged 30 and kindred matters. The taking of a complete count of the population, merely for the sake of obtaining information and without any special purpose in view, is a product of the spirit of scientific inquiry. Such a count is called a census. But to the questions in what country the first census was taken, and what the date of the earliest census was in any given country, no definite answers can be given. It is true that no count deserves to be called a census which does not aim at a complete enumeration. But intention is not enough. In the first place the aim may be only to obtain a rough idea of the total population, and a count made in this spirit hardly deserves to rank as a census. Secondly, though the intention may leave nothing to be desired, the enumeration may be incompletely or inadequately carried out. Certain early total enumerations were to some extent failures because the whole area was not covered. Much more important is the fact that the earlier censuses in many if not most countries, even if the whole area was covered, were inadequately conducted because the machinery was crude, and the results therefore lacking in precision. To this may be added the fact that the object at which a census aims can scarcely be said to be fulfilled unless it provides more than the number of the people. It should also give information about the age and sex of the population, and it is often the case that this information is not collected until the practice of taking a census has been established for some time. It must not be supposed therefore that we can give the dates when the first census was taken in various countries; all we can do is to illustrate the growth and improvement of the practice of conducting total enumerations. Owing to the magnitude of the task, total enumerations are normally conducted by governments. But there are instances where private enterprise has accomplished the task. Dr. Alexander Webster, for example, made an unofficial enumeration of Scotland in 1755 with the co-operation of the ministers and elders of the Scottish Church; it included members of all denominations and is believed to have reached a high degree of accuracy.

The credit of taking the first complete enumeration may be assigned to New France. In 1665 the French authorities in Canada made a count; they repeated it at irregular intervals up to 1754, taking in all sixteen enumerations. Honours for initiating the practice in Europe may be divided between the Scandinavian countries and certain Italian States. An enumeration, supposed to have attained a fair degree of accuracy, was taken in Iceland in 1703; but the practice was not continued, and the three counts of 1762, 1769, and 1785 were somewhat rough. From 1801 Iceland was enumerated with Denmark; in Denmark enumerations were made by the clergy in 1787, 1801, 1834, and thence onwards at five-year intervals until 1870 when the duty was placed upon the municipal authorities. The clergy, acting under government authority, have played an important part in the collection both of population figures and of vital statistics in Scandinavian countries, and from 1834 onwards the Danish figures reach a very fair degree of accuracy. In 1749 the Swedish clergy, who had long been compiling lists of parishioners, were compelled to render returns from which a total for the population was obtained; this was repeated at five-yearly intervals, and the population of Sweden is still enumerated in this unusual but very efficient manner. Until 1809, when Finland fell under the supremacy of Russia, it was united with Sweden, and the same system of enumerating the population obtained as in that country. It is probable that the same degree of accuracy was not reached in the Italian States, many of which conducted enumerations in the eighteenth century; nevertheless the counts in the kingdom of Sardinia in 1773 and 1795, in the duchy of

Parma in 1770, and in the duchy of Tuscany in 1766 are noteworthy achievements. The remaining event of impor- tance in the eighteenth century occurred outside Europe when the United States took their first decennial census in 1790.

In England the first census was taken in 1801, but the methods were rather crude and the objectives limited. So far as machinery was concerned, the duty of collecting the information was assigned in 1801 to the overseers of the poor or failing them to substantial local householders; since the information was collected by questioning from house to house, it was long before the returns came in. There was no central office to direct operations, and the material was placed in the charge of one of the Clerks of the House of Commons for the purpose of being 'digested and reduced into order'. There was little improvement until 1841, when, the office of registrar-general having been created to take charge of the civil registration of births and deaths, the taking of the census was also made a duty of his department. In that year for the first time the census schedules were left with householders to be filled up on census night, thus ensuring a synchronous count. As regards objectives the census of 1801 took particulars of sex but not of age. In 1821 an attempt was made to discover ages, but disclosures of age were volun- tary; the instructions accompanying the schedule stated that age should be given 'if not inconvenient to the parties'. In 1831 age was not required, though a return of males over twenty was made. From 1841 onwards particulars as to age have been required, and from 1851 particulars as to marital status.

The relative success of the first census of Great Britain was not usually achieved elsewhere at the outset. In Ire- land, for example, the census of 1813 was entrusted to the grand juries. The latter were incompetent to perform these duties. The agents employed to collect information were paid by results, a fact which is not unnaturally believed to have swollen the figures. In the end six counties made no returns, twenty-four made defective returns, while the remaining ten made returns which were considered fairly satisfactory. The next census was taken in 1821 and the third in 1831; the second was a great improvement on the first, but the third was not as satisfactory as the second. The fourth attempt in 1841 produced the first trustworthy census of Ireland. In France, again, the first two enumerations of 1801 and 1806 produced very unreliable results, and the enumeration of 1821 is regarded as the first satisfactory census of France. In certain countries the first effort to number all the people merely aimed at a very rough enumeration. In Portugal there were, for example, nine such enumerations between 1801 and 1861, whereas the first attempt to count in such a manner that trustworthy results could be obtained was only made in 1864; in Spain there were enumerations in 1787 and 1797, but the first well-organized count dates from 1857. The practice gradually spread to eastern Europe; an enumeration was made in Russia in 1897, the only occasion during the Tsarist régime.

Mention has already been made of the prominent place occupied by the United States in the history of complete enumeration, and if due allowance is made for later settlement, Australia and New Zealand have not been far behind the United States in furnishing figures of the population. But in Canada, although many counts were taken in various parts, it was not until 1871 that satisfactory figures became available for the whole Dominion. When we come to Central and South America it is a very different story. In hardly any country in these areas has the census habit become firmly established. Argentina, for instance, perhaps the most advanced among them, has conducted no census since 1914. Brazil has a rather better record; figures are available for 1890, 1900, and 1920. The latest figures for Peru date from 1876 and for Bolivia from 1900. It is not merely that in these countries enumerations are infrequent and at irregular intervals; so far as censuses are taken in these countries, they are tributes to the ideal of counting rather than accomplishments. The same considerations apply to many of the figures given by European powers for their colonies. It is more or less a point of honour to provide a figure for the population. The difficulties are very great, and the system, commonly in use in Africa, of requiring the head man in the village or the chief of a tribe to make counts and then of adding them together can only yield very rough results.

Nevertheless, there are cases where Europeans have gradually built up systems of census taking among non-European peoples which reach a high degree of accuracy. This is true of the French in Algeria, the Dutch in Java, and the English in India and in the British West Indies, and the Americans in Hawaii and the Philippines. The first enumeration in India was conducted in 1872, and has been repeated regularly every ten years since 1881—a remarkable achievement since even to-day only 18 per cent. of the population is literate. The Dutch have given figures for Java from the early years of the last century, but the enumeration of 1930 is the first for which they claim a high degree of accuracy.

Among non-European countries which remain independent Japan and Egypt have established censuses. From Japan in recent times there are figures for 1873 and regularly onwards from 1898. But until 1920 the figures were derived from police registers, and the count of 1920 must be regarded as the first census in the stricter meaning of the term. In Egypt there has been an enumeration every ten years since 1897; there was a previous enumeration in 1882 which was organized as a census, the carrying out of which, however, was much impeded by the revolt in that year followed by European intervention.

It is thus erroneous to imagine that in the history of most countries there is a point, marked by the taking of the first census, before which the size of the population is quite unknown, and after which all is clear as daylight. As a rule indirect data first throw some light upon the situation, partial enumerations mark the dawn of real knowledge, while the gradual improvement of the census may be likened to the rise of the sun to the zenith. With regard to our knowledge of births and deaths the position is otherwise. In the absence of direct records we remain entirely ignorant; for there are no means of discovering or estimating the number of births and deaths before they were counted. Early records may be, and generally are, incomplete, and our knowledge gains greatly in accuracy as time goes on. But the first records make a break with the past which finds no parallel in the history of enumeration.

It is a curious fact that, though it has proved to be less easy to obtain accurate records of births and deaths than of population, it was formerly held that the contrary was the case. In 1789 the Chevalier de Pommelles wrote as follows: 'une énumération par tête, qui, en premier aperçu, semble une chose si facile, non seulement serait très dispendieuse, mais, lorsqu'on y réfléchit, elle présente tant de difficultés dans l'exécution qu'il est difficile de ne pas douter au moins de la possibilité et surtout de l'exécution d'une telle opération.' Thus, while European governments long hesitated when faced with the difficulties of counting, they began as early as the first half of the sixteenth century to give orders that baptisms and burials should be recorded in parish registers. But it was not until long after, if at all, that any attempt was made to assemble these data for any country as a whole; in Great Britain, for example, no such attempt was made until 1801, when, in connexion with the census of that year, the clergy were required to make abstracts from their registers for the period 1700 to 1780. Thus, even when the registers were kept in accordance with instructions, they had sometimes perished before their contents were assembled to provide national records.

The keeping of parish registers of baptisms and burials was favoured by the ecclesiastical authorities, both Catholic and Protestant. In 1551 the ecclesiastical authorities in Scotland imposed the duty of keeping records upon the Scottish clergy, and in 1563 the Council of Trent ordered all priests to perform this task. About the same time governments in both Catholic and Protestant countries began to enforce the maintenance of registers. In 1538, at the order of Thomas Cromwell, parish priests in England and Wales were ordered to undertake this function. In 1539 an ordinance of Francis I prescribed that French priests should record baptisms and burials, and in 1574 it was ordered that they should record marriages in addition. It is important to observe that the records, kept at the instance of governments, were of baptisms and burials under the rites of the established church; it follows that in countries where sections of the population did not profess the established religion, these records, even if complete for all births and deaths among members of the established church, were not a complete record of all births and deaths in the country. In England the omissions on this account probably exceeded 10 per cent.; in Ireland, when parish registers were extended over the whole country in 1634, the baptisms and burials of only a small section of the population were recorded. The baptisms and burials of those belonging to all unrecognized denominations may have been recorded by their own organizations, but in that case they were unofficial and seldom survived. But it would appear that in Ireland the Catholic clergy, in spite of the injunction of the Council of Trent, kept no records until the nineteenth century, presumably because they were so harassed by the penal laws as to be unable to do their duty.

Parish registers were kept with very varying degrees of accuracy and continuity; in periods of disorder, as in England during the Civil War, they often lapsed for a time. In a few countries, in Scotland during the eighteenth century for example, the practice was allowed to decay. But in most countries attempts were made to improve the system of ecclesiastical registration; in 1787 the French registers were, for instance, extended so as to include Protestants. In the Scandinavian countries these attempts were so successful that the parish register came in time to perform all that could be required of a system of civil registration. In 1756 a permanent official institution was set up in Sweden, the function of which was to collect and analyse the data recorded in the registers of the whole country. Thus we have a trustworthy series of figures for births and deaths for Sweden from the middle of the eighteenth century. The data were not published at first; indeed in most countries until the beginning of the nineteenth century, and in some, Austria for instance, until the middle of that century, such registration and census data, as the government possessed, were regarded as state secrets, the disclosure of which would be injurious to the interests of the country. In Sweden parish registration, long ago moulded into an efficient instrument for collecting vital statistics, is retained to this day. In Norway parish registration began to be replaced by civil registration in 1906, and in Denmark in 1924. In other countries parish registration was not brought to the same state of efficiency as in Scandinavia, and the introduction of civil registration marks the beginning of a more trustworthy series of figures. Civil registration was introduced in France in 1792, in Belgium in 1803, in England and Wales in 1837, in Scotland in 1855, in Italy in 1862, in Ireland in 1864, in Spain in 1870, in Switzerland in 1874, and in Portugal in 1910. In Russia ecclesiastical registration was retained until the end of the Tsarist régime. Just as in the case of the census, the methods first employed for civil registration were crude and the objectives limited. Thus, for some time in most countries the age of the mother at the birth of each child was not given, and this is for some purposes a very necessary piece of information. While this is now recorded for many countries, England is re-markable in that it still fails to provide it.

In the European settlements overseas there was no system of parish registration except in French Canada. Attempts to set up a system of the civil registration of vital statistics were made in early times in certain North American colonies and districts, in Massachusetts in 1639 and in Nova Scotia in 1782, for instance. But while a mass of scattered information exists, no figures are available for Canada as a whole before 1926. The United States, with their admirable record of census taking, have a poor record for vital statistics. The Bureau of the Census only began to collect information about deaths in 1900, and then only for those States and cities which had an adequate mechanism for reporting deaths. In 1900 the latter comprised about 40·5 per cent., in 1910, 58·3 per cent., in 1920, 82·2 per cent., and in 1929 the whole of the population with the exception of some rural areas. The collection of information about births only began in 1915, when 31 per cent. of the population came under review. By 1929 the whole area had come in with the exception of South Dakota and Texas; to-day the whole country is covered. For Australia we have records from 1860 and for New Zealand from 1870.

Outside Europe and its oversea derivatives vital statistics are scanty. In non-Christian countries no system of parish registration preceded civil registration. As in Europe civil registration has followed the institution of a census, and since the census is generally of very recent origin, there are several countries which have some population figures but no vital statistics. Even where vital statistics are collected they are generally very untrustworthy. From Japan, where the enumeration of 1920 is perhaps the first true census, we have vital statistics, based on family registers kept by the police, which go back to 1874, but it is very doubtful how far the early figures can be trusted. A system of civil registration was inaugurated in India in 1886, and to-day about three-quarters of the population is subject to registration. But the Indian method of recording by the headman of the village is so ineffective that in the official view the records are at least 20 per cent. below the true figure. The Dutch collect figures of births and deaths in Java, but they regard the former as so incomplete that they only publish the latter. In South Africa vital statistics are compulsorily recorded only of those non-Europeans who live in towns. Perhaps the most satisfactory vital statistics for a country outside the sphere of European civilization come from Egypt, where a system of compulsory registration was set up in 1912. In short such figures as we possess for non-European countries extend back at the most for a few decades, and are usually to be regarded as mere approximations.

If we were in possession for the world as a whole of population figures covering a given period of time, and if we possessed vital statistics for the same period, we should have an outline of world population history and should be in a position to analyse it. For the movement of population in the world as a whole is clearly the result of a balance between births and deaths. But the same is not true of particular countries, the population of which may be influenced by migration movements; and there are few countries the population of which has not been affected by movements into and out of their areas. The importance of migration is on the whole greater for countries which have gained than for those which have lost; the reason is that the former are mostly young countries with small populations for which a given absolute gain in numbers is relatively more important than a similar absolute loss from the latter. But there are cases of old countries, such as Ireland, whence loss has been on so large a scale that it has had profound effects on population history. It follows that any sketch of population history must take migration movements into account, and that we require figures for them in order to fill in some important features of the story.

When an attempt is made to count the number of people

in any area or to record the births and deaths in any area, there is little doubt about the aim. There are some difficulties; there is, for instance, the question whether births shall include stillbirths. But for the most part the difficulties relate to execution. It is otherwise with regard to migration. Who is a migrant? One who leaves a country in order to take up a permanent residence in another country, it may be replied. Yes, but intention is not enough. The migrant must fulfil it, and then the question arises how long he must live in the new country in order to be considered as a resident. At a recent international conference on migration statistics it was recommended that a migrant should be defined as a person who resided in another country for more than a year. The governments, however, have not yet accepted this definition, and even if they did the collection of figures would be difficult. For it would be necessary to make elaborate records in order that those who returned within a year could be deducted from the entrants. There are also serious difficulties relating to persons in transit from their country of origin to some distant destination who pass through intervening lands.

The keeping of migration statistics is therefore a formidable task which requires international agreement and co-operation. This is not yet in sight. It is true that under the stimulus of the International Labour Organization migration figures have recently been much improved. But for the most part the figures available are still by-products of the methods of the supervision of migrants undertaken by different countries. Thus in France an immigrant is officially an alien who enters with a contract of employment; the period of the contract does not matter. Moreover, it is officially admitted that many persons have entered France and taken up permanent residence without any contract in recent years. In nine countries at the present time official figures are based on passports; in others they are based on port statistics or on frontier control. It is obvious that the most careful examination of such data can only lead to a very rough estimate of the number of people who now leave one country in order to take up permanent residence in some other country; and it is this that we require to know in order that our understanding of observed population changes should be complete.

It is also obvious that, since our knowledge of contemporary migration movements is so imperfect, it must be still more incomplete for past times. But a vast mass of data exists in the form of passenger lists, port statistics, permits, and so on. The first comprehensive examination of this material was made a few years ago by the National Bureau of Economic Research, and the results were published in 1929. Though much remains to be done, we are now in possession of a most valuable summary of the course of migration movements during the last hundred years. No similar survey has been made as yet of migration during the eighteenth century; but movement was then on a smaller scale, at least so far as Europeans were concerned.

CHAPTER II

GROWTH OF WORLD POPULATION

IF we wish to obtain a picture of the growth of world population it might seem that the first step should be to select a date at which reasonably trustworthy records become available and to tell the story thenceforward to the present time. But the discussion in the last chapter has made it plain that for many parts of the world data are not very trustworthy even for the present day. Therefore, it is better to adopt another procedure and to work back from the present into the past as far as we can reach for the world as a whole.

Having decided to adopt this procedure we require as our starting-point the population of the world at the present day. There are three well-known periodical publications, the *Aperçu de la Démographie des Divers Pays du Monde* published by the Institut International de Statistique, the *Statistical Year-Book* published by the League of Nations, and the *International Year-Book of Agricultural Statistics* published by the International Institute of Agriculture, each of which gives figures for world population. The totals for 1930 are shown in Fig. 1.

FIGURE 1

Estimates of the Population of the World in 1930

Continents	Authority: International Institute of Statistics	Authority: International Institute of Agriculture	Authority: League of Nations
Europe . . .	484,575,000	505,730,000	504,600,000
America . . .	248,772,000	251,500,000	249,800,000
Africa . . .	143,315,000	142,400,000	145,400,000
Asia . . .	1,101,692,000	1,103,300,000	1,118,600,000
Oceania . . .	9,925,000	9,880,000	9,800,000
World Total . .	1,988,279,000	2,012,810,000	2,028,200,000

The difference between the highest and the lowest total is 40 millions; this may seem a large figure, but it is less than 2 per cent. of the average of the three estimates. It is, in fact, at first sight remarkable that three independent tabulations should give results so close together, and we might be tempted to infer that the present population of the world is known to within a small margin of error. But such a conclusion is not justified. For if we examine the way in which these three estimates are constructed, we discover that each of them gives the same figure for many countries of which the population is only known within a wide margin of error. In regard to such countries there is often only one figure available; admittedly it is no more than a rough guess, but, since nothing better is obtainable, every one employs it. Even when more than one figure is available, there is seldom much doubt which is the best figure. One example illustrates what takes place. Up to 1926 the Portuguese government put the population of Angola at 4·1 millions, and all three publications used this figure. In 1926 it revised the figure and gave the population as 2·5 millions; all three publications adopted the new figure. Little importance attaches to the fact that totals are fairly close when they are reached in this manner.

The fact is that our knowledge of the present population of certain important countries is very incomplete, and that in consequence we only know the population of the world within a considerable margin of error. In Mr. Kuczynski's view our knowledge of from one-quarter to one-third of the probable world population is subject to a margin of error of over 10 per cent. either way, and he thinks that it is not possible to say more than that the present population of the world must be between 1,880 and 2,260 millions. Since the population in past times is less well known than that of the present, it is obvious that any attempt to reconstruct world population history must be a very speculative proceeding; according to Mr. Kuczynski it is likely that 80 per cent. of the probable world population in 1800 was not known to within a margin of 10 per cent. either way. But for certain regions and countries for some distance back into the past the facts are fairly well ascertained, and it may be useful to begin by giving some sketch of population history in these places. When doing so what we have in mind are those cases where the figures are based upon direct evidence of a fairly reliable character; these figures seldom reach the accuracy of a modern census, but they are better than the estimates founded upon indirect evidence.

With this object in view let us consider Europe, the present population of which is now known with a high degree of accuracy. The earliest date, for which a figure has been given coming within the required degree of accuracy, is 1770; for that year Mr. Kuczynski puts the population of Europe at 152,500,000. The next earlier date for which a figure is available is 1750, but in this case the evidence is definitely less trustworthy, and in consequence the figure does not deserve inclusion here. For 1800 and each tenth year up to 1900 Sundbärg has given figures which are widely accepted; this series has been continued up to 1930 by Dr. Leybourne. Both Sundbärg and Dr. Leybourne have calculated, not only the figures for Europe as a whole, but also the figures for the three constituent regions of Europe, north-west, south-west, and east; by north-west is meant Great Britain, Sweden, Denmark, Norway, Germany, Switzerland, Holland, and Belgium, and by south-west Europe France, Spain, Portugal, and Italy. While it is not possible to carry the population history of the whole continent farther back than 1770 without descending to the use of data which do not reach the required standard, this can be done for certain European countries. Thus we have figures for England and Wales from 1700, due to the work of Farr and Brownlee who used data provided by the age distributions given in the earlier censuses and by the registers of baptisms and burials. For France we have the reports of the 'intendants' dating from the end of the seventeenth century which were used by Vauban to calculate the total population of the country. There are figures of a similar degree of validity for some other European countries before 1770.

FIGURE 2

The growth of population in Europe

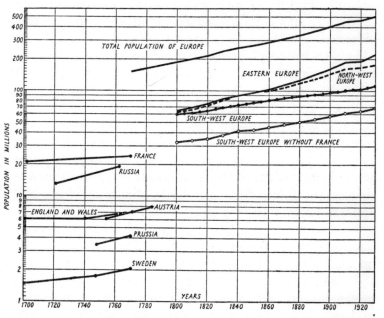

They refer to various dates, but none are earlier than 1700. All these data have been assembled and are shown in diagrammatic form in Fig. 2. In addition the average annual percentage rates of increase have been calculated for each period for every country or part of Europe to which the figures refer and are shown in Fig. 3.

Let us first examine the figures for the period before 1770. The diagram in Fig. 2 makes it clear that all the countries for which we have figures were increasing before that date. There are three countries, England and Wales, Sweden, and Norway, for which we can give average

FIGURE 3

The rate of growth of population in Europe

Average annual rates of increase in percentages

England and Wales	France	Sweden	Norway	Finland	Austria	Prussia	Russia
1701–41: 0·013	1701–70: 0·184	1700–48: 0·362	1735–50: 0·216	1750–70: 1·434	1754–84: 0·862	1748–70: 0·844	1721–63: 0·730
1741–77: 0·456	..	1748–70: 0·664	1750–70: 0·805	..	..	..	..

Period	All Europe	North-west Europe	South-west Europe	South-west Europe without France	Eastern Europe
1770–1800	0·682	..	..	..	..
1800–1810	0·603	0·626	0·369	0·283	0·794
1810–1820	0·703	0·864	0·453	0·311	0·766
1820–1830	0·942	1·142	0·717	0·804	0·940
1830–1840	0·706	0·818	0·551	0·626	0·726
1840–1850	0·581	0·606	0·490	0·530	0·629
1850–1860	0·620	0·655	0·436	0·598	0·734
1860–1870	0·769	0·755	0·455	0·591	1·024
1870–1880	0·831	0·977	0·391	0·535	1·011
1880–1890	0·901	0·811	0·450	0·621	1·292
1890–1900	0·992	1·105	0·412	0·587	1·252
1900–1910	1·114	1·106	0·483	0·698	1·482
1910–1920	0·219	0·272	0·220	0·423	0·172
1920–1930	1·025	0·635	0·709	0·745	1·519
1800–1850	0·707	0·811	0·516	0·510	0·771
1850–1900	0·823	0·861	0·429	0·586	1·062
1900–1930	0·785	0·671	0·471	0·622	1·056

annual rates both for the earlier and the middle decades of the century. In the case of each of these countries the rate for the earlier period is low; it is highest in the case of Sweden with 0·36 per cent. In each case the rate is much higher for the later period, reaching 0·8 per cent. in Norway from 1750 to 1770. In the case of Finland, Austria, and Prussia, for which figures relating to the middle period alone are available, the rate is high, corresponding roughly to the rate in the same period in the three countries already mentioned. For France we can only give the rate for the whole period 1701 to 1770, and it is found to be low. In Russia, on the other hand, between 1721 and 1763 it was high. Though these data are fragmentary, there can be little doubt that the rate of growth of the population of Europe was speeding up during the eighteenth century. Moreover, it looks as though we could almost reach back to a time when the population of Europe was stationary or in any case only increasing very slowly.

Let us now consider the period 1770 to 1930 for which we have figures for Europe as a whole. The average annual rate of increase for the continent was 0·68 per cent. between 1770 and 1800, 0·71 per cent. between 1800 and 1850, 0·82 per cent. between 1850 and 1900, and 0·78 per cent. between 1900 and 1930; in other words the rate of increase was already high in the late eighteenth century, rose slightly until 1900, and then fell back somewhat in the first three decades of the present century. If we examine the rates for ten-year periods which are also given, we find that they show marked variations; the rate was, for example, relatively high during the third decade of the nineteenth century and relatively low in the fifth. The most marked fluctuation occurred in the second decade of the present century and was obviously due to the War. In fact, had it not been for the War the rate of increase in Europe would clearly have been greater between 1900 and 1930 than between 1850 and 1900.

Figs. 2 and 3 also give particulars of the growth of popu-

lation in the three constituent regions of Europe adopted
by Sundbärg, both for the periods 1800 to 1850, 1850 to
1900, and 1900 to 1930, and for each decade. As is well
known, the rate of increase of population in France was
lower than elsewhere, and therefore, in order that the
course of events in south-west Europe should be seen
uninfluenced by France, the rates for south-west Europe
without France have also been worked out. The result is
to show that increase since 1850 has been most rapid in
the east; in each of these three periods the rate is higher
in the east than in Europe as a whole. It has been slowest
in the south-west, even when France is excluded. The
rate for the north-west was higher than for the other two
regions from 1800 to 1850. In consequence, as shown in
Fig. 2, the population of north-west Europe, which in
1800 was slightly less than that of east Europe, grew to
equal that of the latter region. But since 1850 the rate in
eastern Europe has been higher than that in north-west
Europe, with the result that since that date the population
of eastern Europe has drawn ahead. Finally, if we omit
the decade into which the War fell and look at the trend
of the rates of increase in the remaining decades, we find
that in north-west Europe alone is there any sign of a
falling off in the rate of increase. For, while during the
decade 1920 to 1930 the rate of increase in the north-west
was lower than it had been at any time since 1850, it was
the highest ever recorded either in the east or in the south-
west excluding only in the latter case the decade 1820–30.

From Europe we pass to North America; here, as elsewhere throughout this book, the continent of North
America means the territory now included in the United
States and Canada. If we exclude the aborigines the
population of the United States is as well or better known
than that of Europe; for we have figures that will satisfy
our present standards from 1750. But when we consider
the North American continent as a whole we are faced by
the difficulty that, although we have satisfactory figures

for New France from 1665 to 1750, data are incomplete for Canada from the beginning of the period of British ascendancy until at least 1850. It is rather doubtful at what date we should first accept the figures usually given for Canada; but we may perhaps begin with that year. It

FIGURE 4

The growth of population in the United States

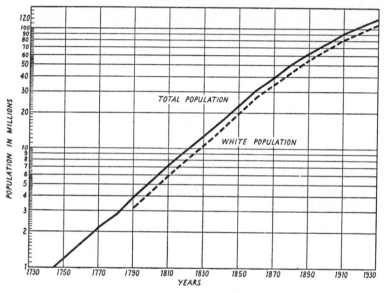

is true, if we again except the aborigines to say that the population history of Australia and New Zealand is well known as far back as 1850, before which date the white population was very sparse. Thus it may be said that the history of population among these Europeans overseas is as well known as that of Europeans at home, having regard to the fact that in Australia and New Zealand all history relating to white men is very recent. The growth of the population of the United States is shown in Fig. 4, and of Canada, Australia, and New Zealand in Fig. 5. From these diagrams it appears that growth was very rapid at

the time when figures first become available for Australia
and New Zealand. But the figures for these two countries
reach back to a time which is relatively earlier in the history of these countries than is the case for any figures

FIGURE 5

FIGURE 5

*The growth of population in Canada, Australia, and
New Zealand*

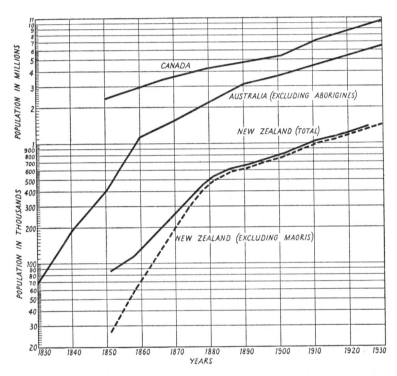

which we possess for the United States and Canada. No
doubt figures for the earlier years of the European occupation of North America would also show very rapid growth;
for, when population is sparse, the arrival of a small number of immigrants results in very rapid increase, whereas
in relatively later times the arrival of the same number of
immigrants would be a negligible matter. The actual

rates of growth are given in Fig. 6. Comparing them with those shown for Europe in Fig. 3, we see that they exceed anything ever known in Europe; the highest rate ever observed in any region of that continent was in eastern Europe between 1900 and 1910 when the average annual rate approached 1·5 per cent. The rate of growth in the United States has steadily declined; in Canada, however,

FIGURE 6

The rate of growth of population in the United States, Canada, Australia, and New Zealand

Average annual rates of increase in percentages

United States	Canada	Australia	New Zealand
1750–1800. 3·01			
1800–1850. 2·99			
1850–1900. 2·4	1850–1900. 1·62	1850–1901. 4·47	1850–1901. 6·8
1900–1930. 1·61	1900–1931. 2·15	1901–1931. 1·84	1901–1932. 2·24

it has been higher in the present century than between 1850 and 1900.

For three out of the six continents, therefore, we have trustworthy population history for considerable periods. For Europe it begins in 1770, though from data which exists for certain European countries we can get some idea of the course of events prior to 1770. For Canada, Australia, and New Zealand trustworthy figures do not extend back as far as a century. But a century ago the population of these countries was so sparse, especially in Australia and New Zealand, that it accounted for a very small fraction of the total world population. Thus the lack of trustworthy figures for these countries in relatively early times is no great matter from the point of view of the reconstruction of world population history. It is a very different matter when we come to the three remaining continents. With the same standard of trustworthiness in mind, it does not seem possible to reconstruct the history of population in any country of Central and South America, to say nothing of this region as a whole. In Argentina, for example, which claims to be regarded as one of the best administered countries in South America, no census has been taken since 1914, and the present population can only be known within a wide margin of error. When we come to Africa and Asia we find ourselves rather better off; there are at least a few countries the population history of which is known with some degree of accuracy for a few decades. In the case of Africa fairly accurate knowledge of the population history of Algeria and of Egypt becomes available in the latter half of the last century; there is some information for certain parts of what now constitutes the Dominion of South Africa dating from before 1900, but for the Dominion as a whole figures begin in 1904. As regards Asia we have data relating to India from 1872, and we also have figures from before the end of the last century relating to Ceylon, Java, and the Philippines. This information is of great importance in relation to these countries and will be used when we come to deal with them; but it is so fragmentary that it affords little guide to world events. It is enough to say here that in the largest of these countries, namely India, the rate of increase is known to have exceeded the annual average of 1 per cent. only during a single decade, but that in the remaining countries the rate in recent decades has been over 1 per cent. per annum. There is also the case of Japan. In the last chapter some reference was made to the system which prevailed of recording population figures from 1721 to 1848. These figures, though in the first place not a complete record of the population, and in the second place not reaching the accuracy of a census for that part of the population which was counted, may perhaps be noticed in this chapter. But between 1848 and 1873 there are no data, and it is uncertain when Japanese figures in recent times rise to the standard of a census. Nevertheless, Japan ranks with those few European countries, the population history of which is fairly well known since the earlier years of the eighteenth century. Taking the data as they are and adding 2 millions for omissions between 1721 and 1846 we get 28·1 millions for 1721, and 28·9 millions in 1846, the highest and lowest figures in the intervening period being 29·2 millions in 1828, and 26·9 millions in 1792. In other words the population of Japan was practically stationary from 1721 to 1846. The next figure is for 1873 when the population was stated to be 33·1 millions, from which it would seem that the population began to grow once more in the first years of the second half of the last century. Since 1873 the average annual rate of increase has been fairly rapid; it was 1·1 per cent. between 1872 and 1898, and 1·2 per cent. between 1898 and 1930.

The figures which have just been mentioned relate to so few countries in Asia and Africa and go back for so short a period (Japan alone being an exception), that we can obtain no picture of the growth of population in these continents based upon this material. These figures are of much interest in relation to very recent times, and will be quoted and discussed when we come to examine the problems of the present day. It has in fact become evident that the scope of the inquiry must be widened if we are to make any reconstruction of world population history.

CHAPTER III

GROWTH OF WORLD POPULATION (*cont.*)

IF we limit ourselves, as in the last chapter, to the use of figures based either upon attempts to enumerate the population which are believed to attain a certain degree of accuracy, or upon calculations, derived from various sources, which are thought to be equally accurate, we can say nothing about the growth of world population as a whole; for in respect to one entire continent and to some important countries in other continents, China for example, there are no figures even for the present day which reach this degree of trustworthiness. Any attempt, therefore, to reconstruct the history of world population must be based in part upon data which yield estimates of a lower degree of accuracy. Even in the case of Europe we must fall back upon such estimates if we are to obtain a figure for a date before 1770. To bring under review the mass of evidence which bears indirectly upon population in past times is an immense task. Fortunately we are absolved from undertaking it on our own account; for Professor W. F. Willcox, a great scholar in the field of population, has recently examined the evidence and given an estimate for the population of the world between 1650 and 1929. Instead of attempting to build up figures of our own, we can take his figures, examine the evidence upon which they are founded, and so arrive at some conclusion as to the amount of confidence which we can place in totals necessarily derived, except in so far as the sort of evidence discussed in the last chapter has been used, from indirect evidence of the kind described in the first chapter.

Willcox's findings are set out in Fig. 7, and to them have been added the figures given by the League of Nations for 1933. The former have been rearranged so as to make the division between North America on the one hand and Central and South America on the other correspond with

that used by the League of Nations. One fact relating to
the figures for 1929 and 1933 will be noticed at once. The
world total is shown as larger by 237 millions in 1933 than
in 1929. It is obvious that this cannot be all due to growth

FIGURE 7

Estimates of the population of the world, 1650–1933

Authorities: 1650 to 1929, Professor W. F. Willcox; 1933, League of
Nations

Millions

Continent	1650	1750	1800	1850	1900	1929	1933
Europe	100	140	187	266	401	478	519
North America	1	1·3	5·7	26	81	133	137
Central and South America	12	11·1	18·9	33	63	106	125
Oceania	2	2	2	2	6	9	10
Africa	100	100	100	100	141	140	145
Asia	250	406	522	671	859	954	1,121
World Total	465	660	836	1,098	1,551	1,820	2,057

Percentage Distribution

	1650	1750	1800	1850	1900	1929	1933
Europe	21·5	21·2	22·4	24·2	25·9	26·3	25·2
North America	0·2	0·2	0·7	2·4	5·2	7·3	6·7
Central and South America	2·6	1·7	2·2	3·0	4·0	5·8	6·1
Oceania	0·4	0·3	0·2	0·2	0·4	0·5	0·5
Africa	21·5	15·1	12·0	9·1	9·1	7·7	7·0
Asia	53·8	61·5	62·5	61·1	55·4	52·4	54·5
	100·0	100·0	100·0	100·0	100·0	100·0	100·0

of population in an interval of only four years. The major
part of the explanation lies in the fact that Willcox has
adopted a much lower figure for China than is assumed in
the League figures; the problem presented by the population of China to-day will be discussed later in this chapter.
It will also be observed that Willcox's total for Europe in
1929 is much lower than the figure given by the League
for 1933, and that again the difference cannot all be due
to growth of population in the interval. In this case the

explanation is that Willcox has not attempted to allocate the present population of Russia between the pre-war divisions of European and Asiatic Russia. The present Russian government does not recognize these divisions, and it is almost impossible to make a satisfactory allocation of the existing figures to one or other side of the line which was formerly drawn between Europe and Asia. The League has made an attempt to do so while Willcox has not, with the result that Willcox places some millions in Asia whom the League puts in Europe.

Europe

In order to understand how Willcox obtains his results we may consider them continent by continent. As far back as 1800 his figures for Europe coincide with those given in the last chapter since they are founded on the same evidence. For 1750 he gives 140 millions. This is based partly on a revision of a contemporary estimate of 130 millions by Süssmilch in the light of knowledge not available to that pioneer of statistics, and partly on the rates of increase in certain European countries the population of which in the eighteenth century is fairly well known. It will be remembered that we accepted a total of 152·5 millions for 1770 in the last chapter, and a total of 140 millions twenty years earlier is not incompatible with the former figure. The total of 100 millions for Europe in 1650 is much less securely based. There is no country in Europe for which a figure can be provided at that date which has the validity of the figures given for certain European countries about 1700 which were quoted in the last chapter. The main evidence for the estimate for 1650 is the work of Julius Beloch, who about thirty years ago made a most careful study of the evidence bearing upon the population of Europe in 1600. Beloch reached a figure of 73·5 millions for Europe omitting some countries in the east for which data were very scanty; he added, however, that the omitted countries probably contained about 25 million inhabitants, and thus arrived at a figure of 100 millions for Europe in 1600. Willcox holds that, owing to war, emigration, and high mortality through disease, the population was no higher in 1650 than in 1600. He finds some confirmation of this assumption in the fact that both Riccioli and Gregory King, the former in 1661 and the latter in 1696, made estimates of the population of Europe and that both reached a total of 100 millions. The agreement between Riccioli and King is however, largely a coincidence as a study of the component parts of their estimates shows, and can hardly afford serious evidence one way or the other. All that can be said is that the figure of 100 millions for Europe in 1650 cannot be improved upon, that it is not incompatible with the rest of our knowledge of European population history, but that there is little substantial evidence for it.

North America

For this continent we have an adequate record of the white population back to the period when their numbers first became significant. It is only concerning the aboriginal population that doubt arises. The size of the aboriginal population before the arrival of white men has often been exaggerated; but the figure of one million for the United States and Canada, adopted by Willcox, now meets with general acceptance. Taking this figure we get the totals given by Willcox from 1650 onwards, and we can repose at least as much confidence in his findings for this continent as for Europe.

Oceania

Though a larger measure of doubt surrounds the population history of Oceania than of either of the other two continents just discussed, it need not cause us much concern. As in the case of North America we have an adequate history of the white population as soon as it became numerous, and it is the aboriginal population which causes trouble. The latter is now estimated to number two millions, and Willcox keeps this figure steady throughout the period from 1650 to 1929. We shall see later that there is evidence for a heavy decline in the aboriginal population of most of the Pacific region during the last hundred years. No adjustment to correspond with this fact has been made by Willcox; but the numbers concerned are relatively so small that adjustment is unnecessary.

Central and South America

The population history of the three remaining continents presents great difficulty. To obtain a figure for the Indian population of Central and South America in 1650 Willcox divided the total area into a number of geographical regions; he then obtained the best available evidence for the density of the aboriginal population in samples of each region, applied the results to the whole of each region, and added the totals. This indirect method is no doubt the best that can be found, but it means that the figure is no more than a careful guess. For 1750 the material upon which to base a guess is even more thin. For Mexico there is an estimate by Humboldt for 1793, and there are late eighteenth-century figures for some of the West Indies. But in respect of South America there seems to be nothing better than to suppose that it held in 1750 that percentage of the population of Central and North America which Humboldt supposed it to contain in 1823. For 1800 Willcox finds some estimates for Central America, but for South America he has again to resort to the use of Humboldt's percentages. It is only when we reach 1850 that direct material becomes available for this continent, but it is scanty and of poor quality. Data become more numerous and more trustworthy up to 1900, but are not as good now as they were two or three decades ago; for, as was related in the first chapter, some South American States, which took censuses towards the end of the last century, have not taken them in the present century. But it would be a mistake to suppose that our knowledge becomes more

D

accurate from 1650 to 1900. The figure for 1650 is founded upon observations of the conditions of native life when it was uninfluenced by Europeans in most parts of the continent. The figures for 1750 and 1800 are more doubtful; for they refer to times when an appreciable but unknown number of Europeans had settled, while the native population had been thinned by war, disease, and general disruption of culture.

Africa

The case of Africa is also difficult. In 1661 Riccioli gave a figure of 100 millions for the continent; it cannot have been more than a guess, but Willcox thinks it a good guess. He points out that 100 millions equals a density of 8·5 persons per square mile, and that this is now the density of those parts of the continent which are not known to have increased in population since the seventeenth century. Therefore, in default of any better evidence he adopts it. He retains this figure until 1850, and gives 141 millions for 1900 and 140 for 1929; he does not discuss at length his reasons for the latter figures. There is no ground for rejecting or amending the figure of 100 millions for 1650. But if it is accepted as the best that can be done, it may be tentatively suggested that the other figures might be somewhat amended so as to bring them more into line with the known facts of African history. There is nothing to suggest an increase in the population of any part of Africa before 1800; the population of Egypt, for example, is assumed to have been about 2½ millions when Napoleon arrived there and can scarcely have been less before. On the other hand, slave raiding must have diminished the population in many regions so that, whatever the population may have been in 1650, it was smaller in 1750 and still smaller in 1800. After 1800 the population of Egypt and of certain other African countries began to increase, and this increase may have more than compensated for the decline which was almost certainly proceeding elsewhere; if so, the population of the continent was rather higher in 1850 than in 1800. During the second half of the last century the growth of population in Egypt, Algeria, and some other African countries was rapid; while decline may have still been in progress in some regions, the net increase in the population of the whole continent was probably about 25 millions. In the present century the number of African countries, in which the population is known to have been growing, has increased; in other parts the population has probably been stationary. Recently, therefore, the rate of increase in the population of the continent has become more rapid, and the absolute increase may have been as much as 25 millions between 1900 and 1933. In any case, it is impossible to accept Willcox's view that the population of the continent remained stationary between these dates.

Since the estimated population of Africa in 1650 forms a large fraction of the estimated total world population at that date, it might seem that the apparently slender basis for the African total of 100 millions renders the foundations for a world figure in 1650 unsubstantial. But this is not so. We may be certain that the conditions of native life in Africa in 1650 were very much the same as when Africa was opened up in the last century. We know that under these conditions population cannot have passed a moderate density. We have, in fact, every reason to suppose that the density was about that prevailing when Africa was exposed to our view in recent times. We do not know this density accurately, but we know it approximately. This means that, while the population of Africa may have been as much as 120 millions or as little as 80 millions in 1650, it can hardly have been much greater or much less. It follows that, in spite of the lack of direct evidence relating to earlier dates, the reasonable measure of doubt about the African figures is not of a magnitude such as to render an attempt to reach an approximate world figure impossible.

Asia

Asia is the crux of the problem; on any computation it contains at least as many inhabitants as all the other continents put together, and no history of world population can be very informative which does not elucidate the main course of events in this continent. In one important respect the history of population in Asia is a more difficult problem than the history of population in Africa and in Central and South America. For, when our period begins in 1650, the Chinese, Japanese, and Indians, not to mention other peoples, had long passed out of the phase of primitive culture. Under the conditions prevailing a fairly dense population was possible; on the other hand, the instability, which accompanied those conditions, implies that the density may have fluctuated, and may at certain times have been reduced to a low level. In other words, it is not permissible to estimate the population in 1650 from evidence of the density which primitive arts make possible in given geographical areas which is the method used by Willcox for Africa and Central and South America. We can only rely upon such direct evidence as may be available.

Willcox gives 250 millions for 1650 and arrives at that total in the following manner. When the enumeration of 1721 was made in Japan certain territorial lords, who had long been in possession of their estates, were ordered to make reports on the population of the areas under their control during the previous eighty years. These reports show that increase had been fairly rapid before 1721, and upon this basis an estimate of 23 millions for Japan in 1650 is founded. This figure for Japan is more solid than for any country in Europe at the same date. For India his figure is 100 millions. This is a mere guess taken from Moreland's description of the state of India at the death of Akbar in 1605. Moreland's figure has been quoted with favour in the census report of India; no better estimate is available, but its factual basis is of the most slender kind.

The population of China is put at 70 millions. In the case of China the trouble is not the absence of records. The *Tung-hwa-Luh*, said by Parker to mean the Eastern Beauty Record, is in seventy volumes and contains population, revenue, and other data for each year from 1651. There are said to be similar records for earlier dynasties. The trouble is to know how to interpret them. Mr. Chang-Heng Chen has worked out the population, assuming first that the figures only included males from 16 to 60 and that such males, after due allowance for those who evaded the poll-tax, amounted to a quarter of the population, and assuming, secondly, that the figures included only heads of families who were subject to the poll-tax and that the average size of family was five. Under the first assumption he gets a total of 57·9 millions, under the second assumption 72·4 millions. Willcox gives 70 millions which he gets by averaging seven different estimates based on attempts to interpret the official figures. Thus, he gets 193 millions as the total population of Japan, India, and China in 1650. He then assumes that these three countries held then, as they do now, about three-fourths of the population of the continent, and this gives him his 250 millions for 1650.

The evidence for the totals for Asia at the later dates which are given by Willcox is best understood if we consider each of the chief countries concerned in turn. As we have seen in the last chapter fairly satisfactory figures are available for Japan from 1721 onwards, and the population history of Asia would be relatively well elucidated if the same was true of the rest of the continent. But this is not the case. For India there are no data upon which to found any estimate for 1750 and 1800. Willcox gets a figure for 1850 by supposing that the rate of increase between 1851 and 1871 was the same as the average of the known rates of increase between 1871–91 and 1891–1901. This gives 205 millions for 1850, which is probably a reasonable approximation to the truth. To get figures for 1750 and 1800 he assumes a uniform rate of increase from

1650 to 1850, that is to say, he 'distributes the increase from 100 millions in 1650 to 205 millions in 1850 evenly over the period. The justification for this procedure may be questioned. There is evidence of a rapid growth of population in India during the hundred years before 1850. Messrs. Thompson and Garratt, for instance, say that 'it is safe to assume a considerable increase of population between 1750 and 1850, especially in southern India. During the latter part of the century it was the subject of frequent comment in official records'. On the other hand, there is no similar evidence of rapid increase between 1650 and 1750. Thus there are grounds for assuming a slower rate of increase between 1650 and 1750 than between 1750 and 1850, and the estimates of the population of India for 1750 and 1800 might be amended accordingly.

There remains the problem of numbers in China which Willcox estimates at 70 millions for 1650. As a basis we possess the official figures to which reference was made above. But, apart from the question what these figures really represent, they are open to grave suspicion. Willcox has noted that of the annual figures for the period 1651 to 1710 thirteen are exact repetitions of those of the preceding year, while in nine cases only one figure, and in eleven only two figures, are different. After 1712 the figures begin to show a rapid increase. Later on they became absurd; those for 1775 show an increase of 44 millions over those for 1774. It would seem that the emperor had observed that the figures for 1774 did not exhibit much advance over the preceding figures, and ordered that in future they should be collected with greater care. The hint was apparently taken, and the total for 1775 was swollen for the emperor's gratification. It is evident that at some date in the eighteenth century the official figures must be abandoned. Chang-Heng Chen, for instance, when making his estimate, no longer uses them after 1741. Willcox abandons them after 1712; his method of getting figures for 1750 and onwards is to obtain a total for the population of China in 1929 by a method described below, to assume that the population has remained stable from 1850 to 1929, and to distribute the increase between 1712 and 1850 at a uniform rate. The view that the population of China did not increase in the second half of the last century is fairly widely held. Chang-Heng Chen, for example, assumes that it was stable from 1850 to 1890 and then began to increase once more. Others believe that it has also remained stable during the present century. Therefore, there is no fundamental objection to be raised against the assumption by Willcox of stability since 1850.

Before we examine the other assumptions upon which the figures, given by Willcox for the population of China at various dates, are based, it should be observed that his results imply a course of events that is scarcely credible. An increase of population from 70 millions in 1650 to 148 millions in 1750 and to 342 millions in 1850 is a fivefold increase in 200 years, and represents an average annual rate of increase of 0·82 per cent. from 1650 to 1750 and of 0·77 from 1750 to 1850. During the 280 years between 1650 and 1930 the population of Europe apparently increased five times, and the average annual rate of increase was 0·71 per cent. from 1800 to 1850 and 0·82 per cent. from 1850 to 1900. But during those 280 years there was an increase in opportunities for employment which has never been paralleled in human history. It is true that from the establishment of the Manchu dynasty in 1644, and especially during long periods in the eighteenth century, China was exceptionally peaceful and prosperous, and that land settlement proceeded fast. But when all allowances are made it is impossible to believe that the population of China increased more rapidly than that of Europe for two centuries.

It follows that Willcox's figures require careful examination. Let us first take his figure of 342 millions for 1850 which he retains until 1929; this figure is for all China and includes 323 millions for China proper. He gets this figure

as a result of a study of the Chinese census for 1910, which he holds to have been more accurate than any other attempt of earlier or later date to ascertain the size of the population. We may note in the first place that Chinese authors will not allow that it possesses any special authority over other data. Further, the census was incomplete and the results never published. Moreover, the interpretation of the data is very uncertain; various categories of persons appear in the data, and it is uncertain whether the total population is to be reached by adding them or whether there is overlapping. Apart from the results of this census there are numerous recent estimates, none of which, it is true, command much respect in themselves. But they all give a much higher figure than that which Willcox extracts from the census of 1910 and, when averaged, suggest a population of about 450 millions. We are faced by the fact that almost every student of the problem believes that the higher figure is more probable than the lower figure. It is impossible to disregard the weight of opinion. But, if we accept a figure of 450 millions for the present population of China, the difficulty is increased and not diminished. For if we assume that the population has been stable since 1850 it implies more than a sixfold increase in 200 years; even if we were to disregard the widespread opinion that the population has been stable since the middle of the last century we should have a more than sixfold increase in 280 years, and we have already found a smaller increase than this to be scarcely credible.

It is obvious that a solution of the difficulty can only lie in a revision of the figure of 70 millions for 1650. This figure is based upon official records. But these records, as already shown, are obviously untrustworthy for the eighteenth century and are open to grave suspicion for earlier times. To this it may be added that Mr. Fitzgerald has recently pointed out that the records do not purport to give a total of persons subject to be taxed but only of persons paying taxes, obviously quite another matter. In

short the official data afford no evidence worthy of consideration and can be left out of account. In that case
what evidence do we possess? Mr. Fitzgerald has recently
conducted a very careful inquiry into the foundation and
history of cities in China; and the growth of urban life may
be taken to reflect the growth in density of population in
such a country as China. The result of this inquiry presents a picture of a state of things in the seventeenth century when the density of population cannot have been so
low as a sixth of what it is now; judging from this evidence
it is difficult to believe that the population in 1650 was
much less than a third of the present population. In other
words the suggestion is that China in 1650 may have had
a population of 150 millions or more. An increase from
150 millions in 1650 to 450 millions at the present day,
spread evenly over the period, implies an average annual
rate of growth of 0·39 per cent., and it may be noted that
the figures which we have accepted for India for 1650 and
1850 imply an average annual rate of growth of 0·36 per
cent. during that period. The most probable solution of
the difficulty is, therefore, that the population of China
in 1650 has been seriously underestimated.

The result of an examination of Willcox's estimate is
to suggest that his figures for Africa after 1650 and for
India in 1750 and 1800 require some amendment in the
directions which have been indicated, and that the figures
for China demand revision at all dates. When making
this revision we start with the fact that the evidence points
to a population of 150 millions in 1650 and of 450 millions
in 1933. We have to take into account the widely held
view that the population of China was not increasing
between 1850 and 1900. Opinion is divided concerning
trends during the last thirty years; since Chinese authorities incline to the belief that the population has recently
increased somewhat, we may perhaps assume that it was
430 millions in 1900. If we keep this figure steady from
1850 to 1900 we have nearly a threefold increase between

1650 and 1850; this implies a high but not an impossible rate of growth during two centuries. If Willcox's figures are emended in this sense the revised estimate works out as in Fig. 8. It follows that world population during the last two hundred and eighty years has increased between three and a half and four times instead of four and a half times as suggested by Willcox. The chief remaining difference between the two estimates relates to the proportion which the population of Asia has formed of world population at different dates.

FIGURE 8

Revised Estimate of the Population of the World,
1650–1933

(millions)

Continent	1650	1750	1800	1850	1900	1933
Europe . . .	100	140	187	266	401	519
North America .	1	1·3	5·7	26	81	137
Central and South America . .	12	11·1	18·9	33	63	125
Oceania . .	2	2	2	2	6	10
Africa . . .	100	95	90	95	120	145
Asia . . .	330	479	602	749	937	1,121
World Total . .	545	728	906	1,171	1,608	2,057

Percentage Distribution

Continent	1650	1750	1800	1850	1900	1933
Europe . . .	18·3	19·2	20·7	22·7	24·9	25·2
North America .	0·2	0·1	0·7	2·3	5·1	6·7
Central and South America . .	2·2	1·5	2·1	2·8	3·9	6·1
Oceania . .	0·4	0·3	0·2	0·2	0·4	0·5
Africa . . .	18·3	13·1	9·9	8·1	7·4	7·0
Asia . . .	60·6	65·8	66·4	63·9	58·3	54·5
	100·0	100·0	100·0	100·0	100·0	100·0

Since a rate of increase of this magnitude cannot have been in operation long before our period begins, it follows that our period is one of unusual, and almost certainly of unprecedented, expansion in numbers. Thus in order to appreciate the position to-day, which it is the main object of this book to examine, it must all the time be borne in mind that the last three centuries have been marked by an unparalleled outburst of population. This is generally recognized, and it is further usual to suppose that the expansion of numbers began in Europe, followed later in other parts of the world, and that an impulse towards expansion was somehow transmitted from Europe to the other continents. But it will be observed that the figures reached in an attempt to reconstruct the story do not altogether bear out this conclusion. A study of Figs. 2 and 3 suggests that we can almost reach back to a time when the population of Europe was stationary. There may have been some increase in the population of certain parts of Europe during the later years of the seventeenth century after the Thirty Years' War; but it seems likely that this was a filling up of gaps created by war and disease in a similar manner to that which had often been observed before. On the whole it is more likely that the definitive increase in the population of Europe began after than before 1700. On the other hand, the population of Japan was in a state of fairly rapid increase from 1650 to 1721, while the population of China expanded swiftly during the eighteenth century and almost certainly also during the last half of the seventeenth century. Thus expansion of population in these two very important Asiatic countries was at least coincident with, and most probably earlier than, expansion of population in Europe. In any case there is no question of the exercise at that time of any influence upon these two countries by Europe. Apart from these two cases, however, increase outside Europe began at a later date than in Europe, and the facts are not only concordant with, but also suggest, the conclusion that the expansion of population in India, Java, Egypt, and elsewhere was due to European influence; in any case it followed closely upon contact with Europe.

In consequence of the different rates of increase the

continents have experienced varying fates. The concentration of population in Europe and Asia is remarkable;
throughout the entire period three-quarters of the population of the world have been situated in these two continents, and the density has been far higher there than
elsewhere. Upon any computation Asia holds over half
the world population from 1650 onwards; Europe's share
has increased from about one-fifth to about one-quarter.
North America has steadily advanced its proportion. At
the beginning of the period Africa and Central and South
America suffered like fates, for their shares of world
population at first decreased. Central and South America
regained their original proportion about a hundred years
ago, and have now nearly trebled it; Africa, on the other
hand, though it has made an absolute gain in numbers,
has continued steadily to lose relatively to other continents.

Since the chief 'races' of mankind were roughly allocated
to certain regions at the beginning of the period, and since,
with the exception of the overflow of white and the transportation of black peoples, they continue to remain for the
most part in their original sites, these conclusions about
the fate of continents have some bearing upon the fate of
'races'. By 'race' is meant no more than the fact that it is
possible to make a very rough classification of mankind
into white, black, brown, yellow, and red. The brown and
yellow peoples have clearly made large absolute gains; it
seems likely that they have about maintained their former
proportions of world population. The black peoples have
suffered heavy relative losses, for they once formed about
a fifth of the population of the world and now form about
a fifteenth. It is impossible to say whether they have
gained or lost absolutely; they have apparently decreased
somewhat in Africa, but against this has to be set the fact
that about a third of all black peoples are now outside
Africa. In any case absolute gain or loss has been slight.
The red peoples numbered about 13 millions in 1650 and
now number well over 20 millions; therefore they have

made an absolute gain but have suffered a relative loss. It is the white peoples who have gained most. In 1650 they numbered about 100 millions; it is probable that persons of unmixed European descent now number about 720 millions. Since the population of the world has increased four times at the most since 1650, it is clear that the white peoples have had a disproportionate share of the world increase.

It is noteworthy that, in spite of these immense changes, three out of the five groups of mankind should have remained in their original homes. Black people have become more widely distributed, but the white peoples alone have expanded not only their territory but also their numbers. They have overflowed, and the vast extent of the areas overseas from Europe now settled by them is very impressive, even if we disregard the other huge areas under European tutelage. Nevertheless, Europeans outside Europe are spread thinly; there are only about 200 millions of them now living outside their former home. This relatively light occupation of these oversea estates by their new masters is one of the most important facts in the present state of world population.

CHAPTER IV

MIGRATION MOVEMENTS

IT follows from what was said at the end of the last chapter that, in order to complete an outline of world population history, something must be added about migration; for although migration movements do not affect the total for the world as a whole, they have had a profound influence upon the growth of population in certain continents. It was pointed out in the first chapter that there are great difficulties in defining a migrant, and that these difficulties have not yet been overcome. In consequence our information about contemporary migration movements is very inadequate, and it is easily understood that our information for past times must be still more unsatisfactory. When dealing with the growth of world population we left all discussion about causes and consequences to future chapters, and we propose to follow the same course in regard to migration. Moreover since, owing to the great importance of migration in the world to-day, the facts will require fairly close attention when we come to consider the situation in various parts of the world, we propose to confine the discussion here to a mere outline of migration history.

It is customary to distinguish between inter-continental and intra-continental movements, and we may adopt this distinction here with the observation that it has more meaning for the movements of Europeans than of non-Europeans. European inter-continental movements have mostly been overseas and for long distances; the chief exception is in the case of the Russian movement into Asia. These movements are thus mostly very different from European intra-continental migration which generally implies short land journeys. But in the case of non-Europeans this distinction is not well marked because there is no close association between inter-continental

movements and long journeys overseas; for a sea journey
may merely mean transfer to another part of the same
continent as in the case of Chinese migration to Malaya.
Nevertheless, it is reasonable to retain the distinction
because migration has mostly been that of Europeans, and
we may begin with some account of inter-continental
movements.

Until after the Napoleonic wars information is of the
most fragmentary kind. The volume of Spanish emigration to the New World is unknown; the records from
Seville, the only authorized port of embarkation, show
150,000 departures between 1509 and 1740. But it is
probable that emigration from Spain was on a much larger
scale than these figures suggest since the number of
Spaniards in the New World in 1800 was considerable.
It may be that the records for departures from Seville are
incomplete and that there was also emigration through
other ports. There were about 55,000 persons in New
France in 1754, and they had been largely recruited by
natural increase. Oversea movements were, in fact, on a
small scale in the seventeenth and eighteenth centuries
except from England and Germany. Soon after the middle
of the seventeenth century there were some 80,000 persons
in New England, about the same number in Virginia, and
perhaps 20,000 in Maryland. In all perhaps a quarter of
a million people left the British Isles for the New World
in that century. In the following century the total may
have been a million and a half, among whom were 500,000
Ulster Presbyterians and 50,000 criminals transported
between 1717 and 1776. It was not until the end of the
century that Irish Catholics began to move long distances
overseas in any numbers; in earlier times they went as
recruits to the armies of continental powers. It is believed
that some 200,000 Germans left for America before 1800;
thus, after the British Isles, Spain and Germany sent the
largest numbers of emigrants overseas from Europe. As
regards non-European movements the only important

emigration was that due to the transportation of Africans to the New World. Estimates of the numbers involved vary greatly, but there is reason to believe that as many as 20 million Africans were taken from their homes. It is well worthy of notice that in any case this movement of Africans must have been on a far larger scale than any other movement during our period until we come to the mass emigration of white peoples from Europe in the nineteenth century. Moreover, it appears that the movement of Africans, relative to their numbers in the eighteenth century, was on a larger scale than the movement of Europeans relative to their numbers in the nineteenth century.

During and for some time after the Napoleonic wars movement was on a small scale, but before the middle of the last century it had swelled into a considerable stream. Thanks to the investigation conducted by the National Bureau of Economic Research, in which all the evidence has been carefully examined, we are able to present figures from 1821 in the case of countries of immigration and from 1846 in the case of countries of emigration. The Bureau brought the figures up to 1924; additions for subsequent years up to 1932 have been included in Fig. 9 from material published by the International Labour Office.

It should be understood that the figures are for gross movements. Until very recent times the magnitude of the return movement is very uncertain, and therefore figures for net migration cannot be given. It is probable that during the seventeenth and eighteenth centuries many of the Spanish and Portuguese emigrants intended at least to come back. But this was not true of the British and German emigrants at that time or of emigrants in general during the nineteenth century until that century was well advanced. For the journey was long and hazardous, and few of those who ventured to take it ever thought that they would return; many of them indeed had reasons for not wishing to do so. But as transport facilities improved, those who failed to establish themselves, or who did not like the new life, were able to repatriate themselves; in addition there grew up a class of temporary migrants who went out with the intention of returning home when they

FIGURE 9

World Inter-continental Migration

Emigration: 1846 to 1932			Immigration: 1821 to 1932		
Country of emigration	Period covered	Total	Country of immigration	Period covered	Total
Europe:			America:		
Austria-Hungary .	1846–1932	5,196	Argentina . .	1856–1932	6,405
Belgium . .	1846–1932	193	Brazil. . .	1821–1932	4,431
British Isles . .	1846–1932	18,020	British West Indies	1836–1932	1,587
Denmark .	1846–1932	387	Canada . .	1821–1932	5,206
Finland . .	1871–1932	371	Cuba . . .	1901–1932	857
France . .	1846–1932	519	Guadeloupe .	1856–1924	42
Germany . .	1846–1932	4,889	Dutch Guiana .	1856–1931	69
Italy . . .	1846–1932	10,092	Mexico . .	1911–1931	226
Malta . . .	1911–1932	63	Newfoundland .	1841–1924	20
Holland . .	1846–1932	224	Paraguay . .	1881–1931	26
Norway . .	1846–1932	854	United States .	1821–1932	34,244
Poland . .	1920–1932	642	Uruguay . .	1836–1932	713
Portugal . .	1846–1932	1,805			
Russia. . .	1846–1924	2,253	Total (America)		53,826
Spain . . .	1846–1932	4,653	Asia:		
Sweden . .	1846–1932	1,203	Philippines . .	1911–1929	90
Switzerland .	1846–1932	332			
Total (Europe)		51,696	Oceania:		
			Australia . .	1861–1932	2,913
Other Countries:			Fiji . . .	1881–1926	79
British India .	1846–1932	1,194	Hawaii . .	1911–1931	216
Cape Verde .	1901–1927	30	New Caledonia .	1896–1932	32
Japan . . .	1846–1932	518	New Zealand .	1851–1932	594
St. Helena .	1896–1924	12	Africa:		
			Mauritius . .	1836–1932	573
			Seychelles . .	1901–1932	12
			South Africa .	1881–1932	852
Grand total .		53,450	Grand total .		59,187

had saved some money. While few figures can be given, it may be mentioned that 30 per cent. of those who entered the United States between 1821 and 1924 and 47 per cent. of those who entered Argentina between 1857 and 1924 are believed to have returned home again.

Two points in Fig. 9 attract immediate attention. The

E

first is that the recorded total of immigrants exceeds the
recorded total of emigrants by about 6 millions. In view
of the very unsatisfactory nature of the material, the failure
of the account to balance need cause no surprise; indeed
it is remarkable that the totals should be so close. There
are various reasons for supposing that the record of immigrants is more complete than that of emigrants; the total
of 59 millions may therefore be taken as a minimum. But
it is certainly an incomplete record, and it is likely that at
least 65 million persons moved overseas in those years.
The second point is that most of those who moved to
another continent were Europeans; under 2 millions of
those recorded in Fig. 9 as moving were non-Europeans.
But the record of the movement of non-Europeans is
relatively more incomplete than that of Europeans; there
are, for instance, no records at all for the movements of
Chinese and some other non-European peoples, and the
total is certainly nearer 3 than 2 millions. Non-Europeans
have thus played no significant part in migration movements during the last hundred years. It is worth noting
that the largest recorded movement of non-Europeans,
namely that of Indians, mostly took place under the indenture system, and therefore that this was not a spontaneous
movement as was the case with Europeans.

It is, therefore, the European inter-continental movement which attracts attention, and we may first examine
the fluctuations which it displays. In Fig. 10 the average
annual emigration from Europe is illustrated; up to 1920
five-year periods have been taken, but since 1920 the
periods are of four years so as to bring the years 1929 to
1932, that is the years of world depression, into a period
by themselves. Wave-like fluctuations are apparent; there
are four peaks before 1920, of which the third and fourth
are especially prominent. Between 1921 and 1924 the
volume of movement rose to the level reached by the third
peak, but instead of expanding between 1925 and 1928,
as might have been expected, it contracted.

The next fact of general interest is the share taken by different countries in the migration movement at different dates. This is illustrated in Fig. 11, which shows for each

FIGURE 10

Inter-continental Emigration from Europe: 1846 to 1932

Annual averages in five- and four-year periods

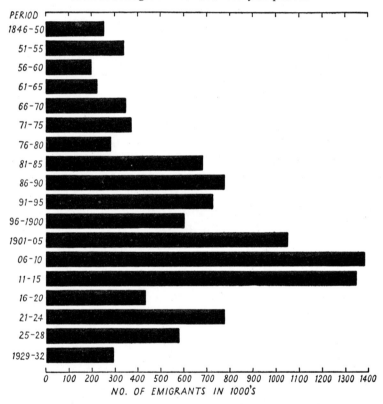

five-year period from 1846 to 1920 and for four-year periods from 1920 to 1932 the percentages which various European countries contributed to the stream of migrants; all those countries are shown for any period whose contribution amounted to more than 2 per cent. of the total; the omission of a country in any period implies that its

contribution, if any, was less than 2 per cent. The Figure
brings out the remarkable changes which have taken place;
the contribution of the British Isles sank from over three-
quarters of the total in 1846–50 to just over a fifth in
1901–5, and then rose again until it exceeded a third.
Germany was the only other country which played a large
part in the earlier phases of the period; but after 1885 the
percentage coming from Germany markedly diminished.
During the last quarter of the last century the share of
other countries became significant, and among them Italy
was prominent; in the period 1901–5 Italy contributed
over 30 per cent. of the whole. The facts indicated in this
Figure should be considered in relation to the history
disclosed by Fig. 10; a small percentage of the total emigrant stream in the later years, when the stream was large,
may have implied an absolutely larger contribution than
a large percentage in the earlier years when the total
amount was small. Thus the 22 per cent. contributed by
the British Isles in 1901–5 represented a larger total than
the 78 per cent. contributed in 1846–50; again the 30 per
cent. contributed by Italy in 1901–5 gave a larger total
than the 78 per cent. from the British Isles in 1846–50.

Neither the gross contribution from any particular
country nor the percentage which this contribution forms
of the total in any year necessarily correspond at all closely
with the intensity of emigration, as measured by the annual
loss per 1,000 inhabitants by emigration. The numbers
leaving Denmark in any year, for example, have never
been large compared with those from bigger countries,
and have never formed a large percentage of the total
movement from Europe; but, nevertheless, emigration
from Denmark has been, relatively to the population of
Denmark, on a large scale. If the loss per 1,000 by emigration is worked out for different countries we find that it
varies very considerably from decade to decade. It is
sufficient to mention that Ireland has stood at or near the
top of the list of countries ranged in descending order of

intensity of emigration for the last ninety years. The
Scandinavian countries, especially Sweden and Norway,

FIGURE 11

Inter-continental Emigration from Europe: 1846 to 1932

Percentage distribution of the average annual emigration from the major
countries of emigration in five- and four-year periods

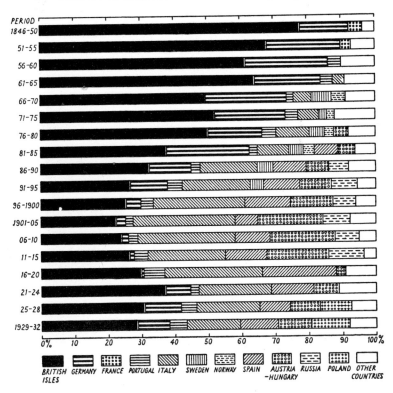

are found high up in most decades, and Switzerland
appears not far behind. Indeed, in most decades up to
1900 the intensity of emigration from Switzerland was
equal to or greater than that from Italy, though numerically Swiss emigration has been of little importance.

It remains to say something about the other side of the
picture. An examination of Fig. 9 shows that out of some

FIGURE 12

*Inter-continental Immigration of Aliens into the United
States, Canada, Brazil, and Argentina: 1856 to 1932*

Percentage shares of each country in the total immigration to these
countries in five- and four-year periods

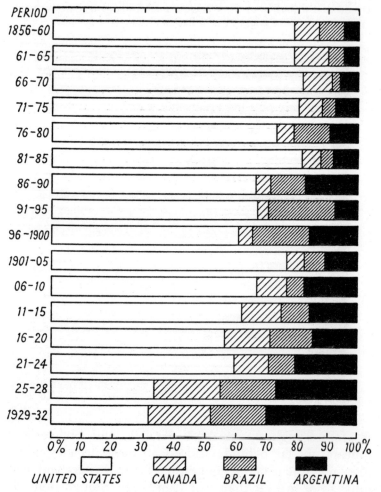

59 million recorded immigrants from Europe nearly 54
million landed in North, Central, or South America.
America as a whole has therefore attracted well over 90 per

cent. of those who went overseas from Europe. In Fig. 12 are shown the percentages which each of the four chief American countries of immigration took of all immigrants to those countries by five- and four-year periods. It will be noticed that up to 1885 the United States more than held their own; thereafter they took a smaller proportion. As the share of the United States sank, that of Brazil rose for three decades; but Brazil has not retained the relative importance which it reached in these years. During the present century the chief feature has been the growth of the importance of Canada as a country of immigration, while Argentina has maintained a percentage in each decade which was only occasionally reached in the last century.

If the above facts regarding changes in the volume of movement, changes in the national origins of the volume, and changes in the relative absorptive capacity of the countries of immigration are considered together, we arrive at the following conclusions about alterations in the national composition of the stream of migrants to the chief countries of immigration. It emerges that the United States alone have been seriously affected by alterations of this kind. Those entering the United States from northern and western Europe constitute what is known as the 'old' immigration, and those from southern and eastern Europe the 'new' immigration. Up to 1880 the 'old' immigration formed over 85 per cent., and up to 1890 over 75 per cent. of the total; but in 1896 the 'new' exceeded the 'old' for the first time, and from 1900 to 1914 constituted over 70 per cent. of the total. Since the War the relative importance of the 'old' has increased once more. It is true that during the two decades preceding the War Canada took a larger proportion than before of southern and eastern Europeans, but there was no dramatic change in the composition of the stream as in the case of the United States. Immigration into Australasia has remained almost wholly British. With the exception of a certain flow of Germans into Brazil, Central and South America have been supplied from Italy, Spain, and Portugal. Argentina has been chiefly recruited from Italy and Spain, Italians predominating in the earlier and Spaniards in the later decades. The predominating element in the inflow into Brazil was Portuguese in the earlier and also in the more recent decades, while Italians assumed first place in the intervening years; Spaniards have formed the only other important element in Brazilian immigration. Spaniards, it may be added, alone have gone in any numbers to Central and South American countries other than Argentina and Brazil.

Compared with oversea movements the other movements of Europeans have been numerically of little account though of much political and social significance, especially in recent times; on that account they will be studied in some detail later, and may, therefore, be passed over here with a few words. One of the most important of European movements, which did not involve passage overseas, is somewhat anomalous in that, while it involved transfer from one continent to another, it took place within the confines of one sovereignty. This was the migration from European into Asiatic Russia which is often loosely called migration to Siberia, though in fact the emigrants settled in the steppe region as well as in Siberia. The movement gathered force after 1860, and between 1800 and 1900 about 3,700,000 emigrants passed into Asiatic Russia. The movement was at its highest point in the earlier years of the present century, and between 1900 and 1914 well over another 3,500,000 left, thus bringing up the total to over 7 millions.

Before 1800 there were continental movements in Europe of some magnitude which mostly took the form of mass expulsions and mass settlements. As an example of the former about a quarter of a million Huguenots are believed to have left France after 1685; as examples of the latter there are the efforts to recolonize Prussia after the Thirty Years' War and the schemes of Frederick the Great and of Maria Theresa. During the nineteenth century European continental movements were at first on a small scale; there was some tendency for skilled workers to move from advanced to backward countries, from Germany to Poland, for instance. After 1880 we begin to notice evidence of a numerically more important movement of unskilled workers from backward to advanced countries; thus Polish labourers began to enter Germany, but the movements were largely seasonal. Movement of unskilled workers into France gradually assumed considerable proportions, and in this case many who entered took up permanent residence. Between 1920 and 1930 no fewer than 2,880,000 foreign workers entered France; and thus France assumed during this decade a prominent place among countries of immigration.

The intra-continental movements of non-Europeans have been on a larger scale than their inter-continental movements, but they have been of no great significance. The movement into Manchuria, which, if Manchuria is regarded as part of China, is an internal migration and therefore outside the scope of this discussion, began when the prohibition upon immigration was raised shortly before the War; the annual figures are believed to have been in the neighbourhood of half a million from 1923 to 1926, and over a million for each of the next three years. Since then the movement has been on a smaller scale. But these are gross figures, and it is said that in seven years more than half the immigrants have returned home. No figures can be given for Chinese emigrants to other destinations. All that can be said is that there was hardly any emigration until 1840, and that there are now some 8 million Chinese, not counting those in Manchuria, living outside China, but nearly all in Asia. They include 2·25 millions in Formosa, 1·75 millions in Java, 1·5 millions in Siam, and a million in the East Indies. Thus most of those Chinese who have emigrated have not gone far afield.

Japanese movements have been of small importance;

there are now about a million Japanese living outside Japan proper but within the Japanese Empire, and another 200,000 in Manchuria. The same is true of Indians; the inter-continental movement, such as it was, ceased to be of importance in the present century, and it was followed by an intra-continental movement towards Ceylon and Malaya, where rather under a million and a half Indians are now to be found.

CHAPTER V

NATURAL INCREASE

IN the last three chapters we have presented in the briefest outline some account of the growth of world population and of migration movements during the last three centuries. We must now begin the work of interpretation. As regards the growth of population one thing is obvious; the growth has been due to a surplus of births over deaths. If we knew accurately the population of the world in 1650 and also to-day, the amount by which the second figure exceeds the first would give us the excess of births over deaths during the period. It is not the object of this chapter to prove that. The object may be explained by saying that we want to discover how this excess has arisen.

In order to deal with this problem we may employ crude birth- and death-rates. These rates are obtained by referring the total births and deaths which occur in any country during a year to the population for that year and expressing the result per 1,000 of the population. Thus the estimated population of England and Wales was 40,467,000 in the middle of the year 1934, the number of live births which took place during the year was 598,084 and the number of deaths 476,853. It follows that the birth-rate was 14·8 and the death-rate 11·8 per 1,000. The difference between them was 3·0 per 1,000. Since births exceeded deaths the difference is called the natural increase; if deaths had exceeded births it would have been called the natural decrease. It is clear that in most parts of the world, since in most places population was increasing, natural increase must have obtained during this period; for that is only another way of saying that births were exceeding deaths. But before this period, since population was either stationary or increasing slowly, there was either no natural increase or only a small natural increase. Thus we may say that before this period birth- and death-rates were running at about the same level, and that during this period the former was running well above the latter. Clearly this divergence can only have occurred either because the birth-rate rose, or because the death-rate sank, or because both took place together. Our problem is to discover what it was that happened.

In order to calculate birth- and death-rates for any area we must know, not only the number of births and deaths, but also the total population of the area in question. The limitations of our knowledge of population became apparent in the second and third chapters. Some idea was given in the first chapter of the extent of our information about births and deaths; it will have been gathered that civil registration followed the setting up of a census, and therefore that in those countries in which no system of parish registration preceded civil registration, birth- and death-rates first became available some time later than the first trustworthy population figures. But in Christian countries, where parish registers were kept, baptism and burial records may be available some time before a census was taken; when this is so, if the population can be reconstructed from pre-census material, it may be possible to make estimates of birth- and death-rates which, though far from accurate, no doubt represent the course of events with some fidelity. We do in fact possess such data for England and Wales, Sweden, and Norway dating from the eighteenth century. They are shown for the two first-mentioned countries in Fig. 13, and are continued to the present day by making use of the increasingly accurate records of the last century.

The figures for Norway date from 1736, those for England and Wales from 1701. There are also Swedish figures from 1700, but they are so unreliable that they have been omitted; if, however, average rates are worked out for Sweden in the first half of the eighteenth century, the birth-rate comes out at 34·25 and the death-rate at 30·4 per 1,000. In the case of each of these three countries, for which alone among the countries of Europe we have evidence from the eighteenth century, the rates had already diverged when information becomes available; but in England and Wales they more or less coincided between 1720 and 1740. Owing to the unreliability of the material in the first half of the eighteenth century, too much stress

FIGURE 13

Birth-rates and Death-rates in England and Wales and Sweden: 1700 to 1930

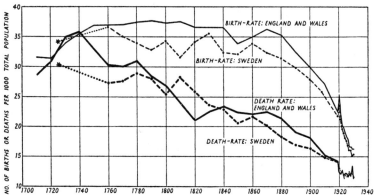

must not be laid upon what they appear to show; but it remains true that the figures, such as they are when they begin, do not coincide. Therefore, since we want to determine how the rates came to diverge, the only course open to us is to examine the trend for the period for which data are available; it may be that we can deduce in this way the probable trend of the rates at earlier dates.

Let us consider the birth-rates first. Omitting for the moment the decades before 1760, the birth-rates in all three countries show fluctuations, in Norway and Sweden very marked fluctuations; but up to the beginning of the fourth quarter of the last century no trend upwards or downwards is to be detected. Then a definite decline sets in. When we turn to the earlier decades we observe in England and Wales and in Norway some sign of an upward

trend; there would also seem to be some evidence of this
in Sweden, because the average birth-rate from 1701 to
1751 was, as already stated, 34·25, whereas from 1751 to
1760 it was 36·57 per 1,000. Thus the history of the birth-
rate seems to show three phases, a first period of some
increase, a second long period when it fluctuated about a
high level, and a third period of sharp decline.

A glance at Fig. 13 shows that the story of the death-
rate is quite different. In the two Scandinavian countries
the story is one of a tendency toward decline all through
the period. The fall was hesitating at first, and there were
occasional checks and even upward movements later; but
in general the marked downward trend is obvious. The
same is true of England and Wales with the exception of
the fact that the death-rate moved up for the first three
decades of the eighteenth century. We shall find reasons
in the next chapter for supposing that this upward movement in England and Wales was due to peculiar circumstances which affected this country only, and therefore
that it was a local phenomenon and not characteristic of
other countries in the same region of Europe.

From these facts there emerges at once one very important conclusion. The gap between the rates, which existed
in 1750 and became larger until late in the nineteenth
century, widened because, while the birth-rate fluctuated
round a high level, the death-rate fell. This means that,
through whatever causes the gap may have come into
existence, it expanded and became large only because of
a downward movement of the death-rate; this is equivalent to saying that the creation of the large surplus of
births over deaths, which was so important a feature of the
history of these countries in the nineteenth century, was
due to a fall in the death-rate and not to a rise in the birth-
rate. During the most recent decades the gap has narrowed. This is not due to any cessation of the fall in the
death-rate, but to the fact that during the last quarter of
the nineteenth century the birth-rate began to fall and has

fallen faster than the death-rate. It remains to refer.to the origin of the gap between the rates.

When information becomes available, the death-rate, though not in England and Wales, where peculiar conditions prevailed, was apparently tending downwards in a hesitating fashion. It may have been decreasing before our figures begin, and the gap may have been wholly created in that way. But there is some evidence that the birth-rate rose for a time, and it is possible, and on the whole likely, that an upward movement in the birth-rate was a contributory factor. It is therefore impossible to say more about this interesting and important point than that in Norway and Sweden, which are more typical of western Europe than England and Wales in the first decades of the eighteenth century, a downward movement in the death-rate may have coincided with an upward movement in the birth-rate to produce the gap, or in other words to cause a surplus of births over deaths.

There are no data available for other European countries before 1800. After 1800 figures begin to come in; they have been assembled by Sundbärg up to 1900. To his data have been added others from an unpublished thesis by Dr. Leybourne for the period 1900 to 1930. The results are given in Fig. 14.

The data are shown for the same areas as in Fig. 2. Those for north-west Europe are from 1820 onwards by ten-year periods. We have in north-west Europe a group of countries which includes the three already examined, and the figures thus illustrate in effect the later part of the same story over a larger area. The birth-rate shows no trend until after 1880, when it begins to decline. The death-rate, which is known to have been declining earlier in three of the countries concerned, keeps about on the level for a time, and then begins to fall again. With one exception an examination of the course of events in individual countries in this area shows merely unimportant departures from the general scheme. The exception is in the case of Ireland. The Irish birth-rate is known to have been declining since 1864, when civil registration began, and was almost certainly declining since 1850; otherwise in this region the decline in the birth-rate first became visible in England in the middle of the seventies. The

FIGURE 14

Birth-rates and Death-rates in Europe: 1800 to 1930

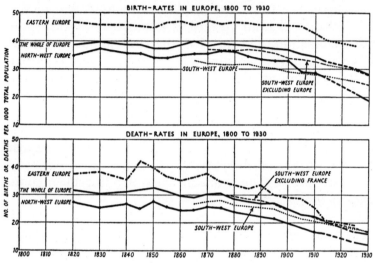

figures for south-west Europe are doubtful until the second half of the century, and only averages for the first fifty years can be given; they work out at 32·4 per 1,000 for the birth-rate and 27·2 per 1,000 for the death-rate. This region includes France, where the course of the birth-rate is anomalous. It therefore seems best also to show south-west Europe excluding France. This brings out the fact that in the remaining countries of the south-west the fall in the birth-rate began later than in the north-west; it was not visible until after 1890. The impression gained from a study of the birth-rate is that in this region, omitting France, events are following the same course as in the north-west, but with a lag of about two decades; and this is borne out by a study of the death-rate. For the countries of eastern Europe figures can be given for the same dates as for north-west Europe; but they must be regarded as merely approximate for the earlier years. The story unfolded is remarkable; a birth-rate, far higher than any which we have yet encountered, remains steady until well into the present century. The death-rate was below the birth-rate at the opening of the century, though it was high in comparison with rates hitherto met with; until 1870 it fluctuated round the same high level, declined with some hesitation to 1890, and then began to fall steadily.

In this chapter we are confined to statistical evidence. From evidence of this kind there emerges a tolerably clear story of events in England and Wales, Sweden, and Norway, though the very earliest phases unfortunately remain rather obscure. When evidence becomes available soon after 1800 for other countries in the same region, events are found to be following a similar course as in the three above-mentioned countries, and it is a reasonable presumption that they were following a similar course in the eighteenth century. For countries of the south-west evidence first comes in at a relatively late date. It is true that, since events in this region were following the same course as in the north-west, though with a lag of some two decades, there is a certain presumption that the story at earlier dates was similar to that unfolded by a study of the north-west region, but with the various phases falling at later dates. This, however, can be no more than a suggestion which deserves examination in the light of such other evidence as may be available. In the next three chapters we shall inquire into the causes of the movement in the birth- and death-rates in Europe. If we can detect the agencies that were at work, it may be that we shall find evidence that they were in operation before vital statistics become available. In that case we shall be able to infer with some confidence how the rates were moving before there is direct evidence. It is in this way that we may also

F

hope to throw light upon the earlier phases of the story in eastern Europe, where, judging from the vital statistics for the later phases, the story was not altogether parallel to that in the west.

The vital statistics of European settlements overseas do not provide any opportunities for investigating the circumstances under which a settled population began to increase. They illustrate what happens in new countries which are attracting a large stream of immigrants. Some reference was made in the first chapter to American vital statistics, and it will be remembered that no report on deaths is available before 1900, that the birth registration area was only organized in 1915, and that it is only in recent years that the data have come to include the greater part of the country. So far as deaths are concerned the gap before 1900 cannot be filled, but the figures since 1900 may be taken as a rough indication of the death-rate among the white population. So far as births go, an attempt has been made by Thompson and Whelpton to reconstruct the white birth-rate since 1800. Their method is as follows: up to 1820 the census gave the number of white children under 10, and from 1830 it gave the number under 5. If these figures are increased to allow for the deaths which occurred under these ages, we can get an approximate birth-rate for each census year. The method is rough, but nothing better can be done and the results deserve attention. For Australia and New Zealand we have figures from 1875. No figures are available for the whole of Canada before 1926; but Mr. Kuczynski has attempted to reconstruct the birth-rate among the Catholic population of Quebec from as far back as the data permit. This information is illustrated in Figs. 15, 16, and 17.

In all these countries the birth-rate was very high when records begin; it was at or above the level in east Europe. In the United States it was above 50 per 1,000 until after 1830, but it was in decline from 1800 and has now reached the level of north-west Europe. In Australia and New

Zealand there was a heavy decline in the first three decades, stability for a short period, and then renewed decline bringing down the rates to the American level. Among the Catholics of Quebec the birth-rate exceeded

FIGURE 15

Birth-rates and Death-rates in the United States: 1800 to 1930

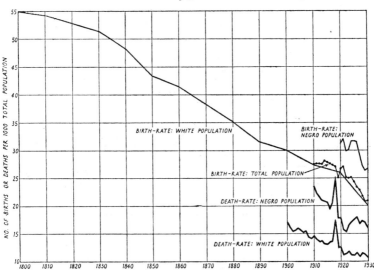

50 per 1,000, except for a few years, for more than a century; data are lacking between 1800 and 1850, but it seems likely that the rate continued at about 50 per 1,000 until 1850 when a slight decline set in. But the rate among the Catholics remains as high as any rate ever recorded in north-west Europe. Information regarding the death-rate is more scanty. But in recent times it has been lower than in north-west Europe and has exhibited no marked changes. The very high natural increase, which obtained in early days in these countries, came about in the only way in which so high a rate is possible—namely by the coincidence of a very high birth-rate with a low death-rate.

Subsequent events have been chiefly due to the heavy fall
in the birth-rate. The death-rate has dropped somewhat,

FIGURE 16

*Birth-rates and Death-rates in Australia and New Zealand:
1875 to 1930*

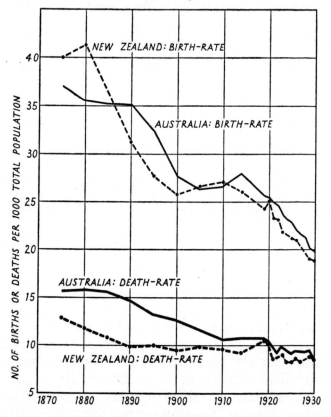

and the result is that the rate of natural increase has fallen
to the level prevalent in north-west Europe.

With regard to non-European peoples we are hampered
by lack of statistical information. For most non-European
countries no vital statistics exist. Where they are available
they are for recent decades only. Moreover, they are

usually very defective. Thus it is officially admitted that Indian vital statistics are deficient by 20 per cent. It

FIGURE 17

Birth-rates in Quebec: 1665 to 1930

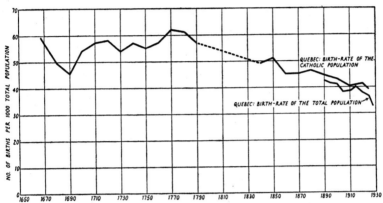

follows that these data can throw little light upon the history of population outside Europe. They are, however, of great significance in relation to the present position and probable future course of population in these countries, and in consequence they will be presented and discussed in future chapters.

CHAPTER VI

DEATHS

THE evidence considered in the last chapter showed that in the earlier part of our period changes in the death-rate were of more significance than changes in the birth-rate in those European countries for which the fullest statistical evidence is available. We may therefore consider the death-rate first, leaving the birth-rate for later treatment. Thus far we have employed the crude death-rate. If the crude death-rate is 20 per 1,000 for any country, it means that on the average out of 1,000 persons alive at the beginning of the year 20 will die within the year. It might seem to follow that the level of the death-rate is governed entirely by the prevalence of death-dealing agencies, and that, if the death-rate rises or falls, it means that the incidence of the death-dealing agencies has increased or diminished. In one sense this is true; the death-rate will only rise if the death-dealing agencies strike more frequently. But it is very important to realize that these agencies may cause more deaths in two quite different ways. Their attack may become absolutely more effective; we may say in this case that the weapons have been sharpened. But if the attack remains at the same level of effectiveness, it may, nevertheless, achieve greater results if the defences weaken. It is obvious that the effectiveness of the attack varies; it increases in times of war and famine, and diminishes with the progress of sanitary measures which prevent people from catching disease. But it is not so obvious that the strength of the defence of the population as a whole against these attacks varies from time to time. This is so, in the first place, because the very young and very old are much more likely to be attacked and to succumb than those of intervening ages, and, in the second place, because the proportion of those most exposed to attack varies from one date to another. Let us suppose,

DEATHS 71

for instance, that the attack of the death-dealing agencies
remains at the same degree of effectiveness, that is to say
that the chance of any person of given age and sex dying
within a year remains the same. Let us suppose further
that the age composition of the population changes in such
a fashion that the old come to form a larger proportion of
the total. Under such circumstances the death-rate will
rise, not because the strength of the death-dealing agencies
has increased, but because the defence of the population
as a whole against them has weakened. Indeed, it is quite
possible for the death-dealing agencies to lose strength
and at the same time for the death-rate to rise, if the composition of the population changes markedly in such a
manner as to expose it more to attack.

The death-rate for any country is in fact the result of
applying the ruling specific mortality rates to the existing
age and sex composition of the population, and by specific
mortality rates are meant the chances of persons of given
age and sex dying within a year. The practical importance
of this is that we must be careful when interpreting changes
in the death-rate in the same country between one period
and another, or differences in the death-rate between one
country and another at the same time. For it does not
follow that, if the death-rate has increased, health conditions have worsened, or that, if the death-rate is lower
in one country than another, health conditions are better
in the country with the lowest rate. Thus the death-rate in
Australia has recently been between 8 and 9 per 1,000 and
in Sweden about 12 per 1,000. But if the true death-rate
is calculated by a method which eliminates the differences
in age composition between the two populations, we find
it to be almost exactly equal for the two countries. The
explanation is that Australia, owing to recent heavy immigration, contains relatively more people than Sweden who
are in the prime of life and therefore well protected against
attack.

The method of calculating the true death-rate, which

gives a correct measure of the strength of the death-dealing agencies, has been recently explained by Mr. Kuczynski who has also worked out the true rates for as many countries and as far back as the data permit. His results are

FIGURE 18

Crude and True Death-rates in England and Wales, Sweden, and France

ENGLAND AND WALES

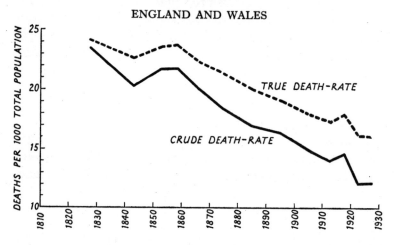

illustrated in Fig. 18, which shows the crude and the true death-rates for England and Wales, Sweden, and France.

It will be seen that in the cases of England and Wales and Sweden the two rates were nearer to one another eighty years ago than they are now. In other words the crude death-rate now gives a less correct measure of conditions than formerly and a much too favourable impression of the present situation. The reason is that the proportion of the population, now in the middle age groups, has become larger and is now high; this has the effect of reducing the number of deaths because it is the young and the old among whom deaths are most frequent. The proportion of children is low because the birth-rate has fallen. The proportion of old persons is also small for two

reasons. The first is that they are the survivors of a population which was about half the size of the present population;

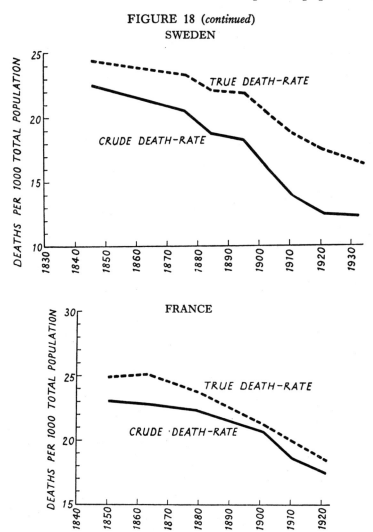

FIGURE 18 (*continued*)
SWEDEN

FRANCE

the second is that mortality among the old was much
higher a few decades ago. In the case of France, however,
the position is the other way about; the rates are closer

together than seventy years ago. The explanation is that in France the birth-rate was falling from the beginning of the nineteenth century. For the same reasons as in the cases of England and Wales and Sweden the crude death-rate fell at one time well below the true death-rate. But from 1840 to 1890 the French birth-rate, though falling slightly, was nearly stable; in consequence the age constitution of the population became more normal, and the crude death-rate was no longer depressed so far below the true death-rate. Recently, however, owing to the fall in the French birth-rate having become sharper, the crude death-rate has diverged again somewhat from the true death-rate. Other European countries resemble England and Wales and Sweden rather than France because their birth-rates only recently began to fall. Thus, in the case of most countries, the farther back we go in time the nearer are the rates, which means that the crude death-rate formerly measured mortality conditions with fair accuracy. In Austria in 1870 and in Italy in 1880, for example, there was no difference between them. The matter is important because we cannot ascertain the true rates for dates more than a century ago. For earlier times we have only the crude rates, but we are justified in supposing that they do not misrepresent the mortality conditions which then prevailed.

The inference to be drawn from the above discussion is that in our search for the causes of the changes in the death-rates we may confine ourselves to changes in health conditions; for in the main it was the latter which governed the former. We may in passing note that evidence concerning the course of the true death-rates, so far as it is available, shows the immense improvement in health conditions which have taken place. Another way of illustrating this progress is to give the mean expectation of life at birth at different dates. In England and Wales it was 39·91 years in 1838–54 and 58·86 years in 1933; in Sweden it was 33·9 years in 1755–75 and 61·91 years in 1926–30; in

Norway it was 45·0 years in 1821–30 and 60·98 years in 1921/2–1930/1. The highest figure is shown in New Zealand, where the expectation of life was 68 years in 1933. The improvement has been rapid and fairly steady, though round about the middle of the last century in Sweden and Denmark, and rather earlier in Norway, there was a check for a time. The true death-rate is now very low and approximately equal in north-west Europe, the United States, and Australasia.

Our aim is to discover why health conditions have improved, why, that is to say, the death-rate has fallen. For the purposes of this discussion the conditions, of which note must be taken, may be classified into four groups, though the boundaries between them are indefinite and though there is much overlapping: (1) political, that is conditions relating to the maintenance of external and internal order; (2) social, including the state of knowledge in relation to the production and use of food, and to the making and use of clothing; (3) sanitary, that is conditions relating to housing, drainage, and water-supply; (4) medical, including both the state of knowledge concerning the prevention and cure of disease and its application to the public at large. Let us review the facts relating to the decline of the death-rate, so far as they are available, for England and Wales in the light of this classification. Since 1838 we can follow the course of the true death-rate; from 1700 up to that date we have only the crude death-rate which gives an indication which, though rough, no doubt represents the general trend of the true rate. The former is shown in Fig. 18 and the latter in Fig. 13.

England had long been free from external aggression; except for the Civil War internal order had been preserved since the Wars of the Roses. Therefore, such changes in the rate as occurred after 1700 were not due to changes in factors falling under the first heading. The course of the rate was thus determined by factors under the other three heads. The rate rose during the first three decades of the eighteenth century. These decades witnessed an unexampled orgy of drunkenness. The control of the sale of beer had become lax towards the end of the seventeenth century; but this was a minor matter compared with the failure to control the sale of spirits, and especially of gin which came into favour at that time. Contemporary accounts abound with descriptions of the degrading scenes which were everywhere enacted. Attempts were made to cope with the evil in 1729 and 1736, but they were ineffective. An Act of 1743 was better designed and the retail distribution of liquor was brought under some control; further improvements were made, among which an Act of 1751 was especially important. This extraordinary episode may be regarded as one in which there was a serious deterioration of conditions falling under (2) which resulted in a rise of the rate through gross abuse of alcohol.

This episode was anomalous in the sense that otherwise there was a slow but continuous improvement during the eighteenth century, not only in conditions falling under (3) and (4), but also in conditions falling under (2) otherwise than in respect to changes in habits of drinking. The adoption of root crops in the place of bare fallow meant more fresh meat during the winter months; the improvement of gardening made vegetables available even to the poor throughout the year. By 1750 scurvy had in consequence become rare. The growing use of cotton garments increased personal cleanliness and reduced the chances of infection. Under (3) we may note the improvement of towns, the paving and cleansing of streets, the substitution of brick for timber in building and the improvement of the water-supply. All these changes were beneficial to health; they were more prominent in some parts of the country than in others, but it is not incorrect to visualize a widespread and steady improvement which resulted in something approaching a revolution when the conditions at the end of the century are compared with those at its beginning.

Improvement under (4) was no less well marked. In order that improvement under this heading should have taken effect, three things were necessary. First, there must have been progress in scientific knowledge, and the eighteenth century abounds with great names in the history of science. In the practical sphere we may notice the introduction of antiseptics and of the practice of segregating infected persons. It is true that the reason for the efficacy of these measures was not understood; but their adoption was the result of the observation that they were efficacious. Secondly, there must have been a profession consisting of practitioners skilled in this new knowledge. This condition was fulfilled by the emergence of the apothecaries, who took to prescribing in addition to compounding medicines, and for whom an adequate system of education was devised during the eighteenth century. In course of time the apothecaries evolved into the 'general practitioners' of the early decades of the next century and were finally incorporated into the medical profession by the Act of 1858. The last condition was made possible by the founding of hospitals and dispensaries. In 1720 there were only two general hospitals in London, whereas in 1764 there were eleven; between 1769 and 1790 thirteen dispensaries were founded in London. Similar progress was made in the provinces at slightly later dates.

There was a rise in the rate about 1780, due apparently to an outbreak of fever. Otherwise the rate decreased until the early decades of the nineteenth century; it then rose somewhat and remained at about the same level for some time. This rise was due to a serious deterioration of conditions under (3). The rapid, unplanned and uncontrolled growth of the industrial towns produced conditions of the most insanitary kind, and though progress continued under (2) and (4), it was more than counterbalanced by the deterioration mentioned. The first step, intended to remedy the state of the towns, was taken in 1835 when the municipal corporations were reformed; there followed a

number of measures dealing with public health, and sanitary conditions were slowly improved. In consequence
the rate began to fall again, and has continued to fall to
the present day.

The course of the death-rate in England and Wales
presents no mystery; though details remain to be illuminated, it is clear that its downward trend was due to the
combined effects of improvements under (2), (3), and (4),
though at certain dates there was a temporary deterioration under one or more of these heads which led to a
check in the fall of the death-rate and even to a rise for
a time. It would further appear that these improvements
may well have been in progress some little time before
1700; if this was so, the death-rate may have been on the
decline when our figures begin. An examination of the
history of the two Scandinavian countries would reveal
a story similar in general outline, that is to say it would
bring to light improvements under the same three heads
which may be held to account for the decline in the death-
rate. The stories would vary in detail from the English
story because the social and economic development of
these countries was very different; but in general there was
a process of improvement in the social, sanitary, and medical factors governing the situation. Improvement of this
kind may well have been in progress in these two countries
before statistics become available, whence we may infer
that the death-rate may have been declining before there
is direct evidence that this was so.

An inquiry into the history of the remaining countries
of north-west Europe would yield similar evidence, though
it would appear that in certain countries, Germany in
particular, improvement was slower. The general result,
however, would be to provide evidence that the death-rate
was declining for the same general reasons as in England.
It is to be inferred, therefore, that the fact that, when
figures become available for these remaining countries,
they follow much the same course as in England and

Wales, Sweden, and Norway, is no mere coincidence, and we may conclude that, broadly speaking, all through this region there was a heavy decline in the death-rate due to similar agencies. Among the countries of south-west Europe we have figures for the death-rate in France from 1800 which show a steady fall; an explanation on similar lines appears to be valid. But for the remaining countries of this region figures are lacking until about 1860, and they show very little fall in the death-rate until 1890 when decline began to be rapid. Indeed, the death-rate was high in these countries in the seventies—higher, for instance, than in north-west Europe in 1800—and the gap between the birth-rate and the death-rate was not large. Improvements under heads (2), (3), and (4) were probably slight before the second half of the last century and were not marked until towards the end of the century. Therefore, whatever may have been the course of the death-rate in these countries before 1860, it is improbable that improvements in the agencies (2), (3), and (4) were tending seriously to decrease it.

When we pass to eastern Europe, whence we have figures for 1800, it is evident that history has not followed the same course as in the countries first examined. The death-rate shows no drop until late in the nineteenth century; this drop must be attributed to the influence of improvements under heads (2), (3), and (4) which began to be felt for the first time after 1870. In this respect the countries of eastern Europe show some resemblance to those of south-west Europe (France excepted), where, as we have just seen, the effect of such improvements seems only to have been felt in relatively recent times. Does this imply that there is no reason for supposing that the death-rate in eastern Europe was no higher before 1800 than in the first half of the nineteenth century? When looking for an answer to this question we may remember that so far we have not attributed any part of the decline in the death-rate in any region to improvements under the first head,

namely, to improvements in internal and external security.
When we examine the history of Russia we find that,
before the accession of Peter the Great in 1689, chaos was
more or less chronic. Thereafter a régime was built up
which, though harsh and crude, at any rate eliminated or
reduced certain important causes of death which formerly
resulted directly or indirectly from lack of internal order
and protection against outward aggression. It is therefore
probable that the death-rate in Russia and other parts of
eastern Europe was reduced during the eighteenth century in this way; then for a century or so it remained at
this level, which, though relatively high, was lower than
formerly, until the factors classed under heads (2), (3),
and (4) came into operation.

This discussion may be summarized as follows. In the
last chapter we found that the growth of population in
three countries of north-west Europe was mostly due to
a fall in the death-rate. In this chapter we have sought the
causes of this fall and have found them in the action of
certain agencies. Since these agencies were also in operation in other countries of north-west Europe and in France
before figures for the death-rate can be given, we may conclude that a fall in the death-rate, brought about by similar
means, was again the main cause of the growth of population. But there is no reason for supposing that in south-
west Europe (excluding France) these agencies were of
great importance before the time when we have figures
for the death-rate, and therefore we cannot suppose that
they had produced any considerable effect upon the death-
rate. The death-rate in this region, however, was not
much below the birth-rate when we first get figures, and
it is possible that these agencies had had some effect, with
the result that the rates had diverged and that the population was increasing though slowly. In the case of east
Europe, these agencies were not in operation before 1800,
the date at which vital statistics begin, or at any rate were
not operating on a scale that could have produced the gap

that then existed. Therefore we can only explain the gap in east Europe by supposing either that the birth-rate had risen or that the death-rate had been reduced by other agencies. We shall find in the next chapter that there is no reason for thinking that the birth-rate had risen significantly; in consequence we are driven to suppose that the death-rate had fallen owing to the operation of other agencies, and the most probable explanation is that it had fallen owing to improvements in security.

When we come to consider non-European peoples we are faced with the difficulty that, even at the present time, vital statistics are scanty and none too trustworthy. We have largely to rely upon indirect evidence in order to decide how far, during periods when population was increasing, the increase was due to a falling death-rate. Let us first take the case of Japan. The evidence is to the effect that population was increasing from 1650 to 1721, was stable from 1721 to about 1850, and then began to increase again. An epoch of internal chaos was brought to an end in 1615, and Japan remained entirely free from civil war until the troubles of 1864; the Tokugawa era was in general a period of peace and prosperity. As in the case of Russia, we may suppose that under such circumstances the death-rate declined. An increase of population followed, and Japan became one of the most densely populated countries in the world. But why did the increase not continue as in Russia, the death-rate at its reduced level running beneath the birth-rate? The explanation is that abortion and infanticide were extensively practised during the eighteenth century in Japan. While these practices may have been inherited from earlier times and may never have died out, they came to be used on a much larger scale during the eighteenth century. Strictly speaking, while infanticide means an increase in the death-rate, abortion means a decline in the birth-rate, and therefore the mention of abortion should be left to the next chapter. But it is so closely akin to infanticide that it may be loosely

G

regarded as a method of increasing the death-rate. So regarded the death-rate may be said to have risen until the gap was closed and the population remained stable for nearly a century and a half. The new era in Japan, marked by the resignation of the Shogun in 1867, saw the gradual abandonment of these practices, with the result that the death-rate sank and the population began to increase once more. When figures become available in 1874 they seem to show a slight increase in the death-rate, but it is possible that this is due to better registration. In any case there is no evidence that improvement under heads (2), (3), and (4) came into operation before the last decade.

For China we possess neither vital statistics nor population figures, but we must infer from indirect evidence that population increased rapidly during the late seventeenth and the eighteenth centuries. The usual assumption is that the population, though fluctuating, was not increasing in the last half of the nineteenth century, and perhaps also in the present century. Our knowledge of conditions in China does not permit us to suppose that, even as yet, factors under (2), (3), and (4) have taken effect, and we are driven back upon the explanation that the increase of numbers in China, as in Japan before 1721, was due to the establishment of a régime which preserved internal order. We know, in fact, that under the Manchu dynasty, which dates from 1644, and especially during the long reign of K'ien-lung (1735–95), order was maintained and that China was exceptionally free from civil war. Once again, therefore, we conclude that the growth of population was due to a decline in the death-rate, which was not, however, due to the same factors which produced the decline in west Europe.

The same conclusion follows from a study of the facts relating to India, Ceylon, Java, and Egypt. The evidence for India points to a large increase of population from the later part of the eighteenth century onwards, that is to say from the time when the British succeeded in pacifying the country and eliminating civil disturbances. So too in Java, where warfare was chronic until the Dutch gained control, the rise of population first became evident after the Dutch occupation had become effective. In Egypt the increase in population dates from the time when Mehemet Ali established his power. In none of these countries is there any evidence that the death-rate has yet been affected by factors under headings (2), (3), and (4). In support of this statement it may be mentioned that, so far as can be ascertained, the expectation of life in India has not increased since about 1890.

At the end of Chapter III mention was made of the fact that in many non-European countries increase of population followed upon contact with Europe. It would appear from the above discussion that the cause of this increase was the reduction of the death-rate owing to the establishment by Europeans of order and security in these countries. It is sometimes supposed that the reason was the introduction by Europeans of sanitation and medicine. But these agencies have hardly begun to affect the lives of non-European peoples. When they do so, their death-rates, which are now, as we shall see later, more or less steady, will decline.

CHAPTER VII

BIRTHS

AT the beginning of the last chapter we entered into some discussion of the crude death-rate, and it will be necessary to make a similar examination of the crude birth-rate. But this may be postponed for the moment; for of the two problems which arise in this chapter the first can be considered without any reference to the complications which an analysis of the birth-rate discloses. This problem relates to the question whether changes in the birth-rate played any part in bringing about the divergence of the birth-rate from the death-rate which caused the expansion of world population.

We may begin with a reference to those non-European peoples who were mentioned in the last chapter. Among the mass of the people in India, China, Egypt, and Java marriage is early and universal, and when marriage has been contracted no steps are taken to limit the size of the family. The same was true until recently of Japan. There is evidence that in the distant past the ancestors of all these peoples limited the size of their families by one means or another; but the habits making for family limitation had long been abandoned before our period opens, and it is clear that we cannot attribute any part of the expansion of population in our period to larger families resulting from the abandonment of such habits and practices. Nor is there any evidence of changes in the other habits or in the situation of these peoples during the seventeenth and eighteenth centuries such as would have caused a large rise in the birth-rate. It is possible that, under conditions of better security and greater well-being, the proportion of live births to conceptions increased; but it is not likely that any rise in the birth-rate so brought about was substantial. Therefore we are driven to conclude that an increase in the birth-rate played no important part in the expansion of these non-European peoples.

Turning to eastern European peoples we find ourselves in the same position as in regard to the non-Europeans just discussed; that is to say we have no direct evidence as to the course of the birth-rate when the expansion of numbers began. Again we discover no indirect evidence suggesting that a marked rise in the birth-rate took place; that is to say there do not seem to have been any changes in habits or circumstances which would have increased the size of the family or the number of families. Once more we conclude that the expansion of population was not due to a rise in the birth-rate. But in England, Sweden, and Norway there is some statistical evidence of a rise in the birth-rate; taken by itself it is not decisive, and we must inquire whether the indirect evidence points to such a rise. To begin with, let us remember that, unlike the position in the European and non-European countries just mentioned, marriage was not universal and was often postponed for a time, especially among the poorer part of the population. Rubin has provided some evidence from Denmark that in the late seventeenth and eighteenth centuries the poorer section of the population began to marry at an earlier age. There is reason to suppose that in several western European countries similar changes took place. In England, for example, under the apprenticeship system a man could not marry until he came oₗ of his time. But during the earlier part of our period the apprenticeship system began to break down, and, more important still, new trades grew up which were not subject to the system. Therefore we may well suppose that people came to marry earlier. In short, so far as certain countries of western Europe are concerned, it is probable that the birth-rate rose somewhat during the first decades of our period. But there is no reason to believe that the rise was large; while in the other countries considered, the expansion of population seems to have been almost wholly due to a decline in the death-rate, in this part of Europe a rise in the birth-rate may have been a contributory factor.

The second problem, to which reference was made in the
first paragraph of this chapter, relates to the decline of the
birth-rate within the sphere of European civilization in relatively recent times. There is no doubt that the decline has
been of the utmost importance in this region; in north-west
Europe it has gone so far that, in spite of a continuing fall
in the death-rate, population will soon cease to increase.
But before we can profitably inquire into the causes of this
decline, we must make some study of the birth-rate.

The crude birth-rate is obtained by referring the births
which occur in any year to the total population and expressing the result per 1,000 of the population. Let us now
observe the conditions under which the rate can change.
(1) Births can only occur among the female part of the
population and only among that section of this part between
the ages of 15 and 50. It follows that, other things remaining the same, if the proportion changes which women of
child-bearing age make of the whole population, the birth-
rate will change. Thus if women of child-bearing age
formed 10 per cent. of the population at one date and came
to form 20 per cent. at a later date, the birth-rate would be
doubled, other things remaining the same. For the sake
of simplicity it may be said at once that in Europe changes
in the proportion which women of child-bearing age form
of the population have played little part in reducing the
birth-rate. Indeed, such changes of this kind as have
occurred in Europe have mostly tended to increase and
not to diminish the birth-rate; thus in England and Wales
the proportion has increased from 25·47 per cent. in 1871
to 28·01 per cent. in 1931. (2) It is well known that when
women approach the end of the child-bearing period they
become less fertile. Therefore, if there is a change in the
age distribution of women within the child-bearing ages,
the birth-rate will be affected. If, for example, the change
is of such a nature that relatively more women of child-
bearing age are found in the age group 35 to 45 than
before, the birth-rate will fall. (3) If we know how many

legitimate children are born in a given year to married women of given age, say 30, we can calculate the chance that a married woman of that age will bear a child within a year. Similarly, we can calculate the chance that an unmarried woman of given age will bear a child within a year if we know the number of women of that age and the number of illegitimate children born to them. In this way we obtain for each year of age within the child-bearing period the chance that a married woman, and also the chance that an unmarried woman, will bear a child within a year. These may be called the specific legitimate and the specific illegitimate fertility rates respectively. But these rates do not remain unchanged. If, for example, women begin to employ birth control, or if they employ it more often or more effectively, the rates will decline, and the birth-rate will fall. (4) Finally, it is obvious that if the proportion of those who remain unmarried changes, the birth-rate will be affected; if, for instance, the proportion increases it implies that relatively more persons are passing their lives subject only to the relatively low illegitimate fertility rate, and this means that the birth-rate will decline. Similarly, for the same reason a change in the average age at marriage will affect the birth-rate; if the age rises, it means that some persons are spending more of their lives subject only to the lower rate.

At this point it is of importance to define the meaning of the specific fertility rate—a term that will be used in later chapters. It is obtained by referring all births, legitimate and illegitimate, which occur among women of a given age, to all women, married and unmarried, of that age. It follows that the specific fertility rate may change either for reasons under heading (3) or for reasons under heading (4). It may also be observed that changes in age at marriage which come under heading (4) will affect the age constitution of married women (heading (2)); but the latter is also affected by changes in the age constitution of all women.

It may be noted that, so far as there was a rise in the birth-rate in certain countries in western Europe in the first half of the eighteenth century, it was apparently due to changes under heading (4). Our task is now to discuss why the birth-rate has fallen in the last century within the sphere of European civilization. The fall was in progress in three countries before 1870, namely, the United States, France, and Ireland, and we may examine them first.

Let us begin with the United States. The calculations of Thompson and Whelpton, illustrated in Fig. 15, show a decline in the birth-rate from 55·0 per 1,000 in 1800 to 20·1 per 1,000 in 1930. We have said that in Europe the fall was not due to any fall in the proportion of women of child-bearing age, and the same is true of the United States. In fact the proportion increased from 20·0 per cent. in 1800 to 23·6 per cent. in 1930. Therefore the changes in this proportion which occurred tended to increase the birth-rate, but were counteracted by other agencies. What were they? It is very probable that there was more marriage, and that those who married did so sooner, in the earlier than in the later decades of the century. There are no figures to show the percentage of persons married before 1890, but since the amount of marriage was in general higher among the rural than the urban population, and since urbanization proceeded rapidly during the century, it is likely that the amount of marriage declined considerably. There are other indications that up to 1890 the amount of marriage was declining; this seems to follow from the increase in the proportion of single persons in the higher age groups which is shown in the census of 1890. Since 1890 the tide has turned the other way towards more and earlier marriages; but up to 1890 changes in marriage habits tended to reduce the birth-rate. We must next examine the changes in specific fertility. No figures are available before 1920, when we get information relating to the fertility of women of child-bearing age by five-year periods. Between 1920 and 1929 specific fertility dropped 5·2 per cent. for the age group 15–19, 17·0 per cent. for the age group 20–4, 20·0 per cent. for the age group 25–9, and still more for the higher age groups. These figures are for all women, married and unmarried, but since the amount of marriage was increasing between 1890 and 1930, the declines would be greater if calculated for married women. Since the average age at marriage was declining since 1890, two factors, namely, amount of marriage and age at marriage, were tending to increase the birth-rate; the birth-rate, however, fell sharply, and this can only be attributed to the heavy decline in the specific fertility of married women. We do not know when the decline in the specific fertility of married women began, but since it was marked in 1890 it must have been in progress for some years previously. It may be that it was in operation from 1800, though this is improbable for reasons to be mentioned in a later chapter; it is more likely that the fall began after the middle of the last century, that before that date the decline in the birth-rate was entirely due to fewer and later marriages, and that after the middle of the century up to 1890 a fall in specific legitimate fertility began to combine with the tendency to fewer and later marriages to reduce the birth-rate. After 1890, as we have said, the fall continued and was the sole cause of the decline in the birth-rate, since marriages became earlier and more numerous.

Apart from the United States France is the only country which shows a fall in the birth-rate since the beginning of the last century. So far back as figures are available there seems to have been little change in the amount of marriage or in the age at marriage in France. It is true that since 1880 there has been a fall in the proportion of women over the age of 15 who were married; but it is slight. Since 1876 the average age of women marrying for the first time has remained almost unchanged. On the other hand, specific fertility is known to have been on the decline since 1892, and, since changes in amount of and age at marriage have

been insignificant since that date, we must conclude that
the decline in the birth-rate has been mainly due to a
decline in specific legitimate fertility. So far as the earlier
part of the last century is concerned there are no reasons
for supposing, as in the case of the United States, that
changes in the amount of or age at marriage occurred

FIGURE 19

Birth-rates and Death-rates in France and Ireland

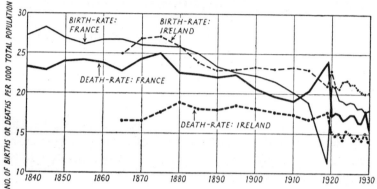

which could have accounted for more than a small part of
the decline in the birth-rate, and we are driven to conclude
that ever since 1800 specific legitimate fertility has been
declining in France, and that during the last fifty years at
least it has been the only important factor in the reduction
of the French birth-rate.

Ireland resembles France in that the birth-rate began
to fall earlier than in the countries with which it is geographically associated. Otherwise, as will appear, the contrast with France is striking. The birth-rate was 26·2 per
1,000 in 1871–81, and 21·1 per 1,000 in 1911–26; it is not
known for earlier dates, but it is probable that it was
nearer 40 than 30 per 1,000 before 1850, and that it began
to fall about that time. So far, we have found a decline in
specific legitimate fertility to be the chief element in the
fall of the birth-rate. But, as shown in Fig. 20, in the

Irish Free State there is no sign of any such decline. The
number of children under 5 years of age per 100 married
women under 45 years of age was 130 in 1861, never fell
subsequently below 130, and was 131 in 1926.

FIGURE 20

*Number of Children under 5 per 100 Married Women under
45 years of age in the Irish Free State and England and
Wales: 1861 to 1927*

Year	1861	1871	1881	1891	1901	1911	1926	1927
Irish Free State .	130	137	134	133	132	135	131	..
England and Wales .	116	118	120	110	98	90	..	71

FIGURE 21

Unmarried Women in the Irish Free State: 1841 to 1926

Year	Unmarried females as a percentage of all females in the same age-group	
	Aged 25 to 35	Aged 35 to 45
1841	28	15
61	39	18
71	38	20
81	41	19
91	48	23
1901	53	28
11	55	31
26	53	29

Therefore in this case we must look to other elements
in the situation for an explanation. In contrast to what
has happened in most European countries the percentage
of women of child-bearing age in Ireland has declined
from 23·4 in 1861 to 21·1 in 1926, and this has tended to
diminish the birth-rate. But the important changes are in
age at and amount of marriage. The average age at marriage for women has risen and is high; it was 29·1 years in
the Irish Free State, as against 26·6 years in England and
Wales, in 1926. Still more remarkable is the decline in

the amount of marriage. As Fig. 21 shows, the percentage
of females aged 25 to 35 who were unmarried in 1841 was
28; in 1926 it was 53. The percentage unmarried is now
far higher than in any other country in Europe; in 1926
the percentage of females aged 25 to 30 who were not
married was 62 in the Irish Free State, 41 in England and
Wales, and 23 in the United States. It further emerges
from Fig. 21 that the percentage unmarried rose rapidly
in the earlier decades, but has remained fairly stable in
later decades. There is, in fact, a correspondence between
the rapid fall in the birth-rate in the earlier decades and
the swift rise in the proportion unmarried, and between
the relatively stable birth-rate in the later decades (1891–
1901, 22·1 per 1,000; 1901–11, 22·4 per 1,000; 1911–26,
21·1 per 1,000) and the fairly constant proportion of
females unmarried. This is not a coincidence; less and
later marriage is the chief cause of the fall in the Irish
birth-rate. When the Irish marry they have as many
children as formerly; and that is the same as saying that
specific legitimate fertility has remained unchanged.

The remaining countries are alike in that the fall in the
birth-rate did not begin until after 1875. The birth-rate
began to fall in England and Wales in 1876 and has fallen
ever since. As a rule it is not possible to give an exact date
for the beginning of the decline, because in most countries
the rate fluctuated for a time, falling for a year or two and
then rising again for a short period. It is enough to say
that a definitive fall in the rate had begun in all the remaining countries of north-west Europe before 1900.

Let us take this country first. Since we do not record
the age of the mother at the birth of a child we cannot
obtain figures for specific fertility. The Registrar-General,
however, has estimated the age distribution of children by
age of mother for one year, namely 1921, but we do not
possess any series of such figures showing the trend of
specific fertility. Nevertheless, we can carry the analysis
of the decline of the English birth-rate to a fairly definite

conclusion in the following way. As we have already noticed, the proportion of women of child-bearing age to the total population has risen in England, and therefore, so far as this factor has operated, it has tended slightly to increase the birth-rate. The age distribution of married women of child-bearing age has altered in such fashion that the proportion aged 35 to 45 is much higher than before the birth-rate began to fall; it was 35·7 per cent. in 1871 and 45·2 per cent. in 1931. At the same time the proportion aged 20 to 24 has fallen; it was 13·4 per cent. in 1871 and is now 9·3 per cent. Changes of this kind have therefore continuously operated so as to reduce the birth-rate. We come next to the age at marriage; this rose until 1920, since when it has tended to fall; for spinsters it was 25·14 years in 1890–1900, 25·81 years in 1916–20, and 25·48 years in 1932. Amount of marriage is not easy to measure, but the proportion for a series of years of unmarried men aged 45 to 54 per 1,000 men aged 45 to 54 gives some indication of the course of events; it was 413 in 1871, rose to 675 in 1921, and fell to 625 in 1931. That amount of marriage should decline when age at marriage rises, and vice versa, is precisely what we should expect, because the more marriage is postponed the greater is the number of persons likely never to marry at all. It is evident that up to 1920 the effect of changes in the amount of marriage and in age at marriage was to decrease the birth-rate, but that since 1920 they have tended to increase it. Since the birth-rate has declined considerably since 1920 we are led to suppose that in this case all, and in previous decades much, of the decline in the English birth-rate must have been due to a decline in specific legitimate fertility.

This conclusion is confirmed by a study of Fig. 22, provided by the Registrar-General, which gives in the second column the general legitimate fertility rate. This is obtained by referring all legitimate births to married women aged 15 to 45. Illegitimate births can be left out of account;

the illegitimate birth-rate has always been relatively low in England and has tended downwards in much the same way as the legitimate rate. We may therefore concentrate our attention on the general legitimate fertility rate; it has

FIGURE 22

Fertility in England and Wales: 1870 to 1933

Period or year	Births per 1,000 married women aged 15 to 45	Ratio to 1931 (1931 = 1,000)	Ratio of actual births to those which would have occurred if the age constitution had been as in 1931
1870–2	292·5	2,380	2,148
1880–2	286·0	2,327	2,117
1890–2	263·8	2,146	1,983
1900–2	235·5	1,916	1,797
1910–12	197·4	1,606	1,592
1920–2	178·9	1,456	1,460
1930–2	122·4	996	999
1931	122·7	1,000	1,000
1932	118·0	962	964
1933	110·4	900	905

fallen from 292·5 in 1871 to 110·4 in 1933. Two things alone can have brought this about, a change in the age distribution of married women and a decline in specific legitimate fertility. We have already seen that the age distribution of married women has altered so as to reduce the rate, and the question is how much of the fall in the rate is to be attributed to this factor and how much to a decline in specific legitimate fertility. The answer to this question is given in the fourth column. This column shows the ratio of actual births to those which would have occurred if the age constitution had been as in 1931. In other words, since in this column the effect of changes in age constitution are eliminated, the figures show how much of the decline is due to lower specific legitimate fertility. It will be seen that by far the greater part of the decline between 1871 and 1921 was due to this agency and that since 1921 the whole of the decline was so due. As in the case of

France since 1800, and as in ᴧne case of the United States from some way back into the last century, the only important cause of the decline in the English birth-rate turns out to be a decline in specific legitimate fertility.

It would be wearisome, and it is quite unnecessary, to analyse the decline of the birth-rate in other countries of European civilization. In every country for which figures are available it appears that the decline has coincided with a fall in specific fertility. The changes in age at marriage and in amount of marriage have varied in direction and in importance, but it is only in the new countries, and then only for short periods, that they have been of any significance. In many European countries, in Sweden and Denmark for example, age at marriage has fallen during the whole period of the decline in the birth-rate, and this has tended to check the decline. Indeed, it is somewhat exceptional to find, as we did in the case of England, that changes in amount and age of marriage have tended, even for a time, to reduce the birth-rate; that is to say in most European countries the decline in specific legitimate fertility has been of even greater importance in accounting for what has happened than in this country.

The conclusion is unescapable. Within the sphere of European civilization, Ireland alone excepted, the only important cause of the decline of the birth-rate is that married women of given age are far less likely to bear a child within a year than formerly.

CHAPTER VIII

THE DECLINE IN FERTILITY

THE next step is obviously to inquire why a married woman of given age within the sphere of European civilization is now so much less likely to bear a child during a year than formerly. There are many possible causes and many ways of classifying them. We classify them here into those which fall under the head of birth-control and those which do not. The term birth-control does not seem to have been used before 1914 and is still loosely employed. It is used here to include practices designed to prevent the birth of a child; these practices are abortion, contraception, and abstention from intercourse. These terms require no explanation. But caution is required; for we must not assume that attempts to control births, by abstaining from intercourse except during the 'safe period' for example, are effective. Evidence that people have tried to control births is not evidence that they have succeeded, and therefore evidence that birth-control practices are common is not evidence that birth-control is a cause of the decline in fertility. We must, therefore, first look into the effectiveness of birth-control methods.

Birth-control methods may be effective in that they achieve their immediate object; they may be additionally effective if they render further births impossible. It is clear that abstention from intercourse does not render future conceptions impossible when intercourse is resumed. As regards abortion and contraception it is possible that certain ways of procuring abortion and the use of particular substances as contraceptives may be injurious either to general health or to particular organs or tissues, and that in consequence future births may be made unlikely or impossible. But in general it is clear that the procuring of abortion and prevention of conception as now usually practised do not have this effect. The question is therefore how far the means usually employed to control births are immediately effective.

Complete abstention from intercourse is of course completely effective. The problem is whether a reduction in the frequency of intercourse has any effect. Intercourse may be reduced equally over the whole menstrual cycle, or it may be unequally reduced in such manner that it is limited to the 'safe period'. In either case the results will depend upon the facts relating to the physiology of reproduction. Unfortunately this is a very obscure subject. The relevant facts, so far as they are known, may be summarized as follows. It is unlikely that human spermatozoa remain alive in the body of the female for more than twenty-four hours; the average duration of life after liberation is perhaps twenty hours. The average duration of life of the unfertilized ovum is probably still shorter. It follows from this that the chance that conception will take place is reduced with diminished frequency of intercourse. It would further appear that, while ovulation may take place at any time in the cycle, it most often occurs between the seventh and the thirteenth day. It follows from this that there is no 'safe period', but that, if intercourse does not take place during this portion of the cycle, the chance of conception will be lowered.

About abortion there is nothing to be said; it is obvious when the methods used to procure it are effective. The effectiveness of contraceptive methods, however, is not so clear. The perfect contraceptive has not been invented. Existing contraceptives are imperfect in two ways. Their use demands more or less care, and even when care is taken there may easily be accidents; secondly, in many cases, when care is taken and no accident happens, success is not always assured. It is quite impossible to give any estimate of the average degree of effectiveness; but there has recently been a tendency to rate the effectiveness of the methods now most practised lower than in all probability represents the true state of the case. This is a reaction

H

against the naïve conclusion that, because contraceptives are employed, they must account for the reduction in fertility. While due allowance must be made for existing imperfections, this does not mean that present practices have not a large measure of success.

The next problem relates to the use made of birth-control methods. If their employment explains in whole or in large part the decline in fertility, their use must have rapidly increased and must now be very extensive. There is no reason to believe that the frequency of intercourse in general has been deliberately reduced, or that there is any widespread restriction to the 'safe period'. Indeed, there seems to have been more interest in the 'safe period' some two or three decades ago than now. There is abundant evidence tending to show that the practice of abortion is very extensive. Its frequency apparently varies much from country to country; it is apparently much lower in England than in Germany. From the nature of the case it is difficult or impossible to give figures, but Burgdörfer has provided data which go to show that abortions were more frequent than births in Berlin in 1929 in the ratio of 103 to 100. Since exact information is lacking for modern times, we cannot say with certainty whether abortion has increased. But if abortion is anything like as frequent in Germany as the above data suggest, it cannot have been equally extensively practised thirty years ago, when the birth-rate was twice as large. The opinion of those most closely in touch with the situation, such as doctors, seems to be that there has been in Germany and some other European countries a considerable, and perhaps a large, increase in this practice. As regards England, where abortion is apparently less frequent, informed opinion is that there has been no very large growth of the practice.

Again, and for obvious reasons, our knowledge of the extent of contraceptive practices is scanty. There have been various small scale inquiries the results of which are mostly subject to the criticism that the persons, among whom the inquiries were made, were already interested in birth-control. An investigation on a relatively large scale, which is free from this criticism, has been made by Dr. Raymond Pearl in the United States. The inquiry related to about 5,000 married women who were divided into four groups on the basis of income. The percentage of white women practising contraception rose from 32·7 in the poorest class to 78·3 in the richest class. It was also ascertained that about half the women had only experienced wanted pregnancies and in this sense had practised contraception successfully, that about a third were unsuccessful because they did not know of effective methods, and that about a sixth were unsuccessful owing to unskilful use of methods. When evidence of this kind is considered along with what is known about the sale of contraceptives and of literature about contraception, there is little doubt concerning the very extensive use of contraceptive methods at the present time within the sphere of European civilization.

Regarding the extent of the use of contraceptives in the past we have only the indirect evidence afforded by literature and propaganda. In 1822 Francis Place published *Illustrations and Proofs of the Principle of Population*, in which he advocated contraception. From 1823 to 1826 there was an active campaign, conducted by Place and his friends, intended to reach the poorer classes; handbills were distributed which advocated coitus interruptus and the use of a sponge. The earliest handbill stated that the methods described 'have long been practised in several parts of the continent'; it seems to have been well known that such practices were firmly established in France. In 1832 Knowlton published a book on the subject in America where it made little impression; but an English edition was printed as a sixpenny pamphlet two years later, and this helped to keep the propaganda alive after Place's campaign had subsided. The English edition was regularly advertised in free-thought journals, and over 40,000 copies were sold by 1876. During the sixties the Malthusian League was founded. Then in 1876 came the Bradlaugh-Besant trial as the result of the republication of Knowlton's book for the sale of which a Bristol bookseller had been imprisoned. The trial was an advertisement for the book, of which some 200,000 copies were sold between 1876 and 1881. Meanwhile, in America Robert Dale Owen, who had arrived there in 1825 ignorant of the propaganda in England, became acquainted with literature on the subject and published his *Moral Physiology* in 1830, which went through nine editions in five years. Thereafter, propaganda in England and America has never ceased. Between 1879 and 1881 175,000 copies of Besant's *Law of Population* were sold in a sixpenny edition, and Allbutt's *Wife's Handbook*, first published immediately after the trial, ultimately sold half a million copies. It has been estimated that between 1879 and 1891 one to two million, and between 1918 and 1927 six to eight million books and tracts were sold giving contraceptive information.

It would seem that there was no organized propaganda in France until 1896, when the Ligue de la Régénération Humaine was founded. But it was chiefly from France that knowledge of contraceptive methods came to England in the twenties of the last century, and small families met with public approval in France before the middle of that century, as will appear in a later chapter. It is not necessary to describe the propaganda in other European countries; it is sufficient to say that it became active towards the end of the last century in western Europe and later in other parts. To show that contraception has been advocated is, of course, not to prove that the advice has been followed. There is no way of discovering the extent of the use of contraceptives in past times; information regarding the sale of contraceptives is, for instance, unobtainable. But there is no reason whatever to doubt that, as a result of all this publicity and propaganda, contraceptives were increasingly used. One other point of some importance may be added when speaking of the history of contraception. We have said that there is, even now, no perfect contraceptive. Improved methods have been introduced from time to time, but no dramatic discovery has ever been made. There is therefore no date after which birth prevention became definitely more easy.

Thus far we have been discussing practices, coming under the head of birth-control, which may have been responsible for the reduction in fertility. To fall under this head a practice must consciously aim at the prevention of birth. No one would employ abortion or contraception who did not want to prevent a birth, but a reduction in the frequency of intercourse might or might not be inspired by this end. We found no reason to suppose that intercourse has been reduced with this aim, but this does not shut out the possibility that it has been reduced. It has been suggested that the increased opportunities for enjoyment, which have been shared by all classes, may have been accompanied by a reduction in the frequency of intercourse. The suggestion cannot be dismissed, though the remarkable improvement in health and vigour, which has been also shared by all classes, might be thought to tell the other way. It has also been pointed out that the discovery that soap, even in very dilute solution, is a powerful spermacide may be significant. For the use of soap has greatly increased during the period in which the birth-rate has fallen. On the other hand, it has not been proved that, during the process of washing, soap is ever left in sufficient quantity and so situated as to act as a contraceptive.

It should not be assumed that the few practices, other than birth-control practices, which have been suggested as possible causes of reduced fertility, are the only alternatives to birth-control which can explain the decline in fertility. It was said above that our ignorance of human reproductive physiology is profound, and it may very well be that the chance that conception will follow intercourse has been reduced by one or more of the innumerable changes in mode of life which have come about in the last few decades. This possibility must be held firmly in mind. It remains true, nevertheless, that birth-control practices are the only practices of which it can be said at present that they are known both to reduce fertility and to have been increasingly employed during the period in which the birth-rate has declined.

The next step is to ask whether birth-control offers an adequate explanation of what has happened. If it does not, we must conclude that other important factors, perhaps undiscovered as yet, have also been in operation. If it does, we are not justified in concluding that no other factor can have played any part; for other agencies may have contributed.

The most promising mode of procedure is to examine some of the more remarkable features of the decline of the birth-rate and then to ask whether they can be attributed to birth-control. (1) There is a correspondence between the date when birth-control propaganda became intensive and the date when the birth-rate began to decline in most countries. It is reasonable to assume that birth-control practices were stimulated by the consumption of birth-control literature. (2) In almost every country the decline began in the upper economic class and spread downwards in such fashion that there has come into being a marked negative correlation between social status and fertility. This is compatible with the spread of contraception if it is supposed that the better-off people first acquired these new practices. It is in general true that fashions spread downwards; moreover, contraceptive appliances are costly, and therefore not easily accessible to the poor. This explanation finds support in Pearl's investigation quoted above, in which he showed that in his sample contraceptive methods were most employed among the rich and least among the poor. He also showed that women of all classes, who did not use birth-control, had about the same number of pregnancies. It has been objected that birth-control propaganda has been directed more to the poor than to the rich; but we may remember that the same is true of educational propaganda and that the poor have not become better educated. It is also held by some that the low fertility of the upper classes is due to a concentration of sterile or relatively sterile persons in those classes. Apart from the fact that this theory finds no support in Pearl's data and that there are other difficulties inherent in it, what we have to explain is not merely the low fertility of the upper class but also the decreased fertility of all classes. (3) In a general way differences in economic class are related to differences in occupations, and the association between manual work and high fertility is merely another instance of the relation between economic status and fertility. But a study of occupational groups brings some curious anomalies to light. For example, textile workers in England have a lower fertility than the class to which they belong. This low fertility can be understood on the hypothesis that it is due to birth-control because, since the proportion of married women among textile workers is relatively high, there is a special reason for keeping the size of family low. (4) In most countries, America and Germany for example, there are very large differences between the fertility of the urban and rural populations. The position in England is peculiar in that this difference hardly exists; but in England the rural population is largely suburbanized. Elsewhere the rural population is more or less isolated and has less opportunity of acquiring birth-control information; moreover, where farms are owned by their occupiers a large family provides a cheap supply of labour. (5) There is an association between religious faith and fertility. Where, as in Holland and Canada, Catholics and Protestants can be compared, the birth-rate is much higher among the former than the latter. Catholics are enjoined not to employ birth-control. It is true that in the Catholic

countries of France and Austria the birth-rate is low; but
France, though nominally Catholic, has long been a centre
of agnosticism, and in Austria fertility is much higher in
the country districts, where Catholicism is powerful, than
in Vienna, where the mass of the population is either in-
different or hostile to Catholicism. It has been objected
that in those American states where there are most Catholics the birth-rate is not higher than elsewhere. But in
America fertility is much lower in the towns than in the
country, and Catholics in the United States are mostly
town dwellers; this would tend to mask any superior
fertility among them apart from the fact that the powerful
American birth-control movement has probably weakened
the obedience of Catholics to their Church in this matter.
It has also been objected that the fertility of Jews is notably
low and that Jews, like Catholics, are forbidden to employ
contraception. But while Jewish fertility is low, it appears
to be a mistake to suppose that Jewish teaching is against
contraception. The authoritative account of Jewish teaching in this matter given by Lauterbach is that, when 'a man
has fulfilled the duty of propagation of the race, as when
he has already two children, he is no longer obliged to
beget children, and the law does not forbid him to have
intercourse with his wife even in a manner which does not
result in conception. In such a case the woman certainly
is allowed to use any kind of contraceptive or preventive.'

All these peculiar features of the decline in the birth-
rate are compatible with the view that birth-control is the
cause. There are additional facts which hardly permit of
any other explanation. Methorst has investigated 21,307
families which were founded in Holland between 1907 and
1911. He discovered that, when no child had died, there
was less than twelve months interval between the birth of
children in only 1·4 per cent. of the cases, but that when
a child had died, another birth took place within twelve
months in no less than 19·7 per cent. The only possible
explanation is that, when a child has died, the parents seek

to replace it and abandon the employment of birth-control for a time. Again, working on English data collected in 1911, Stevenson showed that, whereas in general the fertility of young wives sank from the age of 20 onwards, the fertility of young wives of the professional class rose until they were over 25. Owing to the late age at which professional men begin to earn a living, there are strong motives for using birth-control among very young professional couples when first married; that they do so is the only possible explanation of this curious anomaly. On the other hand, there are no facts connected with the decline in the birth-rate which are inexplicable on the birth-control hypothesis. If the proportion of involuntary sterile marriages had increased, we should have to look to some explanation other than birth-control. The indications are, however, that the proportion has remained unchanged.

So far as we have taken the matter, birth-control can be held to explain sufficiently the facts of the decline of the birth-rate within the sphere of European civilization. Since birth-control methods are known to be effective, to have been increasingly used, and to be employed at the present time on a very wide scale, there is no doubt whatever that their use explains the decline in large part. It may be the whole explanation. But it is possible that other factors, not being practices or habits adopted with the object of reducing the birth-rate, may have been at work. It is possible, for instance, that there may have been some reduction in the frequency of intercourse, and it is possible that unsuspected agencies may have been in operation. However this may be, it would not seem likely that such factors can have been of serious importance. But this discussion does not exhaust the matter; decline in fertility by means of birth-control implies that people have deliberately set a limit to the size of their families. It remains to explain why they have come to desire smaller families.

CHAPTER IX

THE SMALL FAMILY SYSTEM

THERE is abundant evidence that there existed among primitive races what may fairly be called a small family system; that is to say certain customs were extensively and regularly practised which, whether by limiting conceptions through restrictions upon intercourse or by destroying the products of conception by abortion or infanticide, kept the number of living children small. This system, if it may be so called, broke down in Europe and the Near East with the rise of the early civilizations. When at a later date Christianity came to shape the mode of life, large families were encouraged; for on the one hand marriage, though not the most perfect state, was commended for the average man, while on the other hand all practices tending to keep the family small were prohibited. Thus in Europe, when our period begins some three hundred years ago, a situation prevailed which had ruled for many centuries. Under it most people married and married young, while the number of children was dictated by 'nature' alone.

When the situation is examined we find that there was every inducement to marry; only through marriage were companionship, the comfort of a home, and an assured place in the social structure to be attained. But children were the unescapable consequence of marriage. No thought was given to the size of family; size of family settled itself. As things worked out surviving children did little more than replace the previous generation. There were periods when deaths exceeded births and population declined; there were more frequent periods when the opposite condition prevailed. This latter condition dominated in many countries in Europe from the eleventh to the mid-fourteenth centuries, and there was a marked increase in the population of the Continent during that

period. There followed a time when the population of
Europe, though it no doubt underwent considerable
fluctuations in certain countries, apparently remained
fairly stable. Our period begins at about the time when
this stability was brought to an end by a decrease in the
death-rate. Since there was no corresponding decrease
in the birth-rate, which, as we have seen, increased if it
changed at all, the population increased. Thus during the
first part of our period, though important changes took
place in the death-rate, the old conditions prevailed in
respect of size of family.

We may speak of a large family epoch but hardly of
a large family system. The large family was a consequence
of the beliefs, standards, and habits of the time; it was
accepted rather than designed, and it did not lead to any
threatening increase of population which might have
called for some revision of habits and practices. But it
was accepted with resignation as a part of human fate, like
growing old. It was the hard lot of the woman just as
working and fighting were the hard lot of the man. 'The
family is rarely a large one,' remarked J. S. Mill, 'by the
woman's desire, because upon her weighs, besides all
physical suffering and a full share in all privations, the
unbearable domestic toil which grows from a large number of children.' There must always have been among
women a latent desire to be delivered from this burden.
What obstacles stood in her way? Abortion and infanticide were forbidden. We know little about the kind of
contraceptive knowledge available before the nineteenth
century, but we can be certain that there was no widespread acquaintance with such knowledge as existed. It is
probable, however, that it was not so much the absence of
knowledge as the presence of moral sentiments, opposed
to the discussion and even more to the employment of
contraceptives, which kept women in bondage to the large
family.

At the end of the eighteenth century came the French

Revolution, which introduced fundamental and enduring changes in the social and economic structure of France and in the mentality of her people. Feudalism vanished, and its place was taken by peasant proprietorship. The individual became free to secure a situation for himself and was encouraged to do so. But this did not lead to a worship of the self-made man, who has never been a hero in France, but to the desire for social and economic security such as could be attained by taking thought. The peasant aimed at a holding sufficient for himself and his family; the bourgeois wanted a place. It was not that social advancement was out of the picture; quite the contrary, but it was advancement with security and by slow stages. The desire for security from outward aggression, and for internal security with respect to money, have always been prominent. The experience of the 'assignats' went deep down into the consciousness of the people, and we have seen the attitude of the French towards the crisis of the franc and the gold question in our own day.

In addition the Revolution initiated the decline of religious belief which made France the centre of European atheism and agnosticism, and this weakened previously existing moral sentiments. Since contraceptive knowledge was certainly available in France early in the last century, it is not surprising that a beginning should have been made with its use on a wide scale at that time. The logical, realistic, and unsentimental attitude of the people, becoming free from inhibitions about birth-control, made family limitation seem a reasonable and even a necessary practice if the growing desire for individual advancement with security was to be achieved. The provisions of the 'code civil', limiting the freedom of testamentary disposition, tended in the same direction. Varying with the number of his children, a man can only dispose freely of from one-quarter to one-third of his estate. Therefore the financial security of the family, especially the family of the peasant, is threatened if there are numerous children. Thus there grew up in France a movement in favour of the limited family; more than that, the large family became thought of as the mark of bad citizenship. In the department of Allier in 1838, and in the department of Somme in 1842, the prefects advised their officials to limit the size of their families; in 1852 the *conseil municipal* of Versailles created a *prix de tempérance*, and laid down that among the desirable characteristics, which should be taken into account, was the *nombre modéré* of children; in 1851 the Académie française gave a prize for an essay which developed the theme that a county was fortunate when *la sagesse publique et privée* united to prevent a rapid growth of population.

The French Revolution, in spite of all its conquests, left little impression upon the countries which, for a time, were subject to French rule. The result of French aggression was rather to raise a prejudice against all things French. The influence of the Churches was enhanced for a time, and democratic tendencies suppressed. Industrial evolution and the consequential changes in Great Britain did nothing to raise up the ideal of an independence achieved by care in the mind of the mass of the wage earners. Until after the middle of the century nothing occurred which turned thought towards the limitation of the family. The English birth-control propaganda of the twenties, while it may have sown a seed, found the ground too unprepared for any immediate harvest; contrary sentiments were strong and well entrenched, and there was nothing in the practical aims of the day which called them seriously in question. But the knowledge of contraception was there ready for application, and the desire for liberation from the trammels of a large family was present. Queen Victoria, writing to the king of the Belgians in 1841, said: 'I think, dearest Uncle, you cannot *really* wish me to be the "Maman d'une nombreuse famille", for I think you will see with me the great inconvenience a *large* family would be to us all, and particularly to the country, independent of the hardship and inconvenience to myself;

men never think, at least seldom think, what a hard task it is for us women to go through this *very often*.' The great esteem in which the Queen was held by her people was due to the fact that she shared in so many ways the views of her subjects. And in respect of size of family she was no exception.

J. S. Mill, in the passage quoted above, goes on to speak of 'women who to-day would never dare to make such a demand [i.e. for family limitation], but who would do so if they were supported by the moral sentiment of society'. During the last half of the nineteenth century moral sentiments underwent profound changes. There was no dramatic event to which we can trace the impulse to change, but it is now apparent that the sixties of the last century witnessed the end of an epoch, and that thereafter the tone and texture of social life were different. It would be possible, but it would take too long, to attempt to illustrate this statement. What is relevant here is that a change of attitude towards contraception at this time need cause no surprise. The sentiment against family limitation, which had apparently already weakened among the upper classes, ceased to maintain its original strength during the seventies among the people at large. Sentiment, therefore, no longer shut contraception wholly out of the mind, and the advertisement given to the matter by the Bradlaugh-Besant trial reached a public which was not indisposed to listen with sympathetic interest. There were other happenings which, given willingness to listen, made men definitely disposed to consider the matter. Legislation, especially the Education Act of 1870, had reduced the earning capacity of children, and the economic depression, which set in about 1874, reduced real incomes. A large family thus ceased to be financially advantageous, and the pressure to lessen expenditure became urgent as incomes sank.

That contraception, having once become established, should have spread, requires no explanation. There has been unceasing propaganda in its favour; it became associated with the powerful movement for women's rights, and was taken up with religious fervour by some advocates with a gift for publicity. Opposition, except among Catholics, whose views made no impression outside their own community, was half hearted. But it is not likely that the course of events in England would have been very different if there had been less propaganda in the last forty years. The small family fits in, not only with the enduring wishes of the mother, but also with the new mode of life. The last sixty years have seen an immense increase in leisure time, and a still greater increase in facilities for employing that leisure; and children are impediments to those who want to avail themselves of these facilities. In relation to making a living children are now seldom a help and are often an encumbrance. Finally, the effort to rise in the social scale may well be frustrated by a large family. In other words, the particular circumstances of the time through their influence upon both parents have conspired with the enduring disposition of the mother to produce the small family system.

In the following chapter we shall find reason to believe that, owing to the adoption of the small family system, the birth-rate has sunk to a level which creates a serious problem in relation to recruiting the future population. This will make necessary a more detailed investigation of the factors which are responsible for the situation which now rules in England and in certain other countries. Therefore, with this very brief allusion to the main reasons which have led to the adoption of the small family system in France and England, we go on to ask how it came to be adopted elsewhere.

Neither in England nor elsewhere was there any conscious imitation of France, apart from the fact that the early English propagandists derived their methods from that country. Indeed, family limitation came to be adopted at a time when the French were widely stigmatized as immoral and degenerate merely because their population was increasing slowly on account of the adoption of this practice. As regards the United States we do not know when family limitation was first practised on a large scale, and it is therefore uncertain whether events in England had any influence. But we can well understand that there may have been an independent evolution of the small family system on much the same lines as in this country. For propaganda had long been going on; the match was alight and a fire was inevitable as soon as the fuel became sufficiently dry. Sentiment must gradually have changed, and there may have been events which disposed people to take advantage of the new possibility and to listen to the propaganda, such as seem to have influenced the English.

In most, if not all other countries, Ireland excepted, English example was influential. The Bradlaugh-Besant trial was world famous; the English propagandists made every effort to spread their views, and their books were translated into numerous languages. In some countries, Holland for instance, vigorous birth-control movements arose. There is no question that in general the adoption of family limitation, except in the cases of France, Ireland, and probably the United States, was due in part to events in this country. It is unnecessary to attempt to explain the circumstances under which birth-control gained a hold in each country, but there are certain facts concerning the spread of family limitation as a whole which are of much interest. The dates at which the practice became wide-spread in the different countries, as shown by the beginning of the fall of the birth-rate, make it plain that density of population had nothing to do with the matter. Since England was one of the most densely populated countries of the world when the fall began, it might be supposed that the calling of a halt to increase was in some way a response to crowded conditions. But the British Dominions, which are among the countries where the decline began early and has been most marked, are also among the most sparsely populated countries of the world. Again, since the decline began in England, it might be thought that it was in part due to industrialization. But the example of the British Dominions shows that this is also a mistake; for they were almost wholly agricultural when they took to limiting their families. Nor does an examination of the beginnings of the decline show any connexion between a deterioration in economic conditions and the establishment of family limitation. It is true that in England, as already pointed out, the beginning of the decline coincided with a depression, but it has continued regardless of variations in economic welfare; in other countries there is in general no association between the decline and material welfare.

How then are we to explain the spread of the small family system? The countries to which the habit first came were not alike in regard either to density of population or to stage of economic development; nor were they associated in a common experience of economic misfortune. But they were associated in sharing a similar mode of life, a fact sometimes expressed by saying that they had reached a fairly similar level of civilization. They used the same mechanisms and contrivances, they adopted very similar clothes and ate very similar foods. Moreover, they observed similar social conventions and fashions. It would be possible to give numerous examples of the rapid spread over just this group of countries which took early to family limitation of trivial habits or of important changes of opinion. There can be little doubt that the practice of family limitation spread over this group of closely associated countries much as so many other novel habits and new ideas spread. The small family habit came later to southern Europe, and still later to eastern Europe, because the countries in these regions stood, in respect of general level of civilization, rather apart from the group of countries in north-west Europe and in Europe overseas. But they are European also, and just as the more trivial habits and conventions of western Europe were taken up

I

by them in course of time, so the more important novel habits, and among them the small family system, were also adopted by them, though later than in the west.

There remains the case of the Irish Free State. Although figures are lacking there is no doubt that before 1845 the Irish birth-rate was very high. The population in Ireland as a whole exceeded 8 millions and had increased with great rapidity since the later decades of the eighteenth century. The country was admittedly grossly over-populated, and the condition of the people was deplorable. Then came the famine. Since that time the population has steadily declined owing to the combination of heavy emigration with a low birth-rate. Emigration was so heavy that it removed more than the natural increase, but it could hardly have had this result if the natural increase had not been held down by a falling birth-rate. We have already described the mechanism, namely few and late marriages, by which the birth-rate was reduced and kept at a low level. This mechanism implies great self-restraint and much personal sacrifice, and is therefore in sharp contrast with the birth-control mechanism, which, while attaining the same end, permits the enjoyment of married companionship and home life. It follows that the low birth-rate in Ireland could only have come about as the result of a conviction that these painful habits were the only alternative to some worse fate. That fate was the recurrence of over-crowding with all its dangers and horrors. We need not suppose that there was any widespread appreciation of the situation of the country as a whole or of the danger to the community in general. We need only suppose that what happens now (or at least happened until immigration into the new countries was restricted) began to happen soon after the famine. Those with intimate knowledge of the Irish country-side say that there is a conviction that there is room in the village or on the farm only for so many people. Young people must wait until a farm becomes vacant or a place is available for them before they can marry. If there is a surplus, some must leave. It is only by assuming that the experience of the famine bit deeply into the consciousness of the Irish that we can understand the introduction of a mechanism for reducing the birth-rate and keeping it low which runs so obviously counter to normal human wants.

The case of Ireland is anomalous in that, alone among countries within the sphere of European civilization, the small family system was adopted in response to a threatening economic situation and has been maintained primarily to prevent the recurrence of an economic disaster. Elsewhere the motive has been in the main to obtain freedom from burdens, which it is desired to escape whatever the economic situation of the country or of the family may be. This is not so say that outside Ireland the family income is not a factor in deciding upon the size of the family; the point is that, however well able married couples may be to afford the cost of an unlimited family, they seldom wish to bear the physical and social burdens which a large family brings. Nor is it to say that outside Ireland the course of the birth-rate shows no association with the course of business activity. Several investigations, notably that of Thomas on English data, show positive correlation between the marriage rate and business activity, and also a correlation, though a much lower one, between the birth-rate and business activity. The course of business activity can affect the birth-rate in two ways; if conditions worsen, married persons may decide not to have a child, and persons, who would otherwise have married, may not do so.

After 1929 there was a decrease in marriages in the United States and an unusually heavy fall in the birth-rate; in 1933 marriages increased and in 1934 the birth-rate rose, whereas for many years previously it had fallen. The course of events in England has been somewhat similar. But the lesson taught by these facts is not that changes in economic conditions govern the birth-rate in countries outside Ireland, but rather the contrary. At the beginning of the most severe economic depression ever known the birth-rate, already falling before, fell rather more rapidly; at the very first sign of a lifting of the clouds it recovered from this particular downward plunge. The relatively small effect of the depression and short duration of such effect as there was are remarkable. All that seems to happen is that under worsened conditions some married couples postpone having a child, and some who would have married and had a child postpone doing so. But they do so sooner or later, and, if the number of children aimed at in the family is limited, then it makes little difference in the long run whether the children come sooner or later. Indeed, the broad conclusion to be drawn from these observations is that, while changing economic conditions may cause some fluctuations in the birth-rate, they do not affect the general trend.

To this may be added another conclusion of no little importance. So far as the above inferences are true, Ireland would seem to be the only country of which we could predict with certainty that opportunities for further expansion would be followed by a growth of population. For in Ireland alone does the method of keeping the birth-rate down demand self-control; elsewhere the method is agreeable in that it permits the enjoyment of pleasures without adding to burdens. If another Ireland was raised up from the Atlantic, we might expect to see the Irish birth-rate rise and the vacant land peopled. There is little reason to suppose that, if another England was raised up out of the North Sea, we should witness a rise in the English birth-rate.

CHAPTER X

THE BALANCE OF BIRTHS AND DEATHS

WE can balance the births which occur in any year against the deaths which take place in that year, and that is what we did in Chapter IV. The result gives the annual natural increase or decrease. We found that the natural increase, which was formerly high, has been declining in western Europe and in Europe overseas, and that this is due to a fall in the birth-rate, which in recent years has been greater than that in the death-rate. The inference would seem to be that, if these trends continue, if, that is to say, the birth-rate continues to fall at this speed, the population will cease to increase and then decline, unless, which is unlikely, the death-rate falls more sharply than has recently been the case. This inference is correct if all that is meant is that under the conditions stated these results will follow; but it is erroneous if it is implied that the birth-rate will only fall if fertility decreases yet further. The object of this chapter is to show that, in addition to balancing the actual deaths against the actual births, it is important to balance the force of birth against the force of death, and that when this is done it may well be found, and is indeed found for this and some other countries, that, in spite of the present excess of births over deaths, the force of death prevails over the force of birth in one very important sense.

When we speak of balancing the force of birth against the force of death we mean that we ask whether a certain number of people, say 1,000, will, if they exhibit during their lives the present fertility and mortality rates, give rise to another 1,000 or to more or less than 1,000. We are in fact asking whether, if present conditions in regard to fertility and mortality continue to prevail, people will replace themselves. It may seem strange that, although births exceed deaths in a country, yet the population of that country may not be replacing itself. The solution of the puzzle is to be sought in the fact that the number of births and of deaths per 1,000 depends, as we have already explained, not only upon fertility and mortality rates, but also upon other agencies and in particular upon the age constitution of the population. At present in this and certain other countries the age constitution is favourable to births because a relatively large proportion of women are within the child-bearing ages, and unfavourable to deaths because a relatively small proportion are within the youngest and oldest age groups which are most exposed to death. As the age constitution changes, births will tend to decrease and deaths to increase, even if the fertility and mortality rates, that is the forces of birth and death, remain as they are now. The situation may perhaps be illustrated by an analogy. If the school-leaving age was raised from fourteen to fifteen, the school population would increase. We know, however, that, disregarding the results of fluctuations in the post-war birth-rate, the number of children entering school every year is growing less. The school population is not replacing itself because the yearly number of entrants to school is lower than the number of children in the higher age groups in school. Nevertheless, the raising of the school-leaving age would produce a situation in the school world not unlike that in this country, if we liken the temporary check upon the number of school leavers to the temporary check upon deaths due to the peculiarities of the present-age constitution.

Even if this explanation is obscure or unconvincing, there are certain facts about the population of this country which strongly suggest that a decline in numbers is imminent although births continue to exceed deaths. If we use the figures relating to the age distribution of the population which are given in each census, we can easily construct a population pyramid. We put males on the left, and females on the right, and we make each step in the pyramid proportional in area to the number of each sex

within each age group. Fig. 23 shows population pyramids
for 1911 and 1931.

The pyramid for 1911 is so constituted that the lower
steps all project markedly beyond those which come next
above. We can well believe that this population is on
the increase. Let us remember that, in five years from
the date to which the pyramid refers, those composing the
bottom step will compose the second step and so on upwards. But since in the course of five years some in each
block will die, each block will become smaller as it is
raised by the insertion of a new block at the bottom.
Nevertheless, it looks as though in 1911 there was plenty
of margin for wear and tear, and that in 1916 the second
block might well be larger than the second block in 1911.
This was in fact the case. Now look at the pyramid for
1931; it is undercut at the base. Even if there is no wear
and tear the second block in 1936 cannot be as large as the
second block in 1931. Imagine the years to pass and the
blocks to be raised, subject to detrition through the wear
and tear which is in fact inevitable, and it is clear that the
total population will presently be less than it is now.

These facts make it evident that it may be an error to
deduce from an existing surplus of births over deaths that
the population will continue to increase, things remaining
as they now are in relation to fertility and mortality. In
this country there is such a surplus, and yet the population
pyramid makes it evident that decrease is to be anticipated.
We therefore need a method of ascertaining whether a
population is replacing itself. Such a method exists. To
employ it we must have the specific fertility rates in the
first place. They are available for those countries in which
the age of the mother is recorded at the birth of each child.
The information may be tabulated so as to give the number of children born to women in each year of the child-
bearing period; more usually it is tabulated so as to give
the number born to women in five-year age groups. The
latter information, though not ideal, is sufficient. Let us

FIGURE 23

Age and Sex Distribution in England and Wales, 1911 and 1931

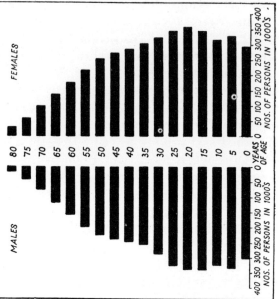

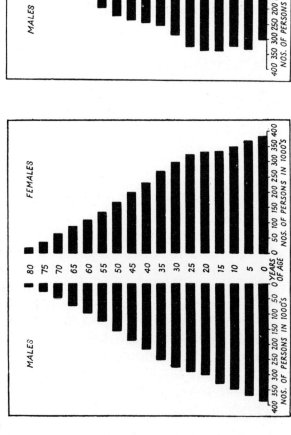

suppose that we possess it; we can then calculate the births per 1,000 women (married and unmarried) in each five-year group, and we get the sort of information that appears in column 2 of Fig. 24. But in that Figure we are supposing that only girl babies are recorded; for since births can occur to women alone we may leave males out of account. Fig. 24, which is purely imaginary and intentionally simplified, tells us that in a certain country in a certain year 1,000 women between the ages of 15 and 19 had 100 girl babies and 1,000 women between 20 and 24 had 400 girl babies and so on.

FIGURE 24

Illustration of the Calculation of the Net Reproduction Rate

Age groups	Number of female children born to 1,000 women passing through each age group	Number of survivors out of each 1,000 female children born	Number of surviving women by whom present women replace themselves
15–19	100	800	80
20–4	400	750	300
25–9	200	700	140
30–4	150	650	97·5
35–9	100	600	60
40–4	50	550	27·5
	1,000		705

Let us now suppose that these specific fertility rates continue to prevail, and that in addition no girl baby dies before the age of 45. It is not difficult to see what will happen. A thousand girl babies will reach the age of 15; when between the ages of 15 and 19 they will have 100 girl babies, when between 20 and 24 they will have 400 babies, and so on; when therefore they reach the age of 45 they will have had 1,000 girl babies. Under these conditions the population is replacing itself, and if they prevail indefinitely the population will remain stationary; for the story of each successive 1,000 girl babies will be the same.

There is an assumption in this imaginary case which does not, and never can, correspond to reality. Some of the girl babies do and always will die each year. Specific mortality rates, that is the number per 1,000 in each age group which die in a year, are more commonly available than specific fertility rates, and we may be fairly sure that if we possess the latter we shall possess the former. Let us therefore suppose that we possess them. In that case we can obtain the number of women who out of 1,000 will reach the age of 15, 16, and so on. While in reality there are complications due to the continued dropping out of some of those who reach 15 and do not reach 20, we may simplify the matter by giving a figure for each age group which represents the average of those who enter and those who pass on from it to the next. The use to be made of these figures is obvious. Let us begin with 1,000 girl babies. Before they reach the age of 15, that is before they enter the child-bearing period, some 200 have died. We may say that 800 of them will live through from 15 to 19 and 750 from 20 to 24. If we follow the slowly reduced group, which originally numbered 1,000, we find that little over 500 live through the child-bearing period. We know that 1,000 women aged 15 to 19 bear 100 girl babies, whence it follows that 800 will bear 80; we know that 1,000 women aged 20 to 24 bear 400 girl babies, whence it follows that 750 will bear 300. In fact we can easily calculate that the original 1,000, reduced to nearly one half in 45 years, will bear 705 girl babies. These 1,000 women are therefore not replacing themselves.

This description, based on imaginary figures, of a method whence it may be ascertained whether a population is replacing itself, is a very simplified description of the Gross and Net Reproduction Rates elaborated and used by Mr. Kuczynski. When fertility alone is taken into account, we obtain the former. In the imaginary case, since 1,000 women leave 1,000 girls, that is 1,000 potential mothers, behind them, we say the rate is 1. If the Gross

Reproduction Rate is as low as 1, the population cannot be replacing itself, because some of the original 1,000 must die before the end of the child-bearing period. But since we want to know how the population does stand in relation to replacement we must take the effect of mortality into account. When this is done in the imaginary case, we find that 1,000 women leave 705 girl babies behind them, and we say that the Net Reproduction Rate is 0·705. When this rate is below unity, the population is not replacing itself.

This simple and beautiful method, which we owe to Mr. Kuczynski, gives precisely what we need. He has applied it so far as data are available. But in order to calculate the net reproduction rate we require data concerning specific fertility as well as specific mortality; and such data are not available for all European countries. They are not available for England and Wales because the age of the mother is not recorded on the birth certificate. But in these cases it is sometimes possible to estimate the distribution of births by age of mother from other sources of information, and an estimated net reproduction rate can then be calculated. Since in all countries the practice of keeping the necessary records is of relatively recent institution, rates can seldom be given for dates more than a few decades ago. Mr. Kuczynski has given a table embodying the results of such calculations as he has been able to make, and they are illustrated in Fig. 25 together with some material from other sources. Some of the rates depend upon an estimation of the distribution of births by age of mother, and some rates are for periods and others for single years.

The anomalous position of France comes out with clarity. Already at the beginning of the century the French were failing to replace themselves. But the gap between the rate and unity was narrow and remained small until recently. So far as information for other countries is available before 1900, we find the net reproduction rate to have been in the region of 1·5, though it was on the decline in Sweden and no doubt also in other countries. Since 1900 dramatic changes have taken place; in north-western Europe the decline has been rapid, and since 1920 the rate has everywhere fallen below unity. It is about 0·9 in Denmark, about 0·8 in France, and about 0·7 in England and Wales, Germany, Sweden, and Austria. For the rest of Europe, when figures are available, they are mostly only for very recent dates; but we can trace the marked decline in Bulgaria from 1·9 about 1900 to 1·3 to-day. We find the rate to be as low as 1·3 in Poland and Portugal and 1·2 in Italy, and we may take it that a heavy decline has been in progress in these countries also. It is worthy of note that the rate in Bulgaria is now lower than in Germany before the War, and that the present Italian rate is lower than the pre-war Swedish rate. If the decline in countries of southern and eastern Europe continues as heretofore, it will not be long before their rates are reduced to unity. The position of Russia is different and of special interest. The rate is now very high at 1·7; that is to say it is now higher than the rate recorded for any country of north-western Europe before 1900. But the Russian rate may have been higher; it was 1·96 in the Ukraine before 1900 and may have been formerly as high in European Russia as a whole. In the Ukraine, however, it is falling with rapidity, and events there may foreshadow what will happen in Russia as a whole. The most striking fact illustrated in Fig. 25 is that the rate in Australia and New Zealand has now dropped below unity. The same is probably true of the United States. The position in Canada is complicated by the contrast between Quebec and the other provinces. According to Mr. Kuczynski the present fertility of Quebec is about the same as that of Germany in 1900, whereas in Ontario and the maritime provinces it is as low as in western Europe.

When these facts are brought to notice it is often said that health conditions will continue to improve and that, even if the present fertility is not sufficient to replace the population, it will become so because deaths will be fewer. It is true enough that much remains to be done in the saving of life, and that we may anticipate large improvements in this sphere. But the only saving of life which can affect the trend of population is the saving of the lives of women before the end of the child-bearing period. The saving of lives above this age will make the population larger at any one time but it will have no effect upon population trend. From the point of view of trend of population it does not matter whether women all die on reaching the end of the child-bearing period or live to be a hundred years old. What matters is whether 1,000 women leave another 1,000 women behind them, and the only improvement which can help here is the decrease in the mortality of women before they reach the age of 45 or thereabouts. If in the imaginary case 900 and not 800 women out of 1,000 survived to constitute the age group 15 to 19, and if 700 and not 550 did so to constitute the age group 40 to 44, the net reproduction rate would be raised. But the scope for decreasing mortality among women before the end of the child-bearing period is much less than is generally believed. From the point of view of the trend of population the ideal would be that every girl baby born should live until the end of the child-bearing period. Let us be generous and put this at the age of 50. Then, if it begins at 15, the ideal would be that every girl baby born should live through 35 years (from age 15 to age 50) in the child-bearing period. Already in this country the average number of years lived in the child-bearing period by each girl baby born is over 30. Clearly the scope for improvement is very small. There will be improvement, but the average number of years so lived can never reach 35 and may never be much over 33. It is much to be desired that the widely current and wholly erroneous notion about the effect of reduced mortality upon the trend of population should be dispelled.

If then it is desired that the population should replace itself, fertility must be raised, since there is little to be hoped from decrease in mortality. The fertility considered when calculating the net reproduction rate is specific fertility, that is the births per 1,000 women, married and unmarried, of given age. Since the unmarried women, though not infertile since there are illegitimate births, are less fertile than the married women, the specific rate would be raised if all women married. On the supposition that the unmarried women married at the same ages as those who now marry, Mr. Kuczynski has calculated that the effect in Denmark would have been to raise the gross reproduction rate, which was 1·166 in 1926–30, to 1·355. This is not a very large effect, and it has to be remembered that there are no doubt among unmarried women a relatively larger number of naturally sterile women than among the married; therefore the true effect would be less than this. Further, Denmark is a country where the effect would be greater than in most countries because there is rather less marriage there than is usually the case. It is true that the effect would be very considerable in the Irish Free State, because, as we have seen, the amount of marriage is much smaller in this country than elsewhere. But Ireland is an exception to most rules. The very important fact therefore emerges that, if the net reproduction rate is to be raised to unity in this and most other countries where it is now below unity, the fertility of marriage must be raised, and that is equivalent to saying that the size of family must be increased.

It remains to ask what conclusions can be drawn from a knowledge of the net reproduction rate as to the probable future course of population. We have seen that a population may be increasing by a surplus of births over deaths even though the rate is below unity; this is the case in this country at the present time. But if the rate remains below unity in any country for any considerable length of time, the population must cease to increase and begin to decrease; furthermore it will continue to decrease so long as the rate remains below unity. Thus, even though we assume that the existing fertility and mortality rates are stabilized, a knowledge of the rate may afford only a general guide to the future course of population. But this is not always the case. It can be shown that, if fertility and mortality rates are stabilized and continue to play upon a population long enough, about a century in fact, a situation will be reached when the future course of population can be accurately deduced from a knowledge of the rate. Under such circumstances, after a century or so, that is to say, of stable rates, the population will move directly in proportion to the rate. If the rate is 0·75, the population will decrease by a quarter in a generation; if it is 1·5 it will increase by a half in a generation, and a generation may be taken as about 30 years. But the circumstances under which the future population can be deduced from the rate are never likely to be met with in practice because fertility and mortality are not likely to remain unchanged for so long a time.

It follows that, if we are interested in future population, another method is required. So-called estimates of future population are now frequently made, but they are often misunderstood. Three kinds of estimates can be distinguished. In the first place, it is possible to calculate what the population will be at a future date on the assumption that existing fertility and mortality rates continue to prevail. The method of making a calculation of this kind is simple. The necessary data are the population, divided into groups by sex and age, and the fertility and mortality rates. In five years' time those aged 0 to 5 will be aged 5 to 10; but some will have died, and to find out how many will have died we must apply the appropriate mortality rate. Thus we get the number aged 5 to 10 in five years' time, and similarly we can arrive at the size of the older age groups. To obtain the number aged 0 to 5 we must first apply the fertility rates to women of child-bearing age, and then deduct those children who will have died in five years' time. In this way we reach the total population five years ahead.

The total reached in this way for the population at any future date hardly deserves the description of an estimate. For the term estimate implies judgement, and in this case there is not necessarily any judgement made by the person who does the calculation. His procedure is like that of some one who, having been told that there are so many balls in a bag and that every day a certain number of balls will be put into the bag and a certain number taken out from it, calculates how many balls there will be in the bag a certain number of days ahead. But the author of the calculation may express the opinion that fertility and mortality rates will continue as at present, in which case his totals become an estimate. If, however, the author is interested in the probable future population, it is almost certain that he will find reason to suppose that fertility and mortality will not remain unchanged. He is thus encouraged to speculate about the probable trend of fertility and mortality and to calculate totals based on the views at which he arrives. A calculation of this kind is a true estimate. The third kind of calculation is a variation of the first. It may be interesting to show what would happen if fertility and mortality rates moved in a certain way. Thus it may be thought illuminating to show what the population of a country would be if fertility and mortality continued to change for a century in the same direction and with the same speed as they have been changing for the last decade. No one is likely to suppose that events would follow this course, and such a calculation is hardly an estimate.

CHAPTER XI

THE SITUATION IN EUROPE

CERTAIN important conclusions, relating to the population situation in Europe, follow from an examination of the net reproduction rates given in Fig. 25. With the possible exception of Russia the rate is falling everywhere, and there is no sign that it is approaching stabilization in any country. In north and west Europe and in Austria and Hungary, where the rate is below unity, the population will presently begin to decline unless there is an immediate and considerable rise in fertility. In the remaining countries the population will continue to increase if fertility is stabilized at its present level; but of stabilization there is, as we have seen, no sign, and these countries are approaching year by year a time when their populations will no longer replace themselves.

These prognostications are rather vague, and the importance of the probable trend of population in Europe is such that it is desirable to be more precise. With this end in view the method outlined at the conclusion of the last chapter is useful. It has recently been employed by statisticians in many countries, and some of their more interesting results are tabulated in Fig. 26. For each calculation the Figure shows its date, the country to which it refers, and the name of the author. The assumptions upon which it is based are briefly indicated, first those relating to fertility, secondly those relating to mortality, and thirdly those relating to migration. In the next two columns the results of the calculations are shown. If the calculation indicates that the population will decline, the size of the maximum population and the date at which it will be reached are given in the first of these columns; in the second are shown any other interesting details which emerge, for instance, the population at some future date. In the last column will be found the present population of each country.

K

It will be remembered that at the end of the last chapter we distinguished three kinds of estimate of future population, and we may examine the estimates in Fig. 26 in order to ascertain the class into which they fall. Those estimates in this Figure which are marked (*a*) and are quoted from the following authors belong to the first class: Dr. Charles for England and Scotland, Gini and Finetti for Italy, Jensen for Denmark, and Burgdörfer for Germany. In each of these cases the calculation shows what the population would be at some future date if the fertility and mortality conditions, prevailing at or about the date when the estimate was made, continued to prevail. The estimate by Sauvy for France, which is marked (*b*) in the Figure, is an example of the third class, that is of a calculation made for illustrative purposes by assuming certain conditions of fertility and mortality, other than those which now prevail, but without supposing that the assumed conditions are likely to be realized. In this calculation Sauvy assumes that the fertility of France sinks at once to the level prevailing in the Département de la Seine and continues at this level. It is an illuminating calculation, but it is merely an illustration since the assumption is impossible.

It is not easy to classify the remaining calculations. They are perhaps best regarded as combining the characteristics of the second and third classes. The authors make assumptions about the direction of the trends of fertility and of mortality which they think are likely to be realized in the near future: this means as a rule that they assume a continuance of the decline in fertility which has been observed during the past decade or so. But, however confident any one may be concerning the general trend of fertility for a few years ahead, the grounds for confidence weaken when it comes to making assumptions about the position more than a few years from now. Nevertheless, the calculations are usually carried forward for several decades, and we may regard the figures for more distant times as falling within the third class of estimate.

If we examine the results of the calculations which fall within the first class, we find that, in the cases of England and Wales, Scotland, France, Belgium, and Germany, the population reaches a maximum at no very distant date and thereafter declines. The calculation for Denmark shows a continuing increase; but the assumptions are a continuance of the conditions which prevailed ten or more years ago. A calculation made on the basis of the present Danish fertility would show a maximum and then a decline. For Italy a continuing increase is shown. These results confirm our expectations based on a knowledge of the net reproduction rates for these countries, but make them more precise. We learn, for example, that the population of Scotland on these assumptions will reach its maximum in 1970, that of England in 1943, and of Belgium in 1940. In none of these countries is the anticipated increment to population more than trivial. These conclusions are of great practical importance. It must be remembered that they are based on the assumption that existing, or more strictly speaking recent, conditions will continue to prevail. Even under these conditions the decline in population will be large. In England and Wales, the maximum having been passed in 1943, the population will have decreased by 2 millions in 1975 and to half its present size in a century. It is of some importance to notice that the decline will be small for a time, and that, after some forty years of relative stability, it will become very rapid. The position is, therefore, not that a problem will be created if fertility continues to fall, but that a problem has been created by the present low level of fertility.

Estimates of this kind do not give us a full measure of the problem. In the first place they are made on the assumption that the fertility existing not less than three years ago, and in most cases rather longer, continues unchanged. But in all these countries fertility has now

fallen farther. If calculations were made on the basis of
the position to-day, they would show the maximum population coming at an earlier date and a more rapid decline
thereafter than is indicated in the Figure. Therefore the
problem is more acute than the calculations in Fig. 26
suggest. In the second place there is no reason to suppose
that the decline in fertility has come to an end or even that
the end is in sight. The reasons for taking this view will
be given at some length in Chapter XV; it is enough to
say here that the time is approaching when all children will
be wanted children and that the proportion of children who
are now unwanted is still very large. It is likely, therefore,
that the problem will become still more acute year by year
for some time to come.

This is evidently the opinion of those authors who have
thought it worth while to calculate the future population
on the assumption that fertility will continue to decline.
No one can form any opinion as to how long the fall is
likely to last, and therefore the date selected for the end of
the fall in any of these calculations should not be regarded
as possessing any special significance. The results are
striking but need little comment. Dr. Leybourne, for
example, who assumes that fertility stabilizes as early as
1945, finds that the population of England and Wales will
have fallen by more than 11 millions by 1976.

As already noted, the calculation for Italy, which falls
within the first class, shows a continuous increase. This is
in accordance with expectations since the net reproduction
rate for Italy is above unity. But another calculation for
Italy is also shown in Fig. 26 which is of much interest.
It assumes a decline in fertility until 1948 and a certain
annual loss by emigration. Under these circumstances the
population would still continue to grow indefinitely, but
the growth would become very slow; by 1961 the population would be larger only by some 4 millions than the
population in 1933.

In the light of inquiries of this kind what is it reasonable to anticipate as regards the probable future course of population in Europe? The future is governed by the trend of mortality and fertility rates. So far as the former are concerned there is very little room for differences of opinion. We may take it as certain that men will continue to desire to live as long as they can, and that, with this end in view, they will continue to press on with research and to apply the results of research for the benefit of public health. We also know that the possibility of saving life among women before the end of the child-bearing period is very limited; the relevant facts were given in the last chapter. The only serious doubt which prevails under this head has reference to the improvement of mortality rates among the persons belonging to the upper age groups; but however much improvement is made it will affect total numbers alone and will not influence trend of population. If the net reproduction rate is below unity, no improvement of this kind will raise it above unity.

If we were as confident about the future course of fertility as we are about the future course of mortality, so far as the latter is relevant to this question, we should not have much doubt about the course of population. But it may seem that, at first sight in any case, we have no grounds for confidence when we attempt to forecast the trend of fertility; for we do not know what size of family men will desire in the future, and whatever they may desire is already in their power to bring about. If married couples want half a dozen children, as a rule they can have them; if they want no children, they can prevent their appearance. This follows if it is correct to hold, as we have argued, that fertility is in the main determined by birth-control. Nevertheless, it is quite erroneous to infer that the trend of fertility is just as likely to be in one direction as in another. If we examine the course of fertility in Europe for the last century we do not find that it has moved erratically; on the contrary it has shown definite and persistent trends. The reason is that we are dealing with a society that is undergoing steady change and is not subject to intermittent catastrophes. Even the Great War was not catastrophic enough definitely to change the trend of fertility; fertility fell during the War and rose afterwards, but if the trend of fertility from 1900 to 1930 is graphed, we gain the impression that the course of fertility after 1920 was roughly what it would have been if there had been no war. Therefore we are not at liberty to say that anything is equally likely in the near future; it is very probable, almost certain in fact, that changes will be gradual. What will be the direction of these changes? As we have observed, the better-off people, some half-century or so ago, came to desire smaller families and found a method of satisfying this ambition which they were willing to use; it is not certain that the size of family, low as it is, has yet been stabilized among this section of society. It is quite certain that the forces making for a smaller family have not worked themselves out among the rest of the population. Therefore the prospect is that fertility will decline steadily for some time to come. The whole problem will receive further attention in a future chapter; the only additional remark which is necessary here has reference to the prospects in different countries. In view of the unity of European civilization and of the evidence that, in respect to size of family as in other matters, the rest of Europe is imitating the west, we may expect that the trend of fertility in the south and east will follow that in the west. In other words, since fertility in the west has fallen below replacement level we may anticipate that in other parts of Europe it will fall in time to about the same low level. Further, since, where fertility has begun to fall latest, it has fallen fastest, we may expect that the time taken to reach this low level will be less in the south and east than in the west.

Let us attempt to translate these considerations into more concrete terms. We may anticipate that in north and west Europe there will be no further increase of population of any importance, and that before 1950 the population will be on the decline in most countries in this region. But in no case will the decline be large twenty years from now. For, assuming fertility to decline still farther, the drop in numbers will only become rapid about 1960. It would be very mistaken, however, to assume that, because even a further decline in fertility would not produce any substantial change in numbers for twenty years, the prospect is such that it need excite no interest during this period. It is of importance for the immediate future, that is for the next two decades, in two ways. First, the prospect of a substantial decline will be common knowledge to all the world, and will (whether for the better or the worse) affect the view taken of these countries, where it is anticipated, by other nations. Secondly, the course of population has its roots in the behaviour of the previous generation. If fertility continues to fall it will be too late to prevent a rapid drop in population if action is delayed until twenty years hence. It is upon our behaviour in the next two decades that the course of population twenty years hence will depend; therefore, supposing, for instance, that we desire a stabilization of numbers, we must remember that, though our present habits will leave the population only 2 or 3 millions below its present level two decades from now, they will inevitably bring about a drastic fall in the more distant future.

In the south and east of Europe the prospects are different. Fertility is declining and is likely to continue to decline; it is probable that the net reproduction rate will fall to unity in south Europe within two decades. But, even if this happens, the population will continue to increase for some time to come; in Italy, for instance, it may be expected to increase by at least an eighth in the next twenty-five years, that is from 40 to 45 millions. In east Europe the fall of the rate to unity will be still longer delayed in all probability, since it is higher than in south Europe; and we may anticipate that in such a country as

Poland the population will increase by a quarter at least in the next twenty-five years, that is from 35 to close upon 45 millions. In the present state of our knowledge these would appear to be outside estimates. There are various reasons for taking this view. It is noteworthy, for instance, that, in every case in which a calculation of future population has been made upon the assumption that fertility will continue to fall, it is found that, if the calculation was made long enough ago to enable the forecast to be compared with actual population, the latter is less than the population forecast. Thus Gini made a number of calculations for Italy, based on different assumptions; if we compare the lowest total arrived at for the present day with the actual figures, we find it to be about 700,000 above the true figures. This means that those who have made these calculations have underestimated the amount by which fertility has fallen, or more correctly that they have not thought it worth while to make a calculation upon the assumption that fertility would fall as fast as it has in fact fallen. Then again, since experience seems to show that, where fertility has begun to fall latest, it has fallen most quickly, we may expect that the decline of fertility in south and east Europe will be rapid.

Russia is in a different position. The net reproduction rate for the whole country is very high, though there are reasons for thinking that it has fallen recently. In the Ukraine, however, the fall has been very rapid; it is also noteworthy that the net reproduction rate was already below unity in Moscow in 1929. But fertility in Moscow has been low for some time; almost alone among the Russian cities figures from Moscow showed resemblances to those from the great cities of central Europe in the pre-war period. It is almost certain that fertility will fall heavily in Russia, and it may fall with very great rapidity. But it is still so high that the population of Russia may well double itself before it stabilizes.

If these are the prospects in Europe, it is appropriate to

ask how far they coincide with needs. For, whatever may have been the case in the past, there is no reason at all to believe that, under the conditions now prevailing in Europe, population automatically adjusts itself to needs interpreted as opportunities for employment. But we must say something about the meaning of adjustment of population to needs so interpreted. The essence of the matter, it is now agreed, is simple. In any country under any given set of conditions there may be too sparse a population in the sense that, if the population was more dense, on the average every one would be better off; this is so because there are benefits arising from co-operation and division of labour, and there may be so few people that these benefits cannot be reaped. On the other hand there may be too many people in the sense that, if there were fewer, every one would be better off. If any one doubts that an increase of population may be a disadvantage, that, in other words, there may be too many people, let him imagine, as Mr. Harold Wright once suggested, that the number of people remains the same and the area on which they live contracts. For to all practical purposes the same population on a shrinking area is equivalent to a growing population on the same area. It must be obvious that, if the area shrank, there would come a time when average incomes would diminish. It follows that in any country under any given set of conditions there must be a density of population which it is best to have—the so-called optimum population.

It must not be assumed that, because we know that there must be a certain density of population which is more desirable than any other in every country at any given time, we can say what it is from our knowledge of the prevailing conditions. We can in fact do nothing of the sort; there is no way by which we can even begin to make such a calculation. If we cannot do that, is it possible to say whether any country, as it is now, is under- or over-populated? There is no infallible and universally applicable test. On the other hand, when dealing with countries the population of which is wholly or mainly engaged in agriculture, we may hope to detect serious maladjustment. Thus if we find that farms are very small, that the amount of labour applied to an acre is large, that living is poor and less than that won in other countries where skill is no higher but farms are larger, we may suspect over-population. Moreover, since agricultural technique, except in certain countries in very recent times, changes very slowly, we may assume that, if over-population exists, it has come about through excessive growth of population and not through any change in the surrounding conditions.

When we come to industrialized countries it is impossible to find even rough tests of this kind. The existence of unemployment is not such a test. If any one believes that unemployment is a sign of over-population, let him consider two facts. Unemployment has come to this country in waves; between the waves it was man-power and not work that was lacking. If we graph the unemployment percentage we get a sharply fluctuating curve, whereas the growth of population is represented by a steadily ascending line, and there is no sign of any relation between them. Any one who thinks that the intermittent unemployment crises have been due to excessive numbers must hold that this country has been over-populated every few years, while in the intervals population has been in adjustment. Secondly, in the United States there has recently been relatively more unemployment than in this country; but in the United States, which are favoured above all other countries by richness in natural resources, geographical location, and an enterprising population, there are less than 50 persons per square mile as against about 700 in this country. There cannot be any over-population in the United States, and yet unemployment has been more severe there than here.

It is evident in fact that there may be over-population

without unemployment, and unemployment without over-population. The United States are an example of the latter, while certain Asiatic countries, which we shall study later, are an example of the former; in those countries men work from before dawn until after dark for a pittance. The one unescapable consequence of over-population is poverty—greater poverty than there need be in view of the resources of the country and the skill available for exploiting them. The nature of unemployment in general may be illustrated by an analogy with a steam-engine in which the steam introduced is the man-power. If the engine is working badly a lot of steam will escape and remain unproductive; this is unemployment. If we reduce the amount of steam entering the engine without improving the mechanism, we may very slightly reduce the amount which escapes; but, however little is introduced, a large proportion will continue to escape. In other words, if we reduce the population without removing the causes of friction in the industrial machine, we shall still have unemployment, though perhaps not quite as much.

This is only to say that unemployment is not necessarily, and in fact is not usually, a consequence of over-population in industrialized countries. But over-population can of course occur in such countries; the difficulty is to detect it. The difficulty arises from the great complexity of the situation. Over-population means that there are too many people in relation to a whole set of facts, including, in the case of an industrialized country, opportunities for external trade. Such opportunities may be suddenly expanded and even more suddenly restricted, and within the last decade rapid changes of this kind have taken place. Changes of this nature adverse to a certain country may cause over-population, at least for a time, in that country; but over-population so caused is in some important aspects not the same as over-population in an agricultural country. First, such over-population is due not to excessive growth of population, but to a recession of conditions leaving the

population stranded; secondly, a restoration of the conditions provides a possible and rapid remedy, whereas in an
over-populated agricultural country, swift improvement
of technique being usually out of the question, the position
can only be restored by the long and painful process of
reducing the population.

Since tests of over-population are hard to come by, it
may be that a general review of certain facts relating to the
various European countries will be suggestive. For that
purpose Fig. 27 has been compiled. Of the various facts
which it is designed to illustrate, the density per square
kilometre alone can be taken as accurate. The other figures
must be used with great caution for various reasons. One
column gives the proportion of total population engaged
in agriculture, but it is not easy to say who is engaged in
agriculture because many people are engaged part time
in agriculture and part time in ancillary occupations such
as forestry, in industry, or in domestic work at home; also
different countries draw the line between agricultural and
other occupations in different places. As to the various
uses to which the land is put, it must be remembered that
temporary pasture is included under arable, though, when
laid down for long periods, it occupies as few people as
good permanent pasture. Then it is difficult to distinguish
between 'permanent grass and pasture' and 'other land';
that is to say, rough hill grazing shades off by imper-
ceptible stages into barren land. The importance of this
latter point can be seen when we contrast Scotland with
England and Wales; both countries are recorded as having
about the same percentage of permanent grass and pasture,
but we know that in Scotland this is largely sheep grazings
on mountain sides, whereas in England much of it is the
finest pasture in the world.

Taking these figures as they are, can we draw any conclusions from them? We observe the very great differences
in density of population, Belgium with 269·8 and Norway
with 8·8 persons per square kilometre, for example. But

in Norway only 2·6 per cent. of the total area is arable and
there is hardly any pasture; most of the country is barren

FIGURE 27

Density of Population and Agricultural Employment in Europe

Country	Number of inhabitants per sq. kilometre (1)	Percentage of total population engaged in agriculture (2)	Percentage of total area in			
			Arable land (3)	Permanent grass and pasture (4)	Wood and forest (5)	Other land (6)
Belgium . .	269·8	19·1 (1920)	40·5	17·7	41·8	
England and Wales . .	267·2	6·4 (1931)	24·5	57·1	18·4	
Netherlands .	239·4	20·6 (1930)*	27·6	40·3	7·4	24·7
Germany . .	139·7	28·9 (1933)*	43·7	17·4	27·2	11·7
Italy . .	134·8	47·3 (1931)	43·5	19·7	16·0	20·8
Czechoslovakia .	106·3	28·3 (1930)	41·6	16·8	32·7	8·9
Switzerland .	99·2	21·3 (1930)	12·1	40·8	21·8	25·3
Hungary . .	94·4	54·0 (1930)	60·1	17·9	11·8	10·2
Poland . .	84·0	75·9 (1921)	47·8	16·7	21·4	14·1
Denmark . .	83·6	34·8 (1921)	60·8	10·4	28·8	
Austria . .	80·4	31·9 (1920)	23·2	27·4	37·4	12·0
France . .	75·9	38·3 (1926)*	40·5	20·6	19·1	19·8
Portugal . .	73·4	51·1 (1930)	..	..	..	..
Romania . .	62·9	..	42·9	13·5	24·5	19·1
Scotland . .	62·2	9·0 (1931)	15·9	62·6	21·5	
Bulgaria . .	57·7	82·4 (1920)	35·6	3·0	61·4	
Yugoslavia .	57·5	82·0 (1921)	28·6	24·5	31·0	15·9
Greece . .	50·3	53·7 (1928)	12·9	..	..	..
Spain . .	47·6	56·1 (1920)	31·5	..	..	..
Irish Free State .	43·2	52·1 (1926)	21·7	46·7	31·6	
Sweden . .	13·8	40·7 (1920)*	9·1	3·0	53·0	34·9
Norway . .	8·8	35·3 (1930)	2·6	0·7	24·3	72·4
Russia (in Europe and in Asia) .	7·8	84·9 (1926)*	..	..	..	..

Note. The figures in column (2) are from the *League of Nations Year Books* for 1933–4 and 1934–5. Those in the other columns are from the *Year Book of International Agricultural Statistics* for 1932–3 and relate to 1932 except in the case of France, where the figures in columns (3) to (6) are for 1931. In column (2) the percentages are for agricultural occupations except where marked by asterisks, when they refer to agricultural industries. The percentages for Yugoslavia in column (2) are incomplete as they omit Dalmatia and a number of other districts for which figures are not available.

and incapable of supporting population, and we have no
reason for supposing either that Norway is under-populated or that Belgium is over-populated on the basis of
these figures. A careful examination of the figures does,
however, bring some facts to light which have a bearing

upon the situation. Germany and Italy have nearly the same density of population, a relatively high density, moreover, since they head the list of countries placed in order of density, if we leave out of account the three very densely populated European countries, England and Wales, Belgium, and Holland. But in Italy nearly half the population is engaged in agriculture as against little more than a quarter in Germany; also less of the total area is 'other land' in Germany than in Italy. Clearly more labour is applied to a given amount of land in the latter than in the former country; and this is no doubt due to the fact that the power and raw materials required for industrial development are much scarcer in Italy than in Germany, thus creating relatively few opportunities for industrial employment. A similar contrast is found between France and Poland. Population is rather more dense in the latter than the former, but in Poland over three-quarters, and in France only rather more than a third, of the total population are engaged in agriculture. Further, the proportion of the whole area devoted to arable and pasture is about the same in the two countries, indicating a much greater application of labour to land in Poland than in France.

These facts prove nothing whatever, but they are sometimes suggestive. There are many other elements in the situation which are relevant, but there is no place to discuss them here. It is probable, however, that, if due weight was given to them, we should find that disparities would remain and that we should be driven to conclude that there must be maladjustment of population in some countries. So far we have found no test, capable of application to industrialized countries, which might indicate the position. But there are facts, such as the average real income at different dates, which may throw light on the situation. Such facts have been subjected to careful examination, and it may be said that the result of these inquiries has been to show that there is no proof that the industrialized countries of western Europe are over-populated. The only qualification to be made is that, owing to a recession of conditions, a purely temporary recession it is to be hoped, the population in some countries may have been 'stranded', to use our previous analogy; this would mean a lowering of the standard of living at least for the time, and might result in unemployment if workers preferred to stand idle rather than accept the lower standard. On the other hand, from southern and eastern Europe there come loud complaints of congestion. Let us examine the situation more closely, taking Poland as an example.

The agricultural density is high over the whole country; it is highest in the south, relatively sparse in the east, and relatively moderate in the west. Where the density is high, dwarf holdings of less than five hectares each are numerous; there are over 2 millions of such holdings out of a total of some $3\frac{1}{4}$ millions. Some of those who occupy dwarf holdings have other occupations which they pursue for part of the time, but there are at least a million and three-quarters of such holders whose entire support comes from the land. It has been calculated that the remaining holdings, consisting either of large estates of more than 100 hectares each or of medium-sized holdings, could support not only their present occupiers but also all the landless agricultural workers if they were redistributed. Thus the problem may be said to centre round the dwarf holdings which do not provide an adequate living for their occupiers. It has been calculated that in 1921 there was on the average over the country a surplus of 5·4 persons per square kilometre; this would mean that in 1931 there was a total surplus of over 3 million persons, or some 600,000 families, and this is probably an underestimate. In the next chapter some account will be given of continental migration in Europe. It may be pointed out here that the powerful stream of emigration from Poland which has been flowing for some time supports the view that Poland is a congested area. Up to 1914 some 600,000 Poles had moved from that part of Poland which was formerly included in Germany, to settle in parts of Germany which were not ethnographically Polish, and over a million Poles had left what was formerly Russian Poland to settle in other parts of Russia. There was in addition a strong seasonal movement of agricultural workers into Germany proper which reached a total of 300,000 in some years.

It would be possible to bring forward facts of a like kind which suggest that Italy is similarly congested. There are signs that Romania, Bulgaria, and Yugoslavia, though not overcrowded to the same extent as Poland and Italy, are over- rather than under-populated; for in these countries the population is fairly dense while the proportion of the inhabitants engaged in agriculture is very high. The evidence therefore goes to show that Poland and Italy certainly, and possibly also south-east Europe to some slight extent, are overcrowded. Moreover, this overcrowding is not of a kind that can be relieved immediately by a resumption of world economic activity as is the case with such western European countries as may for a time in one sense be over-populated. For, owing to paucity of the facilities at present essential to industrial development, no considerable expansion of industrial employment is possible; so long as industry rests upon its present foundations, it is a delusion to suppose that these countries can imitate the example of England and find an outlet for an increasing population in industry. But Russia stands in a different position. The density of population in European Russia is less than a third of that in Poland; the country is no less rich agriculturally and possesses far greater industrial possibilities. The prospects of an increasing population would therefore not seem to be a cause of anxiety to Russia for some time to come. But it is otherwise in the rest of eastern Europe and in Italy where already there is congestion. Nevertheless it is precisely in this region that a considerable increase of population is to be anticipated.

CHAPTER XII

EUROPEAN CONTINENTAL MIGRATION

A DISTINCTION was drawn in Chapter IV between continental and oversea movements; in this chapter we shall be concerned with movements of the former kind in Europe. We tend to overlook them in this country on account of the fact that oversea movements occupy so large a place in our field of view. They are of importance because of their magnitude and because of the light which they throw upon the European population situation. The chief importance, however, of the facts to be given here relates to problems which have not yet been touched, and in this sense this chapter is a prelude to the discussion of the international aspects of population which is to come.

The nature of continental movements in the earlier part of our period was sketched in Chapter IV; it largely took the shape of mass expulsions and mass settlements. Settlers were often encouraged because they brought with them new industries and new techniques. Movements of this kind ceased before the end of the eighteenth century, and it was not until about 1880 that movements of individual unskilled workers from one European country to another took place on a large scale. Until after the War figures of these movements are of the vaguest kind; in the last chapter some guesses were quoted relating to the size of the movement of Poles to Germany and Russia before 1914, and it may be added that the emigration from Italy to other European countries was also large, amounting in some years to a quarter of a million, taking permanent and seasonal emigration together. The chief country of immigration was France, and, in the French census of 1911, 1,133,000 aliens were enumerated. From the time when restrictions upon movement, which lingered on from the eighteenth century, were removed, migration

L

was in general free until after the War. Then we enter upon a period of renewed restriction.

It is this period which demands attention here. There has been a certain flow of skilled labour from west to east called forth by the efforts made in eastern Europe to set up new industries in the search for economic self-sufficiency. This flow, though important in one sense, is numerically insignificant. The numerically significant movement has been from east to west and from south to north-west. But its magnitude is still very imperfectly measured. There are serious difficulties inherent in any attempt to record continental movements; it is less easy to keep records of passage across land frontiers than of a flow through ports. Also there is no uniform system of defining migrants and recording their movements; therefore national statistics are not strictly comparable. That we do possess better figures for the post-war than for the pre-war period is due to the interest which the International Labour Organization has shown in the matter of migration, and to the success which it has achieved in stimulating the improvement of record keeping. The data given in Fig. 28 are derived from the summaries provided by the I.L.O. of government statistics. They relate to the three countries, Poland, Italy, and Czechoslovakia, whence there has been the largest emigration of nationals, and to the three countries, Germany, France, and Belgium, into which there has been largest immigration of aliens in recent years.

These movements have taken place within a complicated system of government regulation. They are the movements which have been permitted; we cannot say what movements would have taken place if movement had been free. For men are free neither to come nor to go. But they are more free to go, that is to leave the country of which they are nationals, than to come, that is to enter a country in which they are aliens. Let us consider restrictions upon outward movement first. It is

EUROPEAN CONTINENTAL MIGRATION

important to note that such restrictions apply, not only
to those going to continental destinations, but also to those
going overseas. Therefore they condition, not only continental migration, which is the subject of this chapter,

FIGURE 28

European Continental Migration: 1922 to 1933

	Emigration of Nationals			Immigration of Aliens		
	Poland	Italy	Czecho-slovakia	Germany	France	Belgium
1922	31,373	170,155	17,935	..	181,472	18,602
1923	72,058	229,854	16,369	27,591*	262,877	22,168
1924	26,136	271,089	19,057	..	223,495	38,104
1925	42,769	178,208	28,679	47,998	176,261	34,734
1926	117,616	141,314	26,480	55,157	162,109	32,944
1927	89,427	91,958	23,272	130,584	64,325	29,973
1928	122,049	79,173	28,845	135,923	97,742	31,034
1929	178,132	88,054	35,063	125,388	179,321	45,006
1930	171,853	220,985	39,972	109,421	221,619	43,217
1931	64,235	125,079	26,434	50,141	102,267	22,018
1932	11,772	58,545	17,410	9,800	69,942	14,881
1933	18,293	60,726	12,468	..	..	..

* Annual average, 1920–4.

but also intercontinental movements, which will be studied
later.

Prospective emigrants are now almost always required
to carry passports, and in order to obtain a passport it is
necessary to present identity papers. This forms a convenient mechanism through which governments can control the exit of their nationals. There is no case of a
general refusal to issue passports and therefore of a general
prohibition upon emigration from any European country.
But it would appear that the conditions under which passports are granted in Russia are so strict that there is what
amounts to a prohibition upon leaving that country, at
least for the ordinary worker. In 1927 regulations were
imposed in Italy which laid down that Italian subjects
could not leave with the intention of settling abroad unless

they were going to join a near relative or possessed a contract of employment. This did not apply to certain classes
of professional workers, but it meant that the permanent
emigration of unskilled workers was rendered very difficult; the effect of these measures is shown in the drop in
Italian emigration in 1927, 1928, and 1929. In 1930, however, the regulations were relaxed and the number of
emigrants rose sharply, as is shown in Fig. 28. Another
important form of restriction is that which makes inability
to comply with the immigration laws of the countries to
which it is desired to go a reason for refusing a passport.
This restriction is in force in most European countries
and operates powerfully to keep down the volume of
emigration. It is imposed in order to avoid the trouble
and expense consequent upon the refusal by countries of
immigration to permit persons to enter; for such persons
may have to be brought home by the country whence they
came. But since in this case the initiative comes from the
country of immigration, and the action taken by countries
of emigration is wholly governed by conditions imposed
elsewhere, it is proper to regard these restrictions as part
of the system of restricting immigration.

There are also numerous other reasons for refusing
passports. They may be refused if legal proceedings are
pending, unless military service has been fulfilled, and
unless, in the case of those leaving dependents behind,
there is a guarantee of support for them. Minors and
young women travelling alone may not be able to obtain
passports, and the reason in this case is to prevent exploitation. Passports are sometimes refused to the aged
and, what is more important, to those who are without
financial resources; the object here is to minimize the
danger of destitution abroad. The offer of financial assistance from foreign sources to pay for the journey is also
sometimes made a reason for refusing the grant of a passport; the motive in this case is presumably again to
prevent exploitation. Thus the motive for restricting emi-

gration in the ways enumerated in this paragraph is not merely the desire to keep nationals at home; the motive is the supposed interest of the would-be immigrants or the demands of social justice. The cumulative effect of this kind of restriction, while not negligible, is probably not numerically considerable; therefore it is only in Italy and Russia that really serious obstacles to emigration exist.

The conditions imposed by European countries upon the entry of aliens are far more severe than those imposed upon the exit of nationals. There is first a large class of restrictions which have as their object to keep out persons who are mentally or physically defective, or whose record, as judged from convictions in a criminal court, is bad. Thus entry into Great Britain is forbidden to lunatics, idiots, and feeble minded, as well as to persons certified by a medical officer as unfitted to land. The number of persons refused admittance on these grounds is apparently very small. The important regulations are those to be discussed next which are intended to safeguard the labour market in each country from foreign competition.

When we come to consider restrictions upon entry into oversea countries, we shall find instances of regulation by means of rigid numerical quotas. Such quotas are not found in Europe; the only approach to them is the German system under which the number of alien agricultural workers who are permitted to enter is fixed at a maximum. But it is not a rigid system, because the number is fixed each year by the Ministry of Labour after consultation with the agricultural interests. The arrangement, which is in force in nearly every European country, takes the form of requiring each alien worker to obtain a permit to take up employment before he can enter. The procedure varies from country to country; it may be said that in general it provides that the Labour or Employment Ministry must consent before a permit is granted. Thus an alien worker may not land in Great

Britain unless he produces a permit for his engagement issued to his future employer by the Ministry of Labour; while Dutch consuls may not visa the passport of any alien, who wishes to enter Holland in order to work, unless he is authorized to do so by the Director of the Unemployment Insurance and Employment Services, and before the Director acts he must consult the employment exchange in the area to which the alien proposes to go.

It is obvious that a system of restriction of this kind can be made very effective, and the influence of nationalism, of trade unionism, and in recent years of unemployment, all combine to ensure that it is effectively applied. It is surprising that under these circumstances there should have been as much movement as the figures show, and we know that the figures are incomplete. The inference would seem to be that, if it was not for these obstacles, continental movements in Europe would be on a very large scale, and this points to maladjustment of population.

The regulation of the movement of individual migrants is, however, only half the whole story of the regulation of migration by governments since the War. The other half relates to the treaties and conventions regulating the collective recruitment and transport of workers. Such agreements were hardly known before the War; they were developed by France immediately after the War. They are usually bilateral; they may be concerned with both individual and collective migration, and it is in so far as they are concerned with the latter that they are of greatest interest. For the attempt to provide for collective migration shows that policy in this matter has not been wholly negative, and that constructive work has been done which at least contains the promise of a rational attempt to solve the difficulties arising from maladjustment of population. These bilateral agreements, whether they take the form of treaties or of conventions, cover the recruitment of labour in one country and the placing of it in the other, model labour contracts, reciprocity in relation to labour

laws and other matters. All these matters may be included in a single agreement, or they may each be the
subject of a special agreement. There are a large number
of such agreements in existence; France alone has agreements with several European countries. The agreements
may contemplate seasonal migration alone, or they may
contemplate permanent migration as well. The agreements between Poland and Czechoslovakia, Germany and
Austria, Germany and Poland are of the former kind, and
we may take the last-mentioned agreement as an example.

The Polish-German treaty of 1927 settled in the first
place certain difficulties arising from the presence of
Poles in Germany. Then it laid down that future movement should be seasonal or temporary only, and that the
migration of agricultural workers alone is contemplated.
The arrangements resulting from the treaty and the
organizations in both countries, which have been set up
to operate it, are most comprehensive. The German
authorities fix a maximum for all seasonal agricultural
workers each year, and distribute quotas to various countries. This is done after a review of the needs of the
agriculturists and is based on the application of German
farmers for permits to employ foreign labour. The number to be recruited from Poland is communicated to the
Polish government together with proposals for the mode
and plan of recruitment. These proposals are considered
by the Polish government and an agreement arrived at.
Elaborate arrangements are made for the transport of
workers by rail; provisions are laid down for the feeding
of workers *en route*, for the provision of sanitary facilities,
and accommodation at junctions until the destination is
reached. The German government guarantees satisfactory
sanitary and housing conditions and the supervision of
moral welfare. The rights of the immigrants to insurance
against sickness and accident and to social assistance in
general while in Germany are laid down. Not least important is the fact that each migrant has a contract of

employment with a specified employer before he sets out, and that this contract is drawn up on the lines of the model labour contract which forms part of the treaty. Arrangements for the return are made in equal detail.

As examples of treaties which contemplate permanent migration we have numerous agreements made by France in recent years. The instrument which governs movement of this sort may deal not only with permanent but also with seasonal migration, and not only with collective but also with individual migration. The Franco-Polish convention of 1919, subsequently modified and enlarged, is an example of a comprehensive agreement. There are first of all certain general provisions which concern all migrants. It is laid down that the competent administrative department of government shall supervise alien workers from the other country, and that complaints or notices of difficulties can be addressed in the language of the immigrant to that department directly or through the medium of the consular representative. Also immigrants are to receive rates of wages not less than those paid to nationals for equal work. Further, the principle of equality is applied to benefits accruing from the domestic legislation of the country to which the immigrant goes. Though in form reciprocal, it was no doubt contemplated that, and in fact it works out so that, these regulations apply only to Polish immigrants in France since there is no movement in the opposite direction.

The most interesting feature of this convention concerns the provisions made for the recruitment of workers whose length of stay is not limited. The two parties pledge themselves to authorize the recruiting of labour for this purpose within the territory of each on behalf of undertakings within the territory of the other; but the government of the territory in which the recruiting is taking place has right to determine the area where recruiting shall be conducted. The parties are to fix the number and class of persons to be recruited in such a way as not to prejudice the economic development of one country or the interests of the workers of the other. For this purpose a commission is set up consisting of representatives of the government, the employers, and the employed. French requests for workers are forwarded to the Emigration Office, and no requests from employers are endorsed if a strike or lockout exists in the undertaking in question and unless working conditions are satisfactory. Polish workers are presented by the public employment offices. A selection is made from among them by a representative of a trade union, or in some other manner under the supervision of the French Labour Mission. Finally, workers must have contracts of employment drawn up in conformity with model contracts agreed between the two countries.

Many other matters are dealt with in these agreements, but enough has been said to show that they are most comprehensive. Their existence shows that constructive efforts have been made to cope with the migration problem, and it is not the case that government action in this matter is summed up in a lengthy list of restrictions upon the movement of workers. For these agreements contemplate movement and are intended to facilitate it. By far the most interesting feature of these agreements is, as has been noticed, the provision for collective migration; for we are witnessing an organized attempt to meet a definite and ascertained need for labour in one country by the recruitment of appropriate workers in sufficient quantity in another country. Through the medium of model contracts, with which the individual contract that each migrant has to possess must conform, social justice is safeguarded on both sides; the home worker is safeguarded against undercutting of wages and conditions by aliens, and the alien worker is not in danger of exploitation in a foreign land where he does not know how to protect himself.

Since France is the chief country of immigration in

Europe, it may help to fill out the picture if we review the main features of the movement into that country, and of French experience in the matter of absorbing aliens. From 1851 onwards we have figures for aliens resident in France at the date of each census; they are shown in Fig. 29. From 1851 to 1881 the number increased rapidly; at the latter date aliens formed 2·7 per cent. of the population. Thence onwards until after the War the number remained nearly stationary, and so also did the percentage, since the population was only increasing slowly. After the War there was a very rapid increase in the number of aliens; nearly 3 millions were enumerated in the census of 1931, when they formed 6·9 per cent. of the population.

FIGURE 29

The Numbers and Percentages of Aliens in France:
1851 to 1931

	(1) Total population of France	(2) Number of aliens	(3) (2) As percentage of (1)
1851	35,783,170	379,289	1·06
1861	37,386,313	506,381	1·35
1872	36,102,921	740,668	2·05
1881	37,672,048	1,000,454	2·66
1891	38,342,948	1,101,798	2·87
1901	38,961,945	1,037,778	2·67
1911	39,604,992	1,132,696	2·86
1921	37,499,769	1,417,357	3·78
1926	40,743,897	2,505,047	6·15
1931	41,834,923	2,891,168	6·91

The contribution made by aliens to the population of France is not fully measured by these figures; for a large number of aliens have been naturalized and therefore absorbed into the French population. As time has passed naturalization has been made more easy. The law of 1889 made naturalization automatic for children born in France to alien parents who were themselves born in France, and optional to children of other alien parents. In 1927 another important change was made; naturalization was rendered possible for aliens who had lived three years in France, and in certain cases for those who had been there only one year. At the same time the automatic naturalization of children was extended. The law of 1889 greatly increased the number of naturalizations; had it not been for the operation of this law the number and percentage of aliens recorded as resident in the censuses between 1881 and 1921 would have been much greater. It would seem that between 1872 and 1911 there were close upon a million naturalizations. Between 1920 and 1926 there were 147,000; in consequence of the increased facilities for naturalization, the number naturalized in 1927 was no less than 86,000 and has remained at a high level ever since. The inflow of aliens has been very irregular; over a quarter of a million have entered in prosperous years since the War, but in years of depression the number has fallen to little over 50,000. But this does not tell the whole story; for in prosperous years relatively few aliens return home, while in poor years returns may exceed arrivals. In 1927 and 1931 the departures exceeded arrivals by 25,657 and 2,700 respectively. In this manner the unemployment problem has been greatly eased; when there is no work, aliens take themselves away. But the adjustment to economic conditions is not purely automatic; it is largely brought about by the control now exercised over immigration. Before the War there was no official control. Difficulties arose early in the present century; French employers complained that alien workers did not respect contracts, and on the part of the aliens there were complaints about wages and treatment. This induced organizations of employers and of employees to take an interest in the problem, and the Syndicat de la Main-d'Œuvre Agricole, in concert with the Comité des Forges, began to attempt to regulate and supervise the introduction of aliens. After experience had been gained in this way by voluntary organizations, the government took charge of the matter and arranged the bilateral agreements, of which there are now eight in force and of which the Franco-Polish agreement has been cited as one example.

Sixty years ago three-quarters of all aliens in France

FIGURE 30

The Percentages of Aliens by country of origin in the Total Alien Population of France: 1851 to 1926

Country of origin	1851	1861	1872	1881	1891	1901	1911	1921	1926
	%	%	%	%	%	%	%	%	%
Belgium .	33·8	41·4	46·7	43·2	41·2	31·3	24·9	22·8	13·6
Italy . .	16·7	15·4	15·2	24·0	25·3	32·0	36·3	29·5	31·7
Germany .	15·0	16·7	14·1	8·1	7·3	8·7	8·9	5·0	2·9
Spain . .	7·8	7·1	7·2	7·4	6·9	7·8	9·2	16·7	13·5
Switzerland .	6·7	7·0	5·8	6·6	7·4	7·0	6·4	5·9	5·1
Russia and Poland .	2·4	1·9	1·3	1·0	1·3	1·6	3·0	5·1	15·7
British Isles .	5·3	5·2	3·5	3·7	3·5	3·6	3·5	3·1	2·6
Austria-Hungary . .	..	..	0·7	1·2	1·1	1·6	2·2	1·6	3·5
Holland and Luxemburg	..	2·6	2·3	2·1	3·6	2·8	2·2	2·4	1·6
Others . .	12·3	2·7	3·2	2·7	2·4	3·6	3·4	7·9	9·8
Total .	100·0	100·0	100·0	100·0	100·0	100·0	100·0	100·0	100·0

came from Belgium, Italy, and Germany; that is to say, France was drawing upon her nearest neighbours for the augmentation of her labour force. But, as Fig. 30 shows, she has come increasingly to draw upon more distant countries. Indeed, as appears from the latest figures, the proportion of aliens coming from beyond the confines of Europe is beginning to be appreciable. If a series of maps is constructed to show the geographical distribution of aliens in France at various dates, it is found that in the earlier years the aliens were concentrated in the departments touching the Pyrenees, the Mediterranean, and the eastern frontier; the Spaniards, Italians, Germans, and Belgians were, in fact, not very far across their own frontiers. At later dates a tendency can be observed for aliens having these origins to spread farther; but when we come to recent times we find that the aliens are much more widely distributed, and this is due, not only to an increased mobility of aliens from the nearer countries, but also to

FIGURE 31

Aliens employed in French Industries

(from sample investigation made in 1928-9)

Industries	Number of firms	Number of employees		Percentage of aliens
		Total	Aliens	
Mines and Quarries .	195	148,800	70,840	47
Lime and Cement Manufacture . .	130	11,100	5,000	45
Chemical Industries .	200	29,050	13,000	45
Public Works Contracting . . .	486	36,722	16,640	45
Sugar Refining . .	126	29,450	12,230	41
Brick and Tile Manufacture . . .	220	8,550	2,900	32
Metallurgical Industries . . .	501	183,280	56,650	31
Light Shoe-making .	43	3,220	977	30
Hotel Industry . .	1,085	34,400	8,200	23
Glass Manufacture .	280	27,100	5,950	22
Textile Industries .	435	111,100	16,120	15
Saw-milling . .	127	2,250	207	9
Leather Manufacture and Tanning . .	126	5,420	507	9
Book Production .	54	2,830	92	3
Total . .	4,008	633,272	209,313	..

the fact that the aliens coming from distant countries, such as Poland, do not cluster near the frontier.

The most remarkable fact, however, about the aliens in France is not their geographical but their occupational distribution. In 1928/9 an inquiry was made in over 4,000 establishments of every size and in every part of the country which in all employed over 600,000 workers. It emerged that 47 per cent. of all workers in mines and quarries were aliens, and that in cement works, chemical works, public works contracting, and sugar refineries over 40 per cent. were aliens. If the industries represented in the sample are ranged in order, with heavy industries at the top and light industries at the bottom, the percentage of aliens steadily decreases. The French are, in fact, abandoning heavy work to foreigners, and this is the basis of the complaint that is sometimes heard in foreign countries that the French are building up a new form of slave state.

Aliens also play a considerable part in French agriculture; in 1927 there were about a quarter of a million alien workers on the land. They are not so widely dispersed as industrial workers from abroad, and their geographical distribution is similar to that of industrial workers several decades ago. That is to say that they are chiefly to be found in the frontier departments of the south and the east. The most interesting feature in connexion with the place of aliens in French agriculture is that they are by no means confined to wage earning. Of the quarter of a million agricultural workers in 1927 over 90,000 were either owners or tenants of land. The land owned or occupied by aliens amounted to 586,000 hectares, that is an area exceeding in size a large department such as Oise or Eure-et-Loir. In certain departments, such as Lot-et-Garonne and Gers, alien occupiers are especially numerous. The population of Lot-et-Garonne about 1850 was in the neighbourhood of 340,000; by 1921 it had sunk below 250,000; the corresponding figures for Gers are 300,000 and 190,000. Since the War Italians have come into these departments, and have veritably recolonized them, with the result that the population is rising again.

It would seem that the assimilation of aliens has created relatively little difficulty and has aroused no great anxiety in France. This is primarily due to the tolerant attitude of the French; they are not animated, consciously or unconsciously, by any racial theory, and the frequency of mixed marriages is evidence of this. The aliens on their side are disposed to adopt French habits and to *copier le Français*. But assimilation would not have been so easy and so rapid had it not been for the work of the schools and of the Catholic Church. As in America, the schools have been the mechanism for turning foreigners into natives. But the work of the Catholic Church should not be underrated. Most immigrants are Catholics and more-over practising Catholics. The Catholic Church has set itself, without noise or fuss, quietly and persistently to care for the welfare of immigrants through numerous organizations specially created for the purpose, and has been very successful in its attempt to initiate them into French life.

CHAPTER XIII

EUROPE OVERSEAS

EUROPEAN continental movements are only one aspect of European migration, and before we can consider the problem of European migration as a whole we must bring the other aspect under review, namely, the movement of Europeans overseas. This demands a preliminary sketch of the population situation in those countries which collectively constitute Europe overseas. But which are these countries? What we have in mind are those oversea estates, which Europeans have not only acquired, but where they do all the work on the fields and in the factories themselves. This excludes all those countries where Europeans are mere supervisors of non-European labour, Ceylon, Java, and the like. The purest examples of European settlement are Canada and Australia, where non-Europeans are negligible in number; with them we may associate New Zealand and the United States in spite of the fact that Maoris form 4·5 per cent. of the population of the former and non-Europeans 11·3 per cent. of the population of the latter. Central and South America and South Africa stand in an intermediate position so far as the proportion of Europeans to non-Europeans is concerned; in the former persons of pure European stock form about 38 per cent. and in the latter about 22 per cent. of the total population. Therefore attention will be concentrated upon the first-mentioned countries.

Some information has already been given relating to the growth of population; in Figs. 4 and 5 the data were shown in graphic form, and in Fig. 6 the rates of increase for successive periods were tabulated. From these figures we learn that population has grown with great, though, except in the case of Canada, decreasing rapidity. The decrease in the rate of growth, as illustrated in Fig. 6, is not surprising; in the early days of a new country, when population is sparse, a small total volume of immigration may cause a rapid increase which cannot be maintained even with a vastly greater absolute volume of immigration. In order to get a fair comparison between the rate of growth in these newly settled countries and the rate in old countries, we may choose the period 1881 to 1921; at the beginning of this period the early rush of incomers had passed, and, if we end at 1921, we exclude the recent period about which there will be more to say later. During these forty years the average annual rate of increase was 2·3 per cent. in New Zealand, 2·2 per cent. in Australia, 1·9 per cent. in the United States, and 1·8 per cent. in Canada. No figures are available for South Africa until 1904; between 1904 and 1911 the average annual rate of increase of the whole population was 2·1 per cent. and of the Europeans 1·9, while between 1911 and 1921 it was 1·5 per cent. for the whole population and 1·8 per cent. for Europeans. As to Central and South America no separate figures can be given for Europeans, and the figures for the total population are subject to a wide margin of error. But it would seem that between 1880 and 1920 the average annual rate of growth was about 1·0 per cent. Between 1881 and 1921 the average annual rate was 1·1 per cent. in Japan and 0·9 per cent. in England and Wales. In other words, when we omit the early years during which growth was almost inevitably very swift, we find that the rate of growth in the United States and the British Dominions has been twice that in the old countries.

Much interest attaches to the part played by immigration in the building up of the population of these new countries. Very careful estimates for the United States have been made by Messrs. Thompson and Whelpton, and Fig. 32 is taken from their work. It refers to the white population only and shows the percentage of growth during each decade which was due to immigration. Column 1 gives the absolute gain in population during each decade from 1800 to 1930; columns 2 and 3 give the absolute gain

M

through natural increase and the percentage of the whole gain due to natural increase, while columns 4 and 5 show the same for immigration. The percentage gain from immigration, which was very high in certain decades of

FIGURE 32

The Contribution of Immigration to the Growth of Population in the United States: 1800 to 1930

Period	Total growth of white population (thousands)	Growth by natural increase		Growth by immigration	
		Thousands	Per cent. of population growth	Thousands	Per cent. of population growth
1800–10	1,556	1,494	96·0	62	4·0
1810–20	2,005	1,934	96·5	71	3·5
1820–30	2,671	2,548	95·4	123	4·6
1830–40	3,658	3,165	86·5	493	13·5
1840–50	5,357	3,937	73·5	1,420	26·5
1850–60	7,369	4,811	65·3	2,558	34·7
1860–70	7,415	5,341	72·0	2,074	28·0
1870–80	9,066	6,486	71·5	2,580	28·5
1880–90	11,581	6,617	57·1	4,964	42·9
1890–1900	11,708	8,019	68·5	3,689	31·5
1900–10	14,923	8,680	58·2	6,243	41·8
1910–20	13,089	10,864	83·0	2,225	17·0
1920–30	15,466	12,131	78·4	3,335	21·6

the eighteenth century, was low in the first three decades of the last century, never amounting to 5 per cent. of the total; in the fourth decade it rose to over 13 per cent. and has since remained at a high figure. It will be seen that the percentage gain from immigration has fluctuated; this is only the other side of the picture shown in Fig. 10 which gave the emigration from Europe since 1846 in five-year periods and brought out the fluctuating nature of the outflow from Europe. Nevertheless, the tendency was for immigration to play an increasingly large part in the building up of the population of the United States until the decade in which the World War fell. The decrease of immigration during that decade needs no explanation; but

it is very noteworthy that during the first post-war decade
the percentage gain from immigration was little more than
half what it was in the decade 1900–10.

FIGURE 33

*The Contribution of Immigration to the Growth of Popula-
tion in Canada, New Zealand, and Australia*

Period	Population at beginning of period (in millions)	Annual natural increase (per cent.)	Annual net immigration (per cent.)	Annual total net gain (per cent.)
	CANADA			
1901–11	5·37	1·59	1·82	3·41
1911–21	7·21	1·60	0·60	2·20
1921–31	8·79	1·51	0·30	1·81
	NEW ZEALAND*			
1871–81	0·26	3·92	4·58	8·50
1881–91	0·49	2·69	0·10	2·79
1891–1901	0·63	1·87	0·45	2·32
1901–11	0·77	1·95	1·06	3·01
1911–21	1·01	1·65	0·44	2·09
1921–31	1·24	1·31	0·50	1·81
1931–2	1·44	0·91	−0·20	0·71
1932–3	1·46	0·87	−0·15	0·72
	AUSTRALIA*			
1871–81	1·70	2·30	1·26	3·56
1881–91	2·31	2·30	1·72	4·02
1891–1901	3·24	1·82	−0·02	1·80
1901–11	3·83	1·62	0·34	1·96
1911–21	4·57	1·71	0·33	2·04
1921–31	5·51	1·37	0·55	1·92
1931–2	6·55	0·82	−0·05	0·77

* The population figures for Australia and New Zealand exclude
aborigines and Maoris.

The contribution of immigration to the growth of
Canada, Australia, and New Zealand is illustrated in Fig.
33. Column 1 shows the population at the beginning of
each period, column 2 the average annual percentage gain
through natural increase, column 3 the average annual net

gain by migration, and column 4 the average annual net gain to total population. The gain through natural increase has remained fairly steady in Canada. The net gain through immigration was very high before the War, remained high during the War, but was markedly lower in the post-war decade. In obtaining the net gain through immigration we have taken account of the loss through emigration. The high average annual loss through emigration has been the remarkable feature of Canadian history; during the two decades 1901–11 and 1911–21 this loss was greater than the gain through natural increase. The explanation is the large drain of population over the frontier into the United States. When we bring the net gain through immigration into relation with the net increase, we see that, whereas in the decade 1901–11, which witnessed an immense expansion of the population of Canada, immigration accounted for about half the growth, in the subsequent decades it has been of much less importance; it is especially noteworthy that between 1921 and 1931 immigration was of less importance than between 1911 and 1921.

The Australian and New Zealand stories are also illustrated in Fig. 33. The fluctuations in net immigration have been far more violent than in the cases of the United States and Canada; that remains true if the very large immigration into New Zealand in the decade 1871–81 is disregarded because it took place at a time when population was still very sparse. Thus, for example, between 1891 and 1901 there was a net loss by migration movements from Australia, while in the preceding decade the gain to New Zealand was negligible. But, taking several decades together, immigration has played a very important part in the building up of the population of these two Dominions; thus, in the sixty-four years between the end of 1860 and the end of 1924, 76 per cent. of the growth of the population of Australia was due to natural increase and 24 per cent. to net immigration. The most striking fact, however, which is brought to light by Fig. 33 is the decrease in the average annual gain by natural increase. Whereas it was well over 2 per cent. up to 1890, it was below 2 per cent. during the next four decades, and since 1930 has been under 1 per cent.; the fall in the gain by births has been dramatic and has not been offset by a corresponding fall in loss by deaths. To pursue the implication of the decline in the rate of natural increase at this point, however, would be to anticipate a discussion of the probable future trend of population in these countries which comes more properly after some further examination of the present position.

FIGURE 34

Apportionment of the White Population of the United States by country of origin: 1790 and 1920

Country of origin	Percentage distribution	
	1790	*1920*
Great Britain and N. Ireland .	77·0	41·4
Germany	7·4	16·3
Irish Free State . . .	4·4	11·2
Holland	3·3	2·0
France	1·9	1·9
Canada	1·6	4·3
Belgium	1·5	0·8
Switzerland	0·9	1·1
Mexico	0·7	1·2
Sweden	0·5	2·1
Norway	0·2	1·5
Czechoslovakia . . .	0·1	1·8
Portugal	0·1	0·3
Spain	0·1	0·2
Poland	..	4·1
Italy	..	3·6
Russia	..	1·8
Other countries . . .	0·3	4·4
Total . . .	100·0	100·0

One interesting feature of the present position in these countries is the origin of the existing population. In Fig. 34 will be found an apportionment by country of origin of

the white population of the United States in the years
1790 and 1920. The figures for 1790, though the result of
a careful survey of the available evidence, are no more
than approximate; those for 1920 were prepared by a committee representing the Departments of State, Commerce,
and Labour in order that the quota provisions of the Act
of 1924, which will be described in the next chapter, might
be put into force. The figures, it need hardly be said, do
not mean that there was a certain percentage of Austrians,
Belgians, and so on in the United States at a given date,
but that Austria, Belgium, and other countries had made
contributions to the population of the United States in
proportion to these figures. In Chapter IV, where Fig. 11
illustrated the changes in the parts played by the chief
European countries of emigration, it was remarked that
the emergence of southern and eastern European countries
as sources of the supply of emigrants had affected the
United States more than any other country of immigration. It was in 1896 that the 'new' immigration from these
regions exceeded the 'old' immigration for the first time.
The resulting changes in the national origin of the white
population are striking; the share of Great Britain and
Northern Ireland has fallen from 77·0 to 41·4 per cent.,
while Italy, Poland, and Russia, who do not appear in the
list for 1790, are now represented.

FIGURE 35

*Apportionment of the Total Population of the United States
between Europeans and Non-Europeans in 1930*

Origin	Per cent. of total population
European	88·7
Non-European	11·3
Negro	9·7
Mexican	1·2
Indian	0·3
Chinese	0·1 (less than)
Japanese	0·1 (less than)
	100·0

It is not possible to analyse the total population in 1790 into whites and others because Indians were not enumerated before 1860. Omitting Indians the whites formed 80·7 per cent. of the population in 1790, and therefore would be found to have constituted a rather smaller proportion if the Indians could be taken into account. In 1930 the whites formed 88·7 per cent. of the total population; in this calculation Mexicans, who were at one time counted as whites, are included as non-Europeans. Therefore the Europeans have gained relatively to the non-Europeans in spite of an influx of Mexicans, Chinese, and Japanese. This is not because the natural increase of the negroes, who constituted about 20 per cent. of the total population in 1790, has been less than that of the whites, but because the latter have been reinforced by immigration whereas the former have not.

FIGURE 36

Apportionment of the Total Population of Canada between Europeans and Non-Europeans in 1881 and 1931

Origin	Per cent. of total population	
	1881	*1931*
European . . .	97·0	97·7
Non-European . .	3·0	2·3
Negro . . .	0·5	0·2
Indian . . .	2·5	1·2
Chinese . . .	..	0·4
Japanese . .	..	0·2
Others . . .	..	0·3
	100·0	100·0

For more than a hundred years the percentage which non-Europeans have formed of the population of Canada has been very small. It was 3 per cent. in 1881 and is now 2·3 per cent. In spite of the fact that between 1881 and 1931 Chinese and Japanese have come into Canada the percentage of non-Europeans has decreased; the reason is that the fall in the percentage which negroes form of the population has not been offset by the arrival of such other non-Europeans as have come in.

FIGURE 37

Apportionment of the Total Population of Canada in 1871 and 1931 and of the European Population of Australia in 1891 by country of origin

	Percentage distribution		
	Canada		Australia
Country of origin	*1871*	*1931*	*1891*
English . . .	20·3	26·4	53·0
Scottish . .	15·8	13·0	13·0
Irish . . .	24·3	11·9	23·0
Other British . .	0·2	0·6	1·5
Total British .	60·6	51·9	90·5
French . . .	31·1	28·2	..
Dutch . . .	0·9	1·4	..
German . .	5·8	4·6	5·2
Italian . . .	..	0·9	..
Polish . . .	..	1·4	..
Scandinavian . .	..	2·2	1·9
Indian and Eskimo .	0·7	1·2	..
Negro . . .	0·6	0·2	..
Others . . .	0·3	8·0	2·4
Total . .	100·0	100·0	100·0

Fig. 37 shows that there has been no striking change in the origins of the white population of Canada as in the case of the United States. The proportion of British has fallen; this is due in the main to a decline in the percentage which the Irish form of the total population; for the part played by the English has increased. But we can also observe, as in the case of the United States, but to a much smaller extent, that a greater share is now contributed by southern and eastern Europeans than was the case in the last century.

In New Zealand Europeans now form 95 per cent. of the total population and are almost all of British origin. The Maoris account for 4·5 per cent., leaving only 0·5 per cent. of other non-Europeans. In 1934 the other non-Europeans included 2,543 Chinese, 1,128 Indians, and 1,000 Syrians. But it is of interest to note that there were 5,000 Chinese in New Zealand in 1880 forming 1 per cent. of the total population; since that time the proportion of Asiatics has sunk. For Australia we have figures for the national origins of the white population in 1891, and they show a smaller proportion of British than in New Zealand; by that date Germans and Scandinavians had made an appreciable contribution to the population. It is probable that the share of the British has fallen slightly since 1891. While immigration from northern Europe has fallen off, Italians and others, not represented before, have come in, though not in large numbers. The largest immigration of Italians in any one year was in 1927 when it reached nearly 8,000. The most significant feature of this aspect of Australian population history, however, relates to non-Europeans. We may leave the aborigines out of account since they have taken no part in the exploitation of the country. They may have numbered 150,000 when Australia was discovered, and now number well under 100,000. The interesting facts relate to Asiatics who at one time were beginning to assume an important part in the opening up of some areas of the country. In 1885 there were about 40,000 Chinese and 10,000 Kanakas in Australia, who together formed 2 per cent. of the population. The Kanakas have been deported, and the number of Chinese has been reduced to half that present fifty years ago. Thus the proportion, which Europeans form of those engaged in exploiting the country, has risen, and this is in line with the experience of the United States, Canada, and New Zealand.

There are two other features of the present situation which deserve attention. It is not infrequently suggested that there are regions in these new oversea countries where the climate is such that Europeans cannot exploit them. This raises an important problem because, whatever the truth of the matter may be, it has a direct bearing upon the question of migration policy which will occupy us later. For it would clearly be hard to defend the retention of regions by Europeans which they could not use.

The suggestion that the major groups of mankind are innately differentiated in such a manner that one group is better adapted to one kind of climate than another, would probably strike most naturalists as more likely to be true than false. For those acquainted with the geographical distribution of species and varieties know that many of them are narrowly restricted in range; it has further been shown in some cases that the limitation of range is due to inability to survive except within definite climatic limits, and it may be suspected the same also holds true in many other cases. While human groups are not as clear cut even as varieties, it is, nevertheless, apparently the case that they have remained for some thousands of years in the same climatic zones, some in tropical and others in temperate regions; and it might on that account be expected that they would have become adapted to these regions. Adaptation need not be so strict that there is inability to survive outside a given climatic zone; it may merely mean that, outside this zone, there are higher mortality rates, less vigour, and perhaps lower fertility, and it is this which those who make the suggestion about the possible adaptation of the larger human groups to climatic zones seem to have in mind. It has, in fact, been supposed that certain physical characteristics of the major groups of mankind are outward signs of such adaptation; the dark skin and wide nostrils of the negro are cited as examples.

The suggestion can only be tested in the light of information that has become available in consequence of the movement of peoples outside their normal climatic zones. American negroes, for example, have moved, especially since the War, into the northern States, and in some such States, Minnesota for example, the cold in winter is very severe. The vital statistics of negroes living under such conditions are therefore of much interest. But they are difficult to interpret; the chances of life or death depend largely upon access to health services, housing conditions, and occupational circumstances. Negroes tend to follow particular occupations and to live in a different manner from the surrounding whites; further, they do not always benefit equally with whites from health and sanitary organizations. So far, however, as the available facts concerning the death-rate among negroes in these northern regions go, there does not seem to be any reason for supposing that they are less well able to survive there than Europeans.

The opposite state of things is found in Queensland. There Europeans live under tropical or semi-tropical conditions. All Queensland is above 29° S. latitude; Brisbane (population over 300,000) is 27° S.; Rockhampton and Townsville, each with over 30,000 inhabitants, are 23° S. and 19° S. respectively. Latitude is not, of course, the only consideration, and geographers have attempted to take all important climatic conditions into account and to construct climographs which summarize them; measured in this way conditions in Townsville are almost identical with those in Calcutta. This means that the white man in Townsville has to face conditions very similar, so far as they are 'natural', to those surrounding the Indian in Bengal. When white men first settled in Queensland they attempted to exploit the country by means of coloured labour, and imported Kanakas from the Pacific region. In those days vital statistics of the whites showed that mortality was high, and lent support to the opinion that white men could not flourish in the tropics. Opinion, however, turned against the use of coloured labourers who were in consequence repatriated; the whites had either to brace themselves up and do the work of the fields and the factories themselves, or leave the province. This seems to have stimulated them to consider carefully what habits of life should be adopted and what precautions taken.

The results have been remarkable; for although Europeans have perforce taken to heavy labour in the sugar plantations and elsewhere, and so made the attainment of healthy conditions less easy than before, vital statistics have immensely improved. There is no evidence at present, judging from length of life, infant mortality, or fertility of women, that Queensland is less healthy than other Australian states; and Townsville, which is the most tropical of the towns in the State, shows as good figures as for the province as a whole. This must not be taken as decisive, for there are many traps and doubtful features in the interpretation of these figures, and, in any case, a sufficient length of time has not elapsed. But while there may be as yet no proof that white men can live and work in the tropics and remain as healthy and vigorous as in a temperate climate, there is no evidence that they cannot do so. There is therefore no basis for saying that these new European estates contain areas of which, for reasons of climate, Europeans by themselves cannot make full use.

The other matter which deserves attention at this point is the population carrying capacity of these new oversea countries. It was pointed out in Chapter XI that there is no way of ascertaining the most desirable density of population in any country, however full our knowledge of all the circumstances may be. On the other hand, we may hope that a survey of existing circumstances will in some cases enable us to detect maladjustment, though certain tests, such as unemployment upon which many rely for this purpose, are not valid. Let us therefore examine the situation in these countries in the hope that some indication as to the position may emerge.

One of the most striking facts about these countries is the low density of population. In the United States, one of the most favoured regions of the world as regards climate, natural resources, fertility, and ease of communication, there are only 41 persons per square mile, whereas in Europe the corresponding figure is 130. There is no reason for supposing that Europe is over-populated as a whole; there are, as we have said, European countries which show signs of congestion, but Russia could no doubt hold a much larger population than it does at

FIGURE 38

Density of Population in certain countries in Europe and of European Origin

Country or Area	Population in 1932 (thousands)	Density per square mile
England and Wales	40,350	695
Ireland . .	2,974	155
Europe (excluding U.S.S.R.) .	383,444	184
United States .	124,822	41
Canada . .	10,506	2·9 (7·7 per habitable square mile)
Australia . .	6,576	2·2 (3·8 ,, ,, ,,)
New Zealand .	1,534	14·7 (18·1 ., ,, ,,)

present, and France is traditionally a country of immigration. On the other hand, there are grounds for thinking that a denser population in the United States would be beneficial because it would tend to reduce the costs of production and of distribution. The density of population is much lower in the British Dominions than in the United States; but it is not easy to obtain a fair measure of the density on account of the large areas of ice-bound or desert land which they contain. Canada is 3,504,688 square miles in extent; if we regard Yukon and the North-West Territory together with the northern parts of the prairie provinces and of Quebec as barren, we are left with a habitable area of 1,354,000 square miles. This makes the present density of population 7·7 per habitable square mile. Australia contains 2,970,000 square miles, of which two-fifths are desert, leaving a habitable area of 1,725,000 square miles, consisting of 1,009,000 square miles of good pasture, 616,000 square miles of land fit for close settle-

ment, and 100,000 square miles suitable for tropical agriculture. The density per habitable square mile is 3·8. If
we deduct from the 104,015 square miles, which forms
New Zealand, the area which is mountainous or covered
with inland water, we are left with 84,500 square miles,
and that gives a density of 18·1 per habitable square mile.
Even when we have made these deductions, the contrast
between these countries and European countries remains
very marked as Fig. 38 shows.

FIGURE 39

*Potential Population of Australia, based on the Population
of Corresponding Rainfall Areas in the United States*

Annual rainfall	Australian areas in rainfall groups (square miles)	United States. All States. Average density (persons per square mile)	Australian potential population based on all U.S.A. (persons)	U.S.A. western States. Average density (persons per square mile)	Australian potential population based on western U.S.A. (persons)
No settlement area	444,777	..	..	..	..
Under 10 in.	625,357	2·4	1,499,000	0·5	312,000
10–15 in.	603,605	4·6	2,597,000	3·0	1,810,000
15–20 in.	358,458	8·5	3,047,000	9·0	3,225,000
20–30 in.	534,766	20·0	10,695,000	19·0	10,161,000
30–40 in.	213,195	50·0	10,660,000	31·0	6,609,000
Over 40 in.	194,423	90·0	17,498,000	38·5	7,486,000
Totals	2,974,581	..	45,996,000	..	29,603,000

If it is correct to assume that it would be beneficial for
the United States to hold a denser population than they
do at present, the advantages of a larger population for
Canada must be still greater. For the habitable part of
Canada is far more sparsely peopled, and the country,
moreover, is richly endowed with mineral resources. The
natural resources of Australia and New Zealand are not
as rich as those of Canada, but it can be shown that even
on a purely agricultural basis Australia is very lightly
peopled as compared with the United States. The comparison rests upon data for rainfall. It is possible to divide
a country into areas, each with a given annual rainfall, and
to ascertain the density of population in each area. This
can be done for the United States as a whole and also for

those States which lie west of the Mississippi. We can then divide Australia into similar rainfall areas, and apply to each Australian area, first the density for equivalent rainfall areas in the whole of the United States, and secondly the density for equivalent rainfall areas in the western States only. If we do the former and add up the totals for each area we obtain a figure which tells us what the population of Australia would be if equivalent rainfall areas were as densely peopled in Australia as in the United States as a whole; if we do the latter we obtain a figure which tells us what the population of Australia would be if it was as densely peopled as the western States. The former calculation gives a total of 46 millions, the second a total of 29·6 millions, whereas the population of Australia is 6,576,000 millions. The first calculation is not very informative on account of the high degree of industrialization in the eastern States; but the American densities in the second calculation are for regions where there is very little industry, and it is a striking fact that, when these densities are applied to equivalent Australian areas, we obtain a total which is nearly five times that of the Australian population. For various reasons it is easy to infer too much from such calculations; it is, for instance, not only the total rainfall, but also the distribution of rainfall over the year which is important. But it is true to say that on a purely agricultural basis Australia is very sparsely peopled when compared with the United States.

Thus there is a good case for saying that a much denser population will be necessary in these new countries if their resources are to be fully employed. But the development of a country cannot proceed beyond a certain speed; roads, railways, and harbours must be built and land must be cleared. All these take time. Therefore, no matter how many people a country could accommodate in time, using existing technical methods for its exploitation, there is a limit to the rate of increase of population which is desirable. We cannot determine this rate of increase theoretically; but experience shows that the population of all these countries has increased at an average annual rate of about 2 per cent. for the sixty years ending in 1924. This is only an average figure. All these countries have known periods when the rate of increase was much lower than this because, owing to economic depression, immigration was very much reduced, or when, as in Australia in the last years of the nineteenth century, the migration stream for a time flowed the other way. They have all also known periods of boom when the inflow of immigrants has swollen to relatively huge proportions. But, taking the fat years with the lean, the average rate of growth has been about 2 per cent. per annum, and we may conclude that the average rate, taking good years with bad, should remain at that level for some considerable time to come. If it does, then, although these countries will still be lightly populated for several decades, there will be no substance in the charge that the owners occupy territory that they do not use; for they will be making all due speed towards full exploitation. But, if it does not, the charge will lie.

We are thus led to examine the prospects of the increase of population in these new countries. Some of the material upon which any opinion must be based has already been provided. We have found that the rate of increase has dropped. There are two reasons for this: the rate of natural increase has been declining for some time, and the contribution of immigration to the building up of the population, which was considerable and in general becoming more important up to twenty years ago, has since that date been on a lower level. In other words one source of supply has been diminishing for a long time, namely surplus of births over deaths, while the other, namely immigration, has begun to show signs of failure. Let us now consider the prospect of growth through natural increase.

In Figs. 15 and 16 the birth- and death-rates for the United States, Australia, and New Zealand were shown in graphic form up to 1930. The latest stages of the story in these countries and in South Africa and Argentina are given in Fig. 40 where the rates are set out, so far as they are available, for periods and single years between 1901

FIGURE 40

Birth-rates, Death-rates, and Natural Increase in Europe Overseas

Country	1901–1905	1911–1913	1921–1925	1926–1930	1931	1932	1933	1934
United States:								
Birth-rate	..	25·1	22·6	19·7	18·0	17·4	16·4	..
Death-rate	..	14·1	11·9	11·8	11·1	10·9	10·7	..
Natural increase	..	11·0	10·7	7·9	6·9	6·5	5·7	..
Canada:								
Birth-rate	..	..	27·1	24·1	23·2	22·5	20·9	20·4
Death-rate	..	..	11·1	11·2	10·1	9·9	9·6	9·4
Natural increase	..	..	16·0	12·9	13·1	12·6	11·3	11·0
Australia:								
Birth-rate	26·4	28·0	23·9	21·0	18·2	16·9	16·8	16·4
Death-rate	11·8	10·9	9·5	9·3	8·7	8·6	8·9	9·3
Natural increase	14·6	17·1	14·4	11·7	9·5	8·3	7·9	7·1
New Zealand:								
Birth-rate	26·6	26·2	22·2	19·7	18·4	17·1	16·6	16·5
Death-rate	9·9	9·2	8·6	8·6	8·3	8·0	8·0	8·5
Natural increase	16·7	17·0	13·6	11·1	10·1	9·1	8·6	8·0
South Africa (European population):								
Birth-rate	..	..	27·1	26·1	25·4	24·2	23·6	23·5
Death-rate	..	..	9·7	9·7	9·4	10·0	9·4	9·7
Natural increase	..	..	17·4	16·4	16·0	14·2	14·0	13·8
Argentina:								
Birth-rate	..	..	32·8	30·4	28·7	28·1	26·0	25·3
Death-rate	..	..	14·6	13·5	12·5	12·0	11·7	11·7
Natural increase	..	..	18·2	16·9	16·2	16·1	14·3	13·5

and 1934. The rapid decline in natural increase in the former group of countries is at once evident. It is least marked in Canada; but when the Canadian position is analysed it is found that the regions inhabited by the French alone still continue to show a considerable natural increase; in 1926–30, for instance, the average annual natural increase was 1·7 per cent. in Quebec but only 0·7 per cent. in British Columbia. Non-French Canada in fact is in much the same position as the United States.

N

Since the death-rates in all these countries are very low already, it would seem that, unless the decline in the birth-rate is halted, natural increase must soon come to an end. We have learnt, however, that crude birth- and death-rates do not tell the whole story, and that it is possible that a population may show a surplus of births over deaths although it is no longer replacing itself. Moreover, in Fig. 25 will be found a table showing the net reproduction rates which have been worked out, and it includes rates for the United States, Australia, and New Zealand. From this it appears that the population of the United States was only just replacing itself in 1931, while Australia and New Zealand were already below replacement rate in 1932.

It is therefore certain that, if present conditions are stabilized, additions to the population of these countries through natural increase will presently cease. The same is almost certainly true of the non-French part of Canada. If conditions change, it is far more likely that they will change in the direction of reducing than of raising the net reproduction rate; for the forces tending to reduce fertility do not seem to have worked themselves out. In the United States, for example, the reservoirs of high fertility are among the foreign born and the rural population; and owing to the slowing down of immigration the foreign born are becoming relatively less numerous, while urbanization is increasing. It would seem likely in fact that annual accessions to population through natural increase, though they may continue for a time, will be relatively unimportant. In order to obtain a more definite forecast of future population the method described at the end of Chapter X must be employed. We owe a number of calculations by this method made on different assumptions for the United States to Messrs. Thompson and Whelpton. Assuming, for instance, that fertility continues to decline, but more slowly than recently, until it stabilizes in 1970 at 67 per cent. of the 1925–9 level, they find that the population of the United States will reach a maximum of 138 millions

in 1955 and will decline to 129·2 millions in 1970. In this
calculation migration movements are left out of account.
If the same hypothesis is adopted concerning the future
course of fertility, but a greater expectation of life is
assumed together with an annual gain by immigration of
50,000 between 1935 and 1939 and thereafter of 100,000,
the maximum population will be 146 millions in 1970; by
1980 it will have declined to 144 millions. If another
100,000 immigrants are assumed annually, the maximum
population will be reached in 1975.

It is therefore probable that, although in the absence
of immigration, population will continue to grow in the
United States, Australia, New Zealand, and non-French
Canada for two decades or more, the maximum population
will not be more than 10 to 15 per cent. larger than the
present population. Thereafter decline will set in assuming
that fertility does not rise. Hence, the great importance of
immigration when the future of these countries is under
review. If they are to continue to grow at an annual
average rate of 2 per cent. or even at a much lower rate,
they will require more assistance from immigration than
before. But, as we have seen, the contribution of immigration to the population has been less during the last fifteen
years than before the War. In part, and in the case of the
United States in very large part, the decline in immigration
has been due to the imposition of legal restrictions upon
entry. The American Act of 1924 laid down that the
maximum annual immigration into the United States
should be 150,000 from quota countries; but we have just
seen that, if present trends continue and immigration adds
no more than this to the population, the population of the
United States will never be more than 146 millions and,
having reached this figure, will then decline. It is thus a
matter of no little interest to ask why these countries
should have adopted a policy of restriction at, what can
without exaggeration be called, a crisis in their population
histories, and why in particular the United States should

have adopted so severe a policy of restriction that, unless
fertility rises, a decline in population will be inevitable.

The answer to this question will be sought in the next
Chapter. It remains only to say something more about
South Africa and Central and South America. After
noting that the population of these areas has been increasing rapidly, though it is still sparse, we left them aside
because other countries are of greater interest as being
wholly or largely European. Three-quarters of the population of South Africa is non-European, and the problems
relating to this section of the population are best considered
together with those of other Africans in Chapter XX. As
to the white population of South Africa the outstanding
facts are that the birth-rate and natural increase are high;
they have fallen, but not to the same extent as in the other
countries for which data are given in Fig. 40. The net
reproduction rate must be well above unity; nevertheless
the indications are that it will slowly fall to unity. Except
in the early days of settlement immigration has played no
large part in building up the white population of South
Africa, and the reason is that the country offers little
attraction to the European wage earner; it is only the
man with some capital who can fit himself into the South
African system. As to Central and South America the position in regard to vital statistics is not unlike that in South
Africa. The birth-rate is high, higher than in South Africa
for every country for which it is recorded with the exception of Uruguay. But it is everywhere falling. In comparison with South Africa the death-rates are still higher,
and in consequence natural increase in most Central and
South American countries is not much above that found
in South Africa. Taking the data as they are (there are no
figures for Brazil and where they exist they can be no
more than approximate), the prospect is that the population of this continent will grow by natural increase for a
long time to come. Moreover, the volume of immigration
does not exhibit a tendency to fall off to the extent which

we noticed in the case of the United States and the Dominions. The facts have been illustrated in Fig. 12. Therefore it is much more likely that this continent will become at least fairly densely peopled than is the case for the other areas considered in this chapter.

CHAPTER XIV

THE REGULATION OF EUROPEAN OVERSEA MOVEMENTS

By regulation is meant any governmental action which brings oversea movements under control whether the aim is to restrict or to promote migration; while it is true that the object of regulation has usually been to restrict movement, this has not always been the case as is shown by the policy adopted by Great Britain since 1922. The aim of this chapter is to outline the action which has been taken and to assess its results. In the next chapter we shall attempt to explain why governments have acted in this way; we shall then be in a position to discuss whether movement should be regulated and, if so, with what purpose and in what manner.

Until the nineteenth century was well advanced, obstacles to emigration from many European countries were in existence. An Act of 1782 prohibited the emigration of skilled workmen from the British Isles; it was not repealed until 1824. Those who wished to emigrate from certain continental countries had to obtain police permits, while serfdom, so long as it obtained in eastern Europe, was a bar to movement. Gradually, however, those who wanted to leave became free to do so. In recent years obstacles have once more been imposed upon emigration; they have been described in Chapter XII, but it will be remembered that, except in the cases of Italy and Russia, the only serious impediment is that those who want to go must usually show that they are in a position to comply with the regulations of the country proposed as their destination.

Obstacles to immigration also existed in earlier times; thus immigration to South America was limited to Spaniards and Portuguese until the revolution which resulted in independence. Round about the middle of the last century, however, men became in general free to come and go between Europe and the European settlements overseas. As we have seen, obstacles were not put in the way of emigration until after the War; the regulation of immigration into the oversea countries, however, began earlier, and, so far as non-Europeans are concerned, was drastic before the end of the century. Since the policy of the oversea countries towards non-European immigration has a most important bearing upon the question of the movements of Europeans, we may extend our sketch of the regulation of the immigration of Europeans by adding some account of the steps taken in regard to non-Europeans.

Chinese began to arrive in California in considerable numbers soon after 1850. Local feeling was roused, and various attempts were made by the Californian legislature to check or prohibit this inflow, all of which were declared unconstitutional. The federal government did not sympathize with the anti-Chinese feeling, and concluded with China in 1868 the Burlingame treaty which recognized the right of Chinese to enter. The agitation continued, and both national parties presently declared themselves in favour of exclusion; in 1879 Congress passed an exclusion Act which was, however, vetoed by President Hayes. But in the following year, in response to continued pressure, a treaty was made with China which admitted the right of the United States to 'regulate, limit or suspend' Chinese immigration, and in 1882 an Act was passed suspending it for ten years. In 1892 suspension was continued for another ten years and in 1902 it was continued for an indefinite period. But the door has been double locked against the Chinese; for the Immigration Act of 1924, of which more will be heard later, declares that persons ineligible for citizenship are excluded from the United States, and Chinese are among those who are ineligible. Chinese were excluded from Hawaii in 1898 and from the Philippines in 1902.

Japanese began to arrive in the United States shortly before 1900, and anti-Japanese feeling soon manifested itself. In 1907 President Roosevelt concluded a so-called Gentleman's Agreement with Japan according to which the Japanese government undertook to refuse passports to Japanese labourers who proposed to go to the United States. In consequence the immigration of Japanese labourers came to an end; but local feeling was not satisfied, partly on account of the entry of 'picture brides', that is of Japanese women who came to marry Japanese already in the United States—a form of immigration not contrary to the Agreement. Agitation in favour of complete exclusion continued, and this was brought about by the Act of 1924 since Japanese, as well as Chinese, are ineligible for citizenship. As to other non-Europeans, Indians and inhabitants of the East Indies are excluded under the Immigration Act of 1917 which laid down that natives of a defined area in Asia, constituting the 'Asiatic barred zone', should not enter. Since natives of India and of the East Indies are not eligible for citizenship, they are also excluded under the Act of 1924. There is no general provision against the entry of Africans, since they are eligible for citizenship and are not natives of any barred zone; but they come under the quota provisions of the Act of 1924 which limits the entry of Africans from independent and mandated countries to 100 each year; immigrants from African colonies are chargeable to the quota of the mother country. Mexicans are also eligible for citizenship, and they are not subject to any quota. The only restrictions to which they are subject are under the Act of 1917; they must obtain a visa, are examined and submitted to tests, and have to pay a head tax of 8 dollars (total cost 18 dollars).

Events have followed much the same course in Canada. Chinese began to move into British Columbia about 1880. In 1885 a poll-tax of $50 per head was imposed; this was raised to $100 in 1901 and to $500 in 1904. Finally, under the Chinese Immigration Act of 1923 the entry of Chinese was prohibited except in the case of those coming as merchants, students, or under one or two other special categories. Japanese began to arrive about 1905, and this led to the conclusion of a Gentleman's Agreement in 1908 on the lines of the American arrangement; the agreement remains in force. The component states of what is now the Dominion of Australia began to impose restrictions upon Chinese immigration at relatively early dates, Victoria in 1855 and New South Wales in 1861. Under the federal Immigration Restriction Act of 1901 entry was prohibited to any person 'who fails to pass the dictation test', that is to write not less than fifty words dictated to him 'in any European language'. In 1905 'prescribed' was substituted for 'European', and in 1931 it was laid down that aliens must obtain a landing permit prior to embarkation. These provisions have been used to exclude Chinese. In 1905 a clause was inserted in the Immigration Act providing that, 'if an arrangement has been made with the government of any country regulating the admission to the Commonwealth of the subjects or citizens of that country,' the latter shall not 'be required to pass the dictation test'. An arrangement has been made with Japan whereby passports are not granted to Japanese who intend to settle. The Pacific Islanders Act of 1901 provided for the deportation with certain exceptions of all Kanakas, the term applied to Pacific Islanders, who were found in Australia after 1906. Thus non-European labourers are excluded from settling in Australia.

In New Zealand the Chinese Immigrants Act of 1881 placed a poll-tax on each Chinaman admitted; under an Act of 1888 onerous conditions were laid upon ships bringing Chinese; under an Act of 1907 a reading test in English was imposed upon Chinese immigrants; finally under an Act of 1920 every person, not of British birth or parentage, is required to obtain a permit to land. This requirement is used to keep Chinese and Japanese out of New Zealand. In South Africa an Act of 1913 prohibits the entry of persons who are undesirable on account of a low standard of living, and thus keeps out all Asiatics, including natives of India. The latter contribute the most important group of potential Asiatic immigrants into the Dominions other than Chinese and Japanese. Indians are excluded from Australia under the dictation test; they are excluded from New Zealand under the requirement of 1920 concerning permits, for a permit must be obtained by Indians and members of other native races within the empire before they can land. They are kept out of Canada partly by the Continuous Passage Ordinance, and partly by an Order in Council of 1923, issued under the Immigration Acts of 1910–24, which prohibit the landing of any Asiatic unless he possesses capital and intends to farm.

Thus there are few gaps in the ring fence which has been erected in the last fifty years by the United States and the Dominions in order to exclude non-Europeans. The Central and South American countries have not all adopted this policy; in general the less advanced among them have been the most exclusive. Ecuador prohibited the immigration of Chinese in 1889, and Peru followed suit in 1909. Panama excluded Chinese and Africans in 1914, and this policy has also been adopted by Uruguay and Paraguay. Costa Rica and Guatemala are among the countries which exclude Asiatics; but it would seem that Argentina, Chile, or Brazil have not discriminated against non-Europeans, and the last-mentioned country has in fact encouraged the settlement of Japanese.

What has been the effect of these measures? It is, of course, impossible to say what would have happened if entry had been free to non-Europeans; but we may hope to discover whether the prospect of a large inflow of non-Europeans was real or imaginary. Fig. 41 has been compiled with this end in view; it shows the number of the more important groups of non-Europeans in some of the larger oversea countries at various dates. Taking the United States first we can leave negroes and Indians aside; the latter are the aborigines, whose numbers are still doubtful, while the former have not been reinforced by immigration though they have never been excluded and now come under the quota provisions. We note the rapid increase in the number of Chinese between 1860 and 1880; in 1882 came the suspension of Chinese immigration, since when numbers have declined with the exception of a slight rise in 1930. The suspension of Chinese immigration resulted in a rapid decline because the number of Chinese women in the United States has always been very small, and therefore there has been little natural increase of the

FIGURE 41

Non-Europeans in European Countries Overseas

(thousands)

UNITED STATES

Date	Negroes	Mexicans	Indians	Chinese	Japanese	Filipinos
1860	4,442	..	..	35	..	..
1870	5,392	..	..	63	..	..
1880	6,581	..	..	105	..	..
1890	7,489	..	248	107	2	..
1900	8,834	171	237	90	24	..
1910	9,828	366	266	72	72	..
1920	10,463	701	244	62	111	6
1930	11,891	1,423	332	75	139	45

CANADA

Date	Negroes	Indian and Eskimo	Japanese	Chinese
1881	21·4	108·6	..	4·4
1901	17·4	127·9	4·7	17·3
1911	16·9	105·5	9·0	28·8
1921	18·3	113·7	15·9	39·6
1931	19·5	128·9	23·3	46·5

NEW ZEALAND

Date	Chinese	Date	Chinese
1881	5·0	1911	2·6
1886	4·5	1916	2·1
1896	3·7	1921	3·3
1901	2·9	1926	3·4
1906	2·6	1934	2·5

FIGURE 41 (*cont.*)

AUSTRALIA

New South Wales		Victoria		Queensland		
Date	Chinese	Date	Chinese	Date	Chinese	Kanakas
1856	1·8	1854	2·3	1861	0·5	··
1861	13·0	1857	25·4	1864	0·6	··
1871	7·2	1861	24·7	1868	2·6	1·5
1881	10·2	1871	17·8	1871	··	2·3
1891	13·2	1881	12·0	1881	11·2	6·4
1901	10·2	1891	8·5	1886	··	10·0
1911	8·2	1901	6·3	1891	8·5	9·2
1921	7·3	1911	4·7	1901	7·7	8·8
1931	5·9	1921	3·2	1911	6·0	··
		1931	3·2	1921	4·1	1·9
				1931	3·4	1·5

South Australia		West Australia	Tasmania	Northern Territory
Date	Chinese	Chinese	Chinese	Chinese
1881	0·3	0·1	0·8	3·8
1891	0·2	0·9	0·9	3·6
1901	0·3	1·5	0·5	3·1
1911	0·3	1·8	0·4	1·3
1921	0·2	1·3	0·3	0·7
1931	0·2	0·9	0·2	0·5

Chinese population. The same is not true of the Japanese who have had their women with them, and therefore, in spite of the virtual prohibition upon immigration since 1907, they have increased considerably. We also note the rapid increase in the number of Mexicans and Filipinos whose entry has not yet been seriously impeded. The inference is that the United States are attractive to non-Europeans of oriental and Mexican origin, and that they would have entered in large numbers if they had been allowed to do so.

This inference is much strengthened by a study of the Canadian figures. It will be seen how much the Chinese population of Canada grew in spite of the Poll-Tax, and how considerably the Japanese have increased in spite of the Gentleman's Agreement of 1908. Between 1901 and 1904 the number of Chinese entering Canada annually averaged about 4,000. The raising of the poll-tax in 1904 from $100 to $500 reduced the inflow to a few hundreds; but in spite of the very high tax Chinese began to flow in again, and in 1913 over 7,000 entered. In 1919 the number of entrants was over 4,000; in fact, it was only the complete exclusion enforced by the Act of 1923 which stopped the flow. Between 1925 and 1934 only seven Chinese entered. In 1908, before the Gentleman's Agreement was made, 7,600 Japanese entered; the effect of the agreement can be seen from the fact that in the following year the number was 495 and has since been kept at an average of about 500 a year.

The experience of New Zealand has been similar. The combined effects of the poll-tax of 1881 and of other measures was to reduce the number of the Chinese; but during the earlier decades of the present century it became evident that the Chinese were climbing over these barriers, and it was not until the Act of 1920 came into force, which requires a permit to land, that the inflow was completely controlled. The evidence from Australia is of special interest. About 1855 a rush of Chinese into New South Wales began which was checked by an Act of 1861. A few years later the restrictive provisions were made rather less severe with the result that the inflow began again; it was brought to an end by the reimposition of restriction. Victoria experienced an invasion at about the same time, and this was brought under control by an Act of 1855. The entry of Chinese into Queensland began later, but was equally rapid. Restrictive measures were imposed in 1875 and were strengthened in subsequent years. Queensland also experimented with indentured Kanaka labour, and this system was brought to an end by the repatriation of the labourers. The other provinces, and especially the Northern Territory, all had a similar Chinese invasion though at rather different dates, and in each case it was brought under control by restrictive measures. In 1901 federal legislation introduced drastic restriction against the entry of Chinese into any part of Australia. The consequence of the existence of independent states in Australia was that the number of Chinese remained high for some time; for as soon as one state took measures, Chinese immigration became directed to a neighbouring state. It would appear that the total number of Chinese in Australia never exceeded 40,000; but it remained near this figure for more than twenty years; in consequence of the federal legislation it declined to 16,000 in 1931. Owing to the fact that Europeans are so greatly outnumbered by Africans the position of South Africa is different. Apart from Indians the number of Asiatics has never been large, and the Indians are mostly the descendants of indentured labourers. In 1921 there were 165,731 Asiatics in South Africa of whom 161,339 were Indians; of the latter 141,336 were in Natal.

The conclusion to which this evidence points is clear. If non-Europeans and especially Asiatics had not been kept out of the United States and the British Dominions, they would have entered in very large numbers. By this time the population of the western seaboard of North America would have been largely Asiatic. It seems that Europeans only established themselves in sufficient numbers beyond the Rocky Mountains just in time to be able to secure exclusive possession of this desirable region for themselves.

Passing to the regulation of the entry of Europeans into the oversea countries mention may first be made of the fact that, since the onset of the world depression, immigration has been brought almost to a standstill either by the enactment of special legislation or by the drastic use of powers under pre-existing legislation. Thus an Act was passed in 1934 in New Zealand which required that all immigrants, including those of British nationality, should be in possession of means to support themselves, while entry into the United States has been reduced to a very low figure by a rigorous use of the provision that persons likely to become a public charge are inadmissible. On the assumption that these extra restrictions will be removed if and when the former standard of prosperity is restored, we may concentrate our attention upon what we may regard as the normal policy of these countries, that is the policy followed before 1930. But it is pertinent to remark that, since, as we shall see, reduction of the volume of immigration is a popular policy, it may turn out that, even with a return of prosperity, there may be a reluctance to relax all these extra restrictions and to permit even that volume of immigration which was taking place before they were imposed.

The first important step was taken by the United States in 1882. The most significant feature of the Act of that year was the exclusion of 'any person unable to take care of himself or herself without becoming a public charge'. Between 1882 and 1917 the law was amended on several occasions and always with the object of strengthening its provisions; in 1885 aliens under a contract to labour and in 1903 paupers were excluded. By 1917 there was a lengthy list of 'undesirable' aliens whose entry was prohibited. To this list there was added in 1917 those over the age of 16 who failed to pass a test of literacy which consisted in reading not less than thirty and not more than forty words in a language designated by the alien.

It was in 1921 that immigration into the United States was first drastically limited. The Quota Act of that year limited the number of immigrants of any nationality who might be admitted in any year to 3 per cent. of the number of foreign-born persons of that nationality resident in the United States in 1910. The Act did not apply to countries whence immigration was already regulated, that is from China, Japan, or countries within the 'Asiatic barred zone', or to aliens who had resided for at least five years in other countries of North and South America. The Act was restrictive since the total admissions from quota countries could not be more than 357,803; it was also discriminatory because the proportion of the total allotted to southern and eastern European countries was less than the proportion of the total inflow which they were contributing before the Act came into force. This Act was superseded by the Act of 1924 which is still in force. This latter Act did two things: it amended the basis of the quota provision of the Act of 1921, and enunciated another and a final basis for a quota which should operate when it had been worked out. The immediate amendment substituted 2 per cent. for 3 per cent. and 1890 for 1910. The result was more restriction and more discrimination; for it reduced the total permitted inflow from quota countries from 357,000 to 164,667, and allowed only a negligible quota to countries such as Italy whose foreign-born representatives were few in 1890. The basis of the definitive quota is laid down in the Act of 1924 as follows: 'The annual quota of any nationality for the fiscal year beginning July 1st, 1927, and for each fiscal year thereafter, shall be a number which bears the same ratio to 150,000 as the number of inhabitants in continental United States in 1920 having that national origin (ascertained as hereinafter provided in this section) bears to the number of inhabitants in continental United States in 1920, but the minimum quota shall be 100.' In order to ascertain the national origins of the population in 1920 it was necessary to attempt to ascertain the contribution made to the building up of the population of the United States by each nationality. This was undertaken by a special committee, and the quotas prepared on this basis were put into force in 1928. The result was slightly more restriction, and a considerable change in the relative sizes of the quotas of certain countries as is shown in Fig. 42.

In Fig. 42 are given first the totals admitted under each of the three systems, secondly, the totals for Asia, Africa,

Oceania, and Europe respectively, and, thirdly, the totals for the principal European countries. The total admitted

FIGURE 42

Numbers admitted from various Countries under American Quota Legislation

Numbers admitted	1921 Act 3 per cent. 1910	1924 Act	
		2 per cent. 1890	National origins
Total	357,803	164,667	153,714
Asia . . .	492	1,424	1,423
Africa and Oceania .	359	1,821	1,800
Europe . . .	356,952	161,422	150,491
Austria . . .	7,342	785	1,413
Belgium . .	1,563	512	1,304
Czechoslovakia .	14,357	3,073	2,874
Denmark . .	5,619	2,789	1,181
France . . .	5,729	3,954	3,086
Germany . .	67,607	51,227	25,957
Great Britain and Northern Ireland .	77,342	34,007	65,721
Greece . . .	3,063	100	307
Hungary . .	5,747	473	869
Irish Free State .	with G.B. & N.I.	28,567	17,853
Italy . . .	42,057	3,845	5,802
Netherlands . .	3,607	1,648	3,153
Norway . . .	12,202	6,453	2,377
Poland . . .	30,977	5,982	6,524
Portugal . .	2,465	503	440
Romania . .	7,419	603	295
Russia . . .	24,405	2,248	2,784
Sweden . . .	20,042	9,561	3,314
Switzerland . .	3,752	2,081	1,707
Turkey . . .	2,654	100	226
Yugoslavia . .	6,426	671	845

under the National Origins provision slightly exceeds 150,000, because no quota country receives a smaller quota than 100, however small its share works out under the method of calculation employed. It will be seen that the differences between the systems affect Europe only, for it is the European total alone which is markedly altered. But

o

it is not only the European total which is changed, for the share which the various countries receive of the European total is also affected. The chief changes occurred when the 2 per cent. provisions of the 1924 Act replaced the 1921 Act; they resulted in drastic reductions in the quotas for

FIGURE 43

Immigration into the United States: 1881 to 1930

(thousands)

Period or year	Number of immigrants			
1881–90	5,247			
1891–1900	3,688			
1901–10	8,795			
1911–20	5,736			
1921–30	4,107			
1921	805 including 174 from Canada and Mexico			
1922	310 ,,	66 ,,	,,	,,
1923	523 ,,	181 ,,	,,	,,
1924	707 ,,	290 ,,	,,	,,
1925	294 ,,	141 ,,	,,	,,
1926	304 ,,	144 ,,	,,	,,
1927	335 ,,	162 ,,	,,	,,
1928	307 ,,	144 ,,	,,	,,
1929	280 ,,	116 ,,	,,	,,
1930	242 ,,	88 ,,	,,	,,

southern and eastern European countries. Thus the Italian quota was reduced from 42,057 to the derisory figure of 3,845. In fact the permitted immigration from southern and eastern Europe was reduced to negligible proportions.

Let us now follow the effect of this legislation upon immigration into the United States. The quantitative effect of the legislation up to 1917 was no doubt negligible, and it does not seem that the literacy test introduced in that year had much effect, since in 1922 only 1,476 and in 1923 only 2,095 persons were excluded under the test. But, of course, some immigrants may have been deterred from presenting themselves by the knowledge that they would be rejected. It is a different matter when we come to examine the effects of the Quota Acts. The facts are set out in Fig. 43, whence it appears that the total immigration during the decade 1911–20 was greater than that during the following decade, although the War fell within the former. When we examine the annual figures for the last decade we can see clearly the results of the quota legislation. The inflow into the United States in 1921 showed signs of reaching the high figures of the pre-War period; then it was cut down until it amounted to about a third of the pre-War annual average. But this is not the whole story. In the first place this low figure was only reached owing to heavily increased immigration from non-quota countries such as Canada and Mexico, themselves expanding countries, the former of which at least was also restricting inflow. Thus Europe was allowed to supply only about half of the actual immigrants, and the actual immigrants were perhaps only a third of the total who would have entered if former conditions had prevailed. It therefore looks as though immigration from Europe was reduced to about one-fifth of the volume to which it would otherwise have attained. In the second place, repatriation was on a more extensive scale than previously, and in consequence the net increase through immigration was small; it was 2,007,575 between 1921 and 1925, and 1,179,737 between 1926 and 1930. The position may be further illustrated by saying that between 1921 and 1930 net immigration accounted only for 21·6 per cent. of the population growth, and that, with the exception of the decade in which the War fell, immigration had not contributed so small a share of the population growth since the decade 1830–40. Moreover, the rate of growth between 1920 and 1930 was the smallest ever recorded for a decade with one exception; therefore immigration contributed an unusually low proportion of an unusually low increase. The restrictive effect of the legislation needs no further illustration. That discrimination is also exercised is sufficiently apparent from Fig. 42. It is enough to add that Italian immigration into the U.S.A. during the decade 1901 to 1910 averaged over 200,000 per annum and that the Italian quota is now 3,845.

Though strict numerical limitation is practised only by the United States, the result of legislation in the Dominions, so far as it affects Europeans, is also restrictive and discriminatory. The Canadian Immigration Act of 1910 excluded 'persons likely to become a public charge', and gave power to the Governor in Council to prohibit by proclamation any person not coming 'by continuous journey' or 'of immigrants belonging to any race deemed unsuited to the climate or requirements of Canada, or of immigrants of any specified class, occupation or character'. In 1919 this last clause was repealed and another substituted giving power 'to prohibit or limit in number for a stated period or permanently the landing in Canada . . . of immigrants belonging to any nationality or race or of immigrants of any specified class or occupation' for, it is roughly true to say, any reason so long as that reason has reference to unsuitability to Canadian conditions; power was also taken to require immigrants to possess a prescribed sum of money. In the same year another amendment added persons over the age of 15 and incapable of reading to the list of excluded persons. Armed with these powers the Canadian government can lay down whom it will admit, and under what conditions. A list has been prepared of 'preferred', 'non-preferred', and 'other countries'. The 'preferred' countries are Belgium, France, Germany, Holland, Switzerland, Denmark, Norway, and Sweden. Their nationals are admitted on much the same terms as British citizens, the chief requirement being that they are proceeding to assured employment or that they have sufficient funds to maintain themselves until they find employment. The 'non-preferred' countries are Austria, Czechoslovakia, Poland, Hungary, Yugoslavia, Lithuania, Esthonia, and Russia. Their nationals may enter only if they are agriculturists or domestic servants. Persons belonging to 'other countries' must obtain special permits.

The dictation test embodied in the Australian Immigration Act of 1901 has already been described; it has also been mentioned that in 1932 a requirement was added that aliens must have a permit to land before they embark. This aspect of Australian legislation is chiefly of importance in relation to non-European immigration. In 1925 clauses were added to the Act on the model of those incorporated in the Canadian Act in 1919; that is to say wide powers were given to the Governor-General to prohibit or limit the entry of persons of any race or nationality on grounds so wide that the power was virtually unlimited. It may be noted that, whereas in Canada prohibition must always be on account of undesirability in relation to Canadian conditions, it is possible to exclude persons from Australia because they 'are unsuitable for admission into the Commonwealth', which implies general rather than special unsuitability; if powers were exercised under this sub-section it would seem to follow that the persons in question had been judged to be in some measure undesirable anywhere. But in fact these powers have not been exercised. The government, fortified, when it comes to bargaining, by the fact that other governments know that these powers are in reserve, has concluded a number of agreements. The governments of Yugoslavia, Greece, and other eastern European countries have agreed to limit the number of passports issued to their nationals who intend to go to Australia; the government of Italy has agreed to restrict the issue of passports to Italians who possess at least £40. The New Zealand Act of 1920 requires all immigrants, other than those of British birth or parentage, to possess a permit to enter New Zealand; in order to obtain a permit, application must be made from the country of origin of the applicant, and the Minister of Customs may in his discretion grant or refuse the request. It would appear that this power is exercised so as to keep the number of non-British immigrants very small.

The South African Quota Act of 1930 limits the

immigration from non-scheduled countries to 50 a year; the scheduled countries are Austria, Belgium, Denmark, France, Germany, Holland, Italy, Norway, Portugal, Spain, Sweden, Switzerland, and the United States. It appears that no country in Central or South America has put legislation into force which either limits the total volume of European immigration or discrimination against particular European nationalities. But the new federal constitution of Brazil lays down that the quota of persons of any nationality authorized to enter in any one year may not exceed 2 per cent. of the number of persons of that nationality who have settled in Brazil in the last fifty years. It is not yet known what the effect of this provision will be.

It is not possible to bring forward conclusive evidence, as it is in the case of the United States, to show that the immigration policies adopted by the British Dominions have reduced the volume of immigration in recent years. The average annual immigration into Canada was 245,000 between 1908 and 1912, and only 121,000 between 1920 and 1929; but the first of these two periods witnessed the greatest boom ever known in Canadian history. Average annual net immigration into Australia was 27,000 between 1911 and 1915, 37,000 between 1921 and 1925, and 26,000 between 1926 and 1930. Immigration into these countries has always fluctuated in a very marked fashion, and it is impossible to deduce from these figures what quantitative effect, if any, recent policy has had. But it is interesting to notice that there is no sign of any marked increase of immigration into Canada following upon the imposition of severe restrictions by the United States, and this is probably to be explained by the fact that Canada was also imposing restrictions. The same is true of Australia. That this explanation is correct seems to follow from an analysis of the figures for immigration into the British Dominions from those countries whose nationals were virtually excluded from the United States after 1921. The number of immigrants from these countries tended to rise slightly after 1921; but the rise was soon checked. We can probably recognize in this fact the working both of quantitative

FIGURE 44

Emigration and Growth of Population in Italy: 1876 to 1929

(thousands)

Period or Year	Excess of births		Net emigration		Actual increase or decrease	
	Amount	Per 1,000	Amount	Per 1,000	Amount	Per 1,000
1876–80	209	7·5	54	1·4	+155	+ 6·1
1881–5	307	10·7	77	2·8	+230	+ 7·9
1886–90	307	10·3	111	3·7	+196	+ 7·6
1891–5	326	10·5	128	4·1	+198	+ 6·4
1896–1900	353	11·1	155	4·9	+198	+ 6·2
1901	343	10·5	265	8·2	+ 78	+ 2·3
1902	366	11·2	286	8·7	+ 86	+ 2·5
1903	306	9·3	241	7·6	+ 65	+ 1·7
1904	387	11·7	145	4·4	+242	+ 7·3
1905	355	10·7	438	13·2	− 83	− 2·5
1906	374	11·2	465	13·9	− 89	− 2·7
1907	362	10·8	384	11·5	− 22	− 0·7
1908	369	10·9	37	1·1	+332	+ 9·8
1909	378	11·0	356	10·4	+ 22	+ 0·6
1910	462	13·4	342	10·0	+124	+ 3·4
1911	351	10·1	155	4·5	+196	+ 5·6
1912	498	14·2	343	9·8	+155	+ 5·4
1913	458	13·0	477	13·5	− 19	− 0·5
1920	476	13·1	414	11·5	+ 62	+ 1·6
1921	476	12·9	57	1·3	+419	+11·6
1922	477	12·1	163	4·2	+304	+ 7·9
1923	482	12·3	265	6·9	+216	+ 5·4
1924	461	11·7	186	4·7	+276	+ 7·0
1925	439	11·0	91	2·3	+348	+ 8·7
1926	414	10·3	86	2·1	+328	+ 8·2
1927	454	11·2	87	2·1	+367	+ 9·1
1928	450	10·5	66	1·6	+354	+ 8·9
1929	376	9·1	47	1·1	+329	+ 7·9

restriction and of discrimination in the immigration policy of the Dominions. For it is reasonable to suppose that, had the people of these countries been free to enter, they would have come in fairly large numbers after 1921.

In order to judge the effect of the immigration policies of the United States and the British Dominions taken together, we may refer back to Fig. 10, which shows how much smaller the volume of oversea emigration from Europe has been between 1920 and 1928 than before the War. The reduction is no doubt due in large part to this legislation. Evidence of discrimination may be found in Fig. 11, which shows that the proportion which the British and other northern and western peoples have contributed since the War to the volume of European oversea emigration has risen, whereas that contributed by the Italians and other southern and eastern peoples has fallen. The picture may be enlarged by an examination of the experience of Italy. The facts concerning the net loss to Italy by emigration, oversea and continental, are summarized in Fig. 44. It will be seen that the actual rate of increase of the population of Italy was kept down to a low figure between 1900 and 1913 because emigration was on so large a scale; in fact in 1905, 1906, 1907, and 1913 the net loss by emigration exceeded the natural increase. In 1920 the loss by emigration was again large. Then the results of American legislation began to make itself felt. The marked diminution of emigration in the last years of the post-war decade, however, is partly due to the action of the Italian government which was described in Chapter XII.

FIGURE 45

Emigration and Number of Assisted Emigrants from Great Britain and Northern Ireland: 1923 to 1929

	Canada	Australia	New Zealand	South Africa
Total emigration	412,783	246,167	66,264	50,929
Total immigration	93,334	57,958	16,787	40,872
Net emigration	319,449	188,209	49,477	10,057
Number assisted	119,230*	166,089	42,244	844

* Excluding 37,140 who sailed under the £10 rate and including 8,000 harvesters who were specially assisted.

It is not, however, the fact that all action taken by governments in relation to migration has been restrictive. Before the War Italy granted reduced railway fares to the port of embarkation for emigrants; after the War Switzerland for a short time gave assistance to emigrants proceeding to Canada. Japan, as we shall see, has assisted emigrants going to South America. But Great Britain has been far more active than any other country in the promotion of emigration. In the third decade of the last century, under the inspiration of Horton, and later under that of Wakefield, the British devised numerous schemes to help emigrants proceeding to the colonies. Soon after 1850 there was a change of policy, and until 1922 the British government did no more for emigrants than to give them free advice. In 1922 the Empire Settlement Act was passed, which permitted an annual expenditure, not exceeding three million pounds, upon schemes for assisting emigrants; these schemes could be made with any Dominion government or with any public or private body either in the Dominions or at home, but the share of the home government must not be more than 50 per cent. of the total cost of each scheme. The number of persons assisted is shown in Fig. 45, which also gives the total outward and inward traffic and the resulting balance between Great Britain and Northern Ireland and each Dominion. Since the number of those assisted who return is not large, we may compare the outward balance with the number who went with assistance. In the case of Canada the proportion which the latter form of the outward balance is not as large as in the cases of Australia and New Zealand. In the latter cases the number assisted is a very large proportion of the outward balance. But some of those who went with assistance would have gone without assistance, and we cannot say precisely what the effect of the Act has been. Nevertheless, it seems certain that the effect has been considerable, and that, if the Act had not been passed, the British emigration to the Dominions would have been far less between 1923 and 1929 than has in fact been the case. Thus the quantitative effect of the discrimination practised by the Dominions against continental Europeans has been counterbalanced by the stimulation of emigration from Great Britain.

CHAPTER XV

THE EUROPEAN MIGRATION PROBLEM

THE peoples who live within the sphere of European civilization are faced by two problems of population which we may call the migration problem and the small family problem. The consideration of the former, which is the subject of this chapter, leads directly to the latter, which is the subject of the two following chapters. In connexion with our present problem it must be remembered that, when the population problems of non-European peoples have been discussed, the conclusions at which we shall arrive here will have to be reviewed.

At the end of Chapter XIII we suggested that, at a time when additions to population by way of a surplus of births over deaths in the European countries overseas are diminishing, it was strange to find that obstacles are being placed in the way of immigrants; for, if the population of these countries is to continue to increase, more reliance must be placed upon immigration in the future than in the past. It is not the case, however, that, when this policy was initiated, the likelihood of a serious diminution in the rate of natural increase was anticipated even by those in the best position to judge. A very few far-sighted persons were discussing this possibility, but they did not obtain sympathetic attention even from experts in the subject. Furthermore, though to-day the decline in the rate of increase is apparent to all, there are few who realize that the net reproduction rate has fallen or is falling below unity; and most people who are troubled about the declining rate of natural increase comfort themselves with the anticipation that, when better times return, the birth-rate will go up, though a close study of the situation does not reveal any substantial ground for this hope. Thus it would be a mistake to suppose that restriction was introduced or is maintained by communities well aware of the probable future course of population.

So far as the future course of population was in mind at all, a belief was prevalent that immigration added nothing to population. This belief, so opposed to common sense, was put forward in the last century by General Walker, an official of the United States census bureau. He held that immigration does not increase population because, 'instead of constituting a new reinforcement to the population, [it] simply results in a replacement of native by foreign elements'. In other words, according to the Walker theory, the arrival of immigrants causes the birth-rate of natives to fall, and the loss by decrease in births thus brought about is as large as the gain by new arrivals from overseas. It is quite possible that in certain places under certain circumstances the arrival of immigrants has depressed the birth-rate; it is not easy to prove this, but it is also impossible to show that immigration never has this result. On the other hand, it is easy to show that the birth-rate in the United States has not fallen to the extent demanded by the theory. An estimate has been made of the American birth-rate at the beginning of each decade since 1800, and we can calculate how many births would have occurred if the birth-rate had remained at that level throughout each decade. By subtracting the actual number of births from the number which would have taken place on this assumption, we discover the decennial loss due to the decline in the birth-rate. It can be shown that in every decade since 1830 the gain by immigration has been larger than this loss. Therefore, even if the whole of the decline in the birth-rate was due to immigration, there was still a net gain from that source. But quite obviously the decline in the American birth-rate was not due wholly, or even chiefly, to the effect of immigration; for in the main it was due to the same causes which have led to a decline in other countries of European civilization. It follows that, even if immigration does at times depress the birth-rate, the result is of small importance, and that, generally speaking, immigration increases population. Thus the common-sense view is correct. It is only possible to explain the prevalence of a theory so contrary to common sense and so lacking in factual support by supposing that it is used as a ready-made argument with a respectable ancestry wherewith to attack freedom of entry, which is disliked for reasons that cannot be conveniently disclosed.

We shall presently suggest what these reasons are. Meanwhile let us note that regulation of migration is widely supported on the ground that it is necessary if population growth is to accord with the expansion of the economic system, that is with the increase of opportunities for employment. It is usually assumed that the danger against which it is necessary to guard is that too many immigrants may come in if there is no regulation. It is possible to obtain some idea as to whether there is any substance in this fear by analysing what happened when entry into the United States was unregulated. As we have seen, there was no serious impediment in the way of immigration from Europe before the War. Shipping companies covered Europe from one end to the other with offers of quick and easy transport to the land of promise, and millions of persons responded to these allurements and entered the United States.

If immigration is ever on a scale that is larger than is desirable, it would be under such circumstances as these. Thanks to Dr. Jerome's admirable study we can ascertain what happened in this case. He has subjected the movement into the United States to a most searching analysis, employing refined statistical methods. His procedure is to analyse with great care the inflow of immigrants, decade by decade, according to age, sex, previous occupation, and so on. At the same time he examines the expansion and progress of the United States, so far as possible, industry by industry. In this fashion it is hoped to discover whether the inflow exceeded the absorptive powers of expanding industry.

The results are startling. Jerome found strong cyclical and seasonal movements in immigration and emigration, and noticed that 'when immigration is not restricted the character of the cyclical variations, at least, is closely similar to the cyclical variations in employment opportunity in the United States. A fairly close similarity is also found in the seasonal movements.' There are some irregularities; but he goes on to say that 'the various irregularities and exceptions which have been noted are by no means adequate to impair seriously the validity of the general conclusion that there is a close relation between seasonal and cyclical fluctuations in employment and the corresponding fluctuations in migration'. This cannot be a coincidence because, 'when the migratory currents are separated into their several elements, it is found that it is just these elements, which one would expect to be swayed in the choice of their particular time of arrival and departure by variations in the prospect of employment, which do show, in fact, the closest correlation with employment conditions'. But the turns in the migration movement do not correspond precisely with reversals in employment opportunity, but 'lag behind the corresponding change in employment, indicating that the passage of some time is required before the full effect of a change in employment is felt upon migration. . . . In a few instances the effect of a change in employment conditions is not seen for almost a year afterward, but in other instances the fluctuations in employment and migration appear to be substantially concurrent. The more common lag in the migration fluctuations is from one to five months.'

When, therefore, there was freedom to come and go, the volume of movement corresponded with changes in opportunities for employment in a fashion that was almost uncanny. During the earlier part of the period surveyed by Dr. Jerome, industry was by no means prosperous or the opposite in all countries at the same time; thus emigrants sometimes left when conditions at home were good and sometimes when they were bad. During the latter part of the period all countries came to be prosperous or the opposite more or less at the same time, and emigration was at its highest when home conditions were relatively good. But men always want still better conditions, as is witnessed by the fact that strikes occur more often in times of prosperity than in those of depression. Therefore men left home, not because things were bad, but because they thought that things would be still better in the United States. How can we explain the fact that they were such excellent judges of the prospects? There was no attempt on the part of the governments concerned to provide information about conditions overseas; such newspapers as were read by the peasants and workmen of Europe were certainly not of much use to them for this purpose, and in bad times as in good the shipping companies were pressing upon their attention the facilities which they provided for emigration. We can only explain the facts by supposing that the continuous stream of letters from emigrants abroad gave an up-to-date and accurate picture of opportunities in the new countries for those at home who contemplated migration.

However we explain them, the facts are a remarkable tribute to the system under which men were free to come and go. For it does not seem to be the case that immigrants came in greater numbers than could be absorbed. But though this investigation goes far to dispose of the case for restriction as it is usually put, it does not dispose of it as it might be put, especially when modern conditions are taken into account. To begin with, it must not be inferred that under the old system migration worked without friction or waste. It was a system of individual migration; most men who went had some information or expectations concerning what awaited them, but this information must have been very vague and incomplete.

They plunged into the emigrant stream, and after much tossing and jostling, mostly managed to climb out eventually on to the bank and establish themselves on dry land. It was inevitably a hit-and-miss affair. More preparation, better information, and skilled guidance would have prevented much economic waste and much individual wear and tear. Though up to a point the old system worked surprisingly well, there was room for improvement.

Since the beginning of this century the situation has changed in such a way as to render the former system less appropriate to present than it was to former conditions. Towards the end of the last century the supply of free land, of a quality that made it desirable for settlement, began to run short in the United States; the same thing happened in Canada at a later date. Enormous areas of land had been freely granted to men who undertook to settle on it and improve it. Under the American Homestead Act of 1862, which was copied by Canada in 1872, 250 million acres, an eighth of the total area of the United States, were transferred into private ownership; it has been calculated that, if account is taken of all other grants of land by way of subsidies, endowments, and rewards, the total amounts to about half the whole area of the country. The old system of migration was not unsuitable for the settlement of new areas under these conditions. The Swedish or Norwegian peasant knew what he was about; he settled down to do more or less what he was doing before, but with greater elbow room and as his own master. Still more important was the fact that he did not appear as a competitor to those already settled; he appeared rather as a fellow pioneer taking his share of the hard task of the clearance and improvement of land. As the process of land settlement came to an end and as industry developed, a larger proportion of immigrants, many of whom had always gone into industries, found employment in the towns. Organization of labour followed the expansion of industry, and the aim of trade unionism, there as here, was to safeguard and raise wages. The most obvious method of attaining this end in the new countries was to reduce the supply of labour by cutting down immigration and so putting up wages. Therefore the whole force of organized labour was behind all proposals for restriction. The power of organized labour in Australia is well understood because it is shown in industrial disputes; its potency in the United States and Canada is less obvious, because it is chiefly exercised in exerting political pressure by lobbying and similar methods. To a very considerable extent in all the new countries the restriction of immigration has been due to the political activities of organized labour. It was only prudent, of course, not to emphasize the dominant motive unduly; and any convenient argument against immigration has been used, such as the Walker theory, the supposed flooding of the labour market, and the alleged difficulties which arise from failure of immigrants to become fully assimilated.

This is not to say that organized labour has no case and no grievances. In the United States since 1890, and later in the Dominions, the inflow, actual or threatened, of southern and eastern Europeans has endangered the standards of living of the workpeople in these oversea countries. There is no question but that immigrants from these parts will accept, for a time at least, lower wages than the native-born consider reasonable. The latter have every right to attempt to safeguard themselves. But the true remedy is not mere restriction of numbers, but some system under which undercutting is prevented. We may remember that the prevention of undercutting is one of the objects of the bilateral treaties which have been concluded between many European countries since the War and which were described in Chapter XII. These treaties always provide that immigrants shall possess contracts drawn up in conformity with model contracts; and this provision seems to have satisfied organized labour in the European countries of immigration.

P

There are strong reasons, in fact, for the view that oversea movements should be regulated, as continental movements are regulated, by such treaties. In the first place they afford a way out of the difficulty which arises from undercutting. Secondly, they provide for regulation, but do not aim at mere restriction, of movement; for the essence of the system is that the needs of industry and agriculture for additional labour shall be ascertained, and measures taken to satisfy it. This does not imply any government control of industry or agriculture; all that happens is that the government, by some system whereby employers requisition for alien labour, exerts itself to supply it. The initiation of development schemes by governments and the introduction of labour for their prosecution are unwise on the general ground that governments are not sensitive to the movements of the economic barometer and may embark on schemes at unpropitious moments; this has happened in connexion with certain land-development schemes in Australia. Then again the European schemes provide just that form of regulation the lack of which was the cause of the waste and disappointment which, as we have noted, was inevitable under the old hit-or-miss individual migration. For an integral aspect of these schemes is not only that the right number of persons shall be recruited, but also that the right kind of persons, that is persons of the appropriate age, sex, skill, and experience, shall be chosen. It may be added that recent changes in the social conditions in countries of emigration make this aspect of any scheme of regulation more necessary than in the past. Potential emigrants are now better educated, have higher standards than formerly, and enjoy social services at home. They are less willing than in old days to plunge into the emigrant stream, with the vague hope of getting somewhere; they are coming to demand a more modern form of transport, some vessel which will land them at a given spot where a welcome and a job awaits them. It seems that at present there is only one example of a treaty between a European and an oversea country on these lines, namely that between Poland and Brazil (State of São Paulo) signed in 1927. It contains most of the important points found in the European bilateral treaties, and also the interesting provision that the competent government department of São Paulo shall transmit regularly to the Polish emigration office information concerning land in the state which is becoming ripe for colonization.

The argument most often used to justify restrictive measures is based on the difficulty presented by assimilation. It is alleged that some peoples cannot be assimilated and that others can only be assimilated with difficulty. This implies the belief that the average representatives of different peoples are unlike, that in some cases the unlikeness persists and that in others it only passes away after a considerable period. Let us briefly examine such facts as may throw light upon the validity of this belief.

It may first be observed that no one can doubt the existence within any community or nationality of huge differences between the members. In every community there are some whose inborn or genetic aptitudes fall markedly below the average for the community; for everywhere we find that a proportion of the population is afflicted with genetic mental or physical disabilities, such as feeble-mindedness. Again there are others whose mental or physical capacities have been reduced to a subnormal level by disease or accident. All countries now exclude sub-normal persons, and it may be allowed at once that there is ample justification for this procedure. There is no reason why any country should take upon itself to support persons belonging to another community who cannot earn their own living, and who, in some cases of ill health, might infect the native born and reduce them to a similar low level. Indeed it may be said that there is a clear duty to exclude such persons in the interests of the inhabitants of the country of immigration. This is so obvious and so widely admitted that no controversy is aroused except occasionally in relation to the definition of moral sub-normality. The conception of 'moral turpitude' has sometimes been widened to include trivial offences; and convictions before a criminal court are by no means always a sufficient proof of immoral tendencies. But these are small matters.

The real problem is the nature and implications of the differences between the average or normal representatives of the various peoples or groups of mankind. If we take into account every kind of difference, including for instance speech and habits, it is obvious that the differences are very large. These differences may have their roots either in unlike genetic constitutions or in unlike acquirements, or of course in both at the same time. Let us consider genetic differences first. It is clear that the easily distinguishable physical differences between the main groups of mankind, such as pigmentation, are for the most part due to unlike genetic constitutions; for babies born to black parents are black whether they are born in temperate or in tropical climates. But, if we consider all the ascertainable physical differences which are of this nature, we do not find that any of them justify exclusion from any country. It does not appear, as we have noted, that members of certain groups cannot thrive, and would therefore become physically enfeebled, in particular climates; nor does it seem that, in spite of some evidence of varying liability to contract certain diseases, the members of any group are so susceptible to serious disease that their exclusion is justified on that account. Fertility is a physical attribute, and if members of one group were not fertile with those of another there would be good cause for maintaining geographical separation; for harmony could hardly exist in a community the members of which were not fertile one with another. But unions between all the major groups of mankind are fertile. As to the implications of so-called racial mixture it is perhaps enough to say that mixture in itself is neither good nor bad; the results depend upon what is put into it.

It does not follow from this that the existence of genetic physical differences is unimportant. In the first place their existence implies that the major groups of mankind have been geographically isolated long enough to enable these average differences to appear. The past history of mankind is therefore such that other and possibly more important differences may have evolved, and it follows that we must approach the question of the existence of mental and temperamental differences with this fact in mind. In the second place the existence of physical differences is very important because a section of a community which conforms to a recognizable physical type is conscious of its distinctness, and this consciousness may tend towards the preservation of acquired differences.

From physical we pass to average mental differences between groups, and we may take intelligence first among mental qualities. During the last thirty years methods of measuring intelligence have been elaborated which under certain conditions yield very trustworthy results. But when these methods are used in order to compare the intelligence of people belonging to different groups, the conditions are such that satisfactory results are very difficult to obtain. For intelligence tests must involve some reference to acquired knowledge or habits; and even when testing persons belonging to different social strata of the same community for comparative purposes, it is difficult to ensure that the results will not be vitiated by the fact that members of the different strata possess different acquirements, and it is much more difficult to escape this source of error when testing persons belonging to different national groups. So far, however, as the evidence derived from intelligence tests goes, there is no reason whatever to suspect the existence of differences in intelligence between the major groups of mankind, with the possible exception of Africans. Some investigators are of opinion that the intelligence of the latter is on an average below that of the other main divisions of mankind; the question deserves further inquiry, and in the meantime the possibility of some degree of inequality in this connexion must be borne in mind.

Intelligence is the faculty upon which the construction and maintenance of the mechanical aspects of civilization chiefly depend, and we may say that all the major groups of mankind appear to have an equal capacity for this aspect of civilization, with a possible reservation in the case of Africans. There remains temperament, a faculty no less important than intelligence. There is no reason to doubt that temperament has a basis in the genetic constitution equally with intellectual and physical characteristics. But no means have yet been devised for measuring it. In order to assess the qualifications of candidates for a post, a medical examination is conducted to test the physical characteristics, and written questions are set to test intelligence; but in order to test temperament nothing better than the interview has been invented. Moreover temperament, as assessed in this rough-and-ready fashion, is the product of the impact of circumstances upon the genetic constitution; the relative importance of these two factors is of no interest in the ordinary affairs of life because all that is required is an estimate of the temperament as it is. But for our purposes we require to know how far average temperamental differences are the result of the existence of average genetic differences, and how far to different experiences. There is no doubt about the existence of average temperamental differences between the major groups of mankind, and in some cases between the lesser groups also, as for instance the groups found within the British Isles. There is also no doubt that, in part at least, these differences are due to different circumstances; that is the clear lesson of history which shows that in the course of years a group, the average genetic endowment of which cannot have changed significantly, passes from one

attitude or outlook to another, from a mood of depression
to one of self assertion, for example. The question which
remains is whether groups differ in respect of their genetic
temperamental endowments.

The answer to this question must depend upon the
interpretation of history. All our knowledge of the behaviour of groups is relevant as evidence. We can note
the temperamental characteristics of the same group at
different times, and of different groups at the same time
as manifested in their culture, mode of life, and artistic
expression. We find some cases of apparently rapid transformation and others of the age-long persistence of certain
traits. We observe the enduring differences between the
English and the Irish; we can investigate the profoundly
interesting evidence offered by the presence of a hundred
thousand Japanese in the midst of American civilization;
we can ask ourselves why Jewish characteristics remain
distinguishable. It is unnecessary to multiply examples of
the evidence which is relevant, and it is impossible even
to begin to discuss it. All that can be said is as follows.
Since the major groups of mankind show some genetic
physical differences, it is possible that genetic temperamental differences may also exist; for if circumstances
have been such that the former could evolve, it is possible
that the latter may have evolved at the same time. The
view which we hold about the position must depend
whether we believe that a satisfactory explanation can be
given of the known facts without recourse to the hypothesis that average genetic temperamental differences have
played a part in bringing them about. A number of
observers find that explanations which exclude this hypothesis are not wholly satisfactory, and are therefore inclined to postulate the presence of such differences. It is
evident that we cannot exclude this possibility. At the
same time few if any observers imagine that the genetic
temperamental differences, the existence of which they
suspect, are such that groups can be graded as relatively

superior or inferior on account of their presence. But this does not imply that the differences, if they exist, are unimportant; for the supposed differences are of the kind which colour and shape the whole pattern of life. Thus the culture which is the appropriate expression of the temperament of one group may differ profoundly from that which is the appropriate expression of another.

What practical inferences are we entitled to draw from these considerations when the problem of regulating migration movements is under review? The government of any country has not only the right but also the duty to attempt to ensure that the composition of the population is such that harmonious co-operation is possible between all its elements. It may be urged that harmony does not demand uniformity and that diversity is a source of vitality. While this is true, it is also clear that diversity may be such as to render harmony impossible; if this is so, members of diversely gifted groups should remain geographically separate. There is at least a sufficient possibility that diversities of this kind may exist as to make it doubtful whether the mingling of members of the major groups of mankind in one community is wise. In other words governments of European oversea countries are entitled to hesitate before they permit the entry of non-Europeans.

With this in mind, let us pass on to consider the importance, from the point of view of the regulation of migration, of the undoubted existence of acquired differences. Theoretically these differences, since they are all acquired since birth, need not be shown in the native born, that is in the children of immigrants; for the latter could acquire the culture and habits of the country which their parents had adopted. The immigrants themselves, on the other hand, however anxious they may be to turn themselves into typical citizens of the country of their choice, can never shed all that they acquired in the country of their birth. Thus there is a case for ensuring that unassimilated immigrants do not form too large a fraction of the population.

Again, while the complete assimilation of the children is theoretically possible, it does not happen in practice; for alien traditions linger in the households of foreign-born parents. This strengthens the case for regulation. It was very relevant to the problem, as it presented itself in America, that notice should have been taken in the United States of the fact that in 1924 1,500 newspapers in thirty different languages were being published in that country. In other words assimilation takes time, and it is proper that the inflow should be restricted to allow sufficient time.

Nothing can be said, however, about the precise time which is required for assimilation. It will be long or short according to the attitude of the two parties. The process can be greatly hastened by the deliberate adaptation of schools and other agencies with the object of assisting assimilation; it will be helped by a tolerant and welcoming attitude on the part of the natives. On the other hand, if the alien is made to feel that he is an undesired and inferior intruder, and if opprobrious epithets are applied to him, the process will be lengthy. It is worthy of note that the French, whose tolerance in these matters is well known, have experienced little difficulty with aliens. The same was true of the Americans until recently. No doubt the Americans in the last few decades have had to deal with a class of alien whom it is not very easy to assimilate; but that this difficulty should have become acute at a time when racial theories involving the superiority of 'Nordics' became popular, is not a mere coincidence. The trouble which the Australians experience with aliens is not unconnected with their attitude towards foreigners which cannot be regarded as welcoming or encouraging.

The attitude of the alien immigrant is no less important; he can assist or resist the process of assimilation. For the most part, until the last few years he was almost pathetically anxious to cast off his old clothes and to *copier le Français* or to Americanize himself as the case might be.

But things have changed with the rise of aggressive nationalism; and the change is all the more significant when it is fostered by the action of governments. The Italian government, for instance, has recently adopted measures which aim at keeping alive the loyalty of Italians abroad to Italy and at strengthening their attachment to Italian culture. In 1927 the General Directorate of Italians Abroad was set up, and it is significant that it is officially regarded as having 10 million Italians living overseas under its charge. It attempts to stimulate Italian patriotism by organizing schools, fascist groups, and dopolavoro institutions, and to organize visits of Italian children born abroad to Italy; it co-operates on the cultural side with the Dante Alighieri Society. It is evidently true to say that the object of the Italian government is to hinder or prevent assimilation.

To these considerations, which, it is suggested, should guide any regulation enforced with the assimilation question in view, may be added another. When discussing genetic differences between groups, it was said that there is no doubt about the existence of genetic physical differences between the average representatives of the major groups of mankind, whether or not there are also other genetic differences. Though there are no grounds for exclusion or discrimination directly on account of such differences, their existence is indirectly of some importance in relation to the question of assimilation. For until a physically demarcated group loses its identity through intermarriage, the members are conscious of the possession of common characteristics. This fact hinders assimilation and makes complete assimilation unlikely, though it does not render it impossible. Supposing that physical differences alone separate average members of the major groups, there is nothing to make it impossible, let us say, for Japanese in California to become fully Americanized; nevertheless the fact of physical differentiation will very probably stand in the way. For the physical differences will on the one hand form a rallying-point round which ancestral traditions may shelter, and on the other hand will engender sentiments, derived from the consciousness of constituting an easily recognizable and peculiar group, which are not shared by the ordinary American.

The discussion which has occupied us in this chapter up to the present may be summarized by saying that it is not only the right but also the duty of the government of any country to regulate immigration on two grounds. In the first place it is proper, in order to avoid the waste, friction, and disappointment which are inevitable under the old system of individual, hit-or-miss migration, to substitute a system of collective migration. In the second place it is proper to take such steps, as experience may prove necessary, to ensure that such immigrants as are admitted become assimilated. This may involve limiting the annual volume of immigration, special restrictions upon the entry of members of certain groups because they become assimilated more slowly than others, and exclusion of other groups because they cannot be assimilated. But when we examine what has been done we do not find that it can all be justified on the above grounds. The exclusion of non-Europeans from European countries overseas is probably wise because the very different traditions of non-Europeans, possibly expressing genetic temperamental differences, are likely to be very persistent owing to physical differentiation which makes it unlikely that the process of assimilation can be satisfactorily accomplished. But the restriction of the total volume of immigration, at any rate to the low point fixed by the United States, cannot be justified on the grounds that larger numbers cannot be absorbed by the normal expansion of the opportunities for employment. Nor can the virtual exclusion of southern and eastern Europeans from the United States and the British Dominions (Canada is somewhat more liberal than the other countries mentioned) be fully justified on the ground of the difficulty of assimilation. The action of these countries can partly be explained as due to genuine misapprehension as, for instance, the belief that, when inflow is unregulated, more enter than can be absorbed. But the major part of the explanation is to be sought in motives which are not often openly expressed. Organized labour approves any policy that will make labour scarce; nationalism and the accompanying fear and dislike of foreigners, partly the result and partly the cause of pseudo-scientific 'racial' theories, support everything that tends to restriction. Moreover, as is very important to note, the growth of these sentiments itself makes assimilation more difficult; in no small degree, in other words, the assimilation difficulty, which troubles those who are of this frame of mind, is their own creation.

Let us attempt to bring this discussion down to the concrete aspects of the situation. As we saw in Chapter XIII, in order that full use should be made of the European settlements overseas, it is apparently necessary that their populations should continue to increase for some decades to come at an average annual rate of 2 per cent. At present the *average* annual absorption capacity (the absorption capacity may vanish in times of depression and expand enormously during booms) of the United States and the British Dominions must be between half and three quarters of a million, and of the Central and South American countries over 150,000. The average absorption capacity is almost certainly nearer the upper than the lower limits. But the rate of natural increase, especially in the former group of countries, is declining sharply; therefore, if growth at, or even approaching, an annual average of 2 per cent. is to be maintained, immigration must play a larger part in the future than in the past. But immigration must not merely supply a larger proportion of a given increment of population; as the population increases, a given rate of growth, whether it be 2 per cent. or something less, implies a larger increment each year. Therefore immigration will be called upon each year on the average to supply a larger proportion of a rising volume. In other words the absorption capacity of these countries will expand continuously for some time to come, assuming always that the present depression is followed by conditions which permit migration to be resumed once more.

These countries have decided, except in the case of some South American states, that they will not permit immigration from non-European countries and will draw only from Europe. The countries of northern and western Europe now have an annual surplus of about 600,000 births over deaths, but it is rapidly diminishing. Already in France, Belgium, Sweden, and Germany there is widespread public concern about the future course of population, and no doubt a similar concern will soon manifest itself in other countries belonging to this group. It cannot be shown that any country of north or west Europe is suffering from congestion of population in the sense that it is experiencing troubles which can only be alleviated by a change in its population situation. It is true that certain of these countries, Norway and Denmark in particular, are troubled by the contraction of opportunities for emigration. They have become adjusted to a position under which in normal times they lose on the average every year a number of citizens which is large relative to their natural increase, but small absolutely. The closing down of opportunities for emigration has been followed by the economic depression, and in consequence much is heard about the difficult situation in which they are placed by the policy of the oversea countries. But the source of the trouble will presently vanish with the fall in natural increase, and in any case would never have become prominent if it had not been for the depression. Turning to southern Europe, Italy, Portugal, and Spain now have an annual surplus of about 780,000 births over deaths, and though this surplus will diminish slowly, additions to population will remain considerable for some time to come. The countries of eastern Europe, omitting Russia which does not permit emigration and can apparently absorb its own surplus, now have an annual surplus of about 1,200,000. The position in south and east Europe is different from that in west Europe. It will be remembered that, as a result of the discussion in Chapter XII, we were led to believe that some countries in this part of Europe, and especially Italy and Poland, are already congested. They are already suffering, that is to say, from difficulties which can only be alleviated by population changes. To the extent that population increases, these difficulties will become more serious. Therefore they would benefit if the loss by emigration was equal to the natural increase, and they would benefit even more if it exceeded the natural increase.

From what has been said it would appear that the average annual absorption capacity of all the oversea countries taken together is such that they could take about half the natural increase of the countries of south and east Europe. As time goes on the absorption capacity of the oversea countries will grow while the natural increase of the European countries will diminish. Since France and certain other European countries are also countries of immigration, the difficulties arising from congestion in some parts of Europe are soluble on paper. But there are practical difficulties. It does not follow that the assimilation capacity of a country is equal to its absorption capacity. The upshot of the discussion of assimilation, however, was to show that the degree of difficulty which is occasioned depends largely upon the attitude of the country of immigration, and that the attitude of the United States and of the British Dominions has lately been such as to magnify these difficulties. It may be that the unescapable difficulties of assimilation are such that only a partial solution of the European emigration problem is possible. But the path even to this partial solution is blocked by the virtual refusal of the United States and the British Dominions (though Canada is rather more liberal than the other countries concerned) to take immigrants from south and east Europe. Thus the problem of congestion in south and east Europe remains. Moreover countries in this region suffer under a sense of grievance in that they are not permitted to share in the building up of the most favourably situated of the new European oversea communities. But when nationalism assumes an aggressive form, it may not be desired that emigrants should go to a country under another flag. This is so in Italy at present, and it is accompanied by a desire to annex areas where Italians may settle. Hence arise problems that we shall consider when we come to deal with non-European countries. It is, however, not only the European situation which is made more difficult by the policy of the United States and the British Dominions. In the absence of immigration from those countries where natural increase will continue for some decades to come, the annual rate of increase of the oversea countries will not be maintained at an average of 2 per cent.; indeed it will soon be difficult to maintain it 1 per cent. This raises the issues involved by the decision to exclude non-Europeans from these countries. The justice of closing these countries to non-Europeans, even if admitted while Europeans are making all speed to develop resources, will certainly not remain unquestioned should it become apparent that the process of development is not going to be carried through.

It remains only to say something about the policy of assisting emigration. In this connexion it is relevant to remember that, when a person emigrates, it is implied that one country bears the cost of his maintenance and education while another gets most of the benefit of his productive activities. At the present time the cost to public and private funds of putting a boy on to the labour market in this country cannot be less than £300. Incidentally it may be remarked that the value of the gift which Europe has made to the oversea countries in the shape of millions of ready-made workers is not generally appreciated. As to the other consequences of emigration it may be said that they depend upon the sort of person who goes. If they are a random sample of the population, it probably makes little difference to the amount of unemployment; if they are drawn from the unemployable or sub-normal, unemployment will be decreased, but if they are drawn from the young, active, and intelligent section, the employment position may be made worse in the long run. For there is no fixed amount of employment in any country; some people increase unemployment and others, by their enterprise, activity, and resilience, are in a position to lessen it, and it is in the latter class that the young and intelligent fall. This raises the question as to the type to which emigrants usually belong. All that can be said is that in the case of any country they may be below the average at one time and above it at another; when 'remittance men' left England for the Colonies it was for England's good, whereas without question the assisted emigrant of to-day is above the average. Again the position may be different as between two countries at the same time. In Scotland, as the result of an ample provision of scholarships, the brighter school children receive professional training in such numbers that many of them have to leave the country in order to find occupations in these professions; in consequence there is a drain out of the country of persons who are above the average both in education and in native ability. Those who know the Irish country-side best say that, before emigration was brought to an end by the depression, there was a universal tacit understanding that a surplus of men must not be allowed to accumulate in the village or on the farm. But those who left were not on the whole those of most value to the farm or the village; somehow places were found for the more promising at home, while the others went overseas. In consequence Irish emigration may not have been a drain upon the human resources of the country.

With these considerations in mind let us examine the British policy of assisting emigration. If those who were assisted to go belonged to the classes whom it was impossible to employ, such as the mentally or physically subnormal, or for whom it was very difficult to find employment, such as the men in the special areas of some age and trained only in a declining industry, this country would benefit. If they belong to other classes, no benefit necessarily follows, and in fact those who are assisted mostly conform to the latter and not to the former type. Assisted emigration, therefore, is not likely to profit the home country. It will no doubt be of advantage to the Dominions to receive immigrants carefully selected as to physique, mentality, and character. But the object of the policy is not stated in this way; the intention is said to be to find a remedy for the unequal distribution of the white population within the Empire. But this is not a matter which in itself demands a remedy; the unequal distribution is the result of the fact that the Dominions are recently settled countries. Their populations have grown until recently as rapidly as could be expected. It is very desirable, and probably essential, that growth should continue with the same rapidity if white occupation is to remain effective. But the contribution which the home country can make to this growth will rapidly decline, and relatively to the needs of the Dominions for immigrants will in any case be small. If the populations of the Dominions are to continue to grow, they will have to look elsewhere for most of their recruits. Under these circumstances it is a question whether it is wise to subsidize emigration from this country which is not only a part of, but much the most important part of, the Empire, a fact which sometimes seems to escape the notice of those who in their enthusiasm for the Empire advocate an expansion of assisted emigration.

Q

CHAPTER XVI

ATTEMPTS TO RAISE THE BIRTH-RATE

IT is obvious that the migration problem is of immediate importance, and that it will not be easy to solve; furthermore, as we have observed, obscurity surrounds some scientific questions, such as the possible existence of genetic differences between national groups, which are directly involved. When we turn to the small family problem it is clear that it is fundamentally of more importance than that of migration; for, if families remain so small that communities die out, there will be an end of migration and of all other population problems. No one could refuse assent to this proposition; but in all probability most people would say, if the matter was presented to them, that the small family problem was not urgent and could wait for a time, and also that its solution, when the time comes to consider it, will offer no great difficulties. This, however, is not true. It will certainly be found that the small family problem is of the most intractable nature, and largely because the problem will be so difficult to solve it is urgent that the whole question should receive immediate attention. The reasons for taking this view rest upon the evidence to be given in this chapter and upon the discussion in the first part of the following chapter; we shall then be in a position to suggest possible lines of solution.

In this chapter we shall be concerned with the efforts which have been made in certain countries to raise the birth-rate. We may begin with Italy and Germany because in those countries measures have been put into force with the direct object of increasing population; then we may pay attention to some legislation in certain other countries which was initiated primarily for reasons unconnected with the population problem, but which has been supported and expanded largely with the hope that it would also stimulate the birth-rate. These attempts to raise the birth-rate have recently been described and analysed in a most valuable book by Mr. Glass, and in this chapter his work is closely followed.

Ever since the establishment of the Fascist régime in Italy the declining birth-rate has been a matter for comment and a subject for anxiety. Certain measures were taken in the early days of the régime; but it was not until 1927, after a speech by Mussolini on the 26th May of that year, that legislative and administrative action was initiated on a large scale. Action has been both repressive, that is designed to discourage celibacy and childlessness, and positive, that is designed to favour large families. As examples of the former there are taxes on bachelors, first introduced in 1926 and doubled in 1928, and extra rates of income tax on bachelors and childless couples. But the burdens imposed are not heavy; the tax on bachelors aged 35 to 50 years is 100 lire a year, and this is said to be less than the cost of a dog licence. More important is the preference given to married candidates with children for posts in government service and for state subsidized houses and flats; men with families are also preferred in private industry. The most important positive measures have taken the form of reducing or abolishing taxes falling on 'large families'; thus the income tax is graduated so as to fall lightly on 'large families' which are also entirely exempted from taxes levied for education and from certain communal contributions. But a family must be really 'large' in order to qualify for favours; state employees must have seven children, and other employees must either have ten children, or have had twelve of whom six remain to be provided for. Mr. Glass calculated that about 15 per cent. of the population of Italy benefits under the measures which were introduced in 1928.

In addition to these schemes, the sole object of which is to raise the birth-rate, there are others which have this as one of their objects. Thus family allowances or cost of living bonuses in proportion to the number of children have been paid to state employees since 1929. In 1934 family allowances were extended to industrial workers; they are paid out of a fund to which both employers and employees contribute. The social services for mothers and children have been much expanded since 1925. Finally, an attempt has been made to counteract the tendency towards urbanization partly on account of the fact that the birth-rate is lower in the towns than in the country. It must also be remembered that, apart from material help for large families, every effort has been made to represent parents of large families as those most worthy of honour and esteem.

FIGURE 46

Marriages and Births in Italy: 1921 to 1934

Year	No. of marriages	No. of marriages per 1,000 total population	No. of live births	No. of live births per 1,000 total population
1921	438,535	11·0	1,163,213	29·2
1922	365,460	9·6	1,175,872	30·8
1923	334,306	8·7	1,155,177	30·0
1924	306,830	7·9	1,124,470	29·0
1925	295,769	7·6	1,109,761	28·4
1926	295,566	7·5	1,094,589	27·7
1927	302,564	7·6	1,093,772	27·5
1928	285,248	7·1	1,072,316	26·7
1929	287,800	7·1	1,037,700	25·6
1930	303,214	7·4	1,092,678	26·7
1931	276,035	6·7	1,026,197	24·9
1932	267,771	6·4	990,995	23·8
1933	289,915	6·9	995,979	23·7
1934	312,662	7·4	992,975	23·4

It is not easy to attempt to trace the influence of these measures owing to the lack of the necessary statistical data. Taking marriage first we notice a decline in the annual number of marriages from 1921 to 1928, a slight rise in 1929 and 1930, a fall to an unprecedentedly low level in 1931 and 1932 followed by a marked rise in 1933 and 1934. We may perhaps recognize the effects of penalizing bachelors in the events of 1929 and 1930. The subsequent events, a decrease of marriage in the early years of the depression and an increase in the last year or so, can be paralleled in countries, such as the United States, where there are no measures against bachelors in force. It is thus doubtful whether any noteworthy result has followed from the action which has been taken to encourage marriage. As to the birth-rate we find that it fell steadily to 1929, rose in 1930, and has fallen ever since. The total number of live births, however, was larger in 1933 than in 1932, and larger in 1934 than in 1932, though not as large as in 1933. The increase over 1932 was small and, since the population was increasing, it was not enough to raise or even to maintain the birth-rate. It seems likely that this increase was due to the greater number of marriages, and that the latter was due to the contraction of marriages which were postponed at the onset of the depression. Figures prepared by Professor Mortara and quoted by Mr. Glass show that, when 1921–5 is compared with 1930, legitimate live births per 1,000 married women aged 15 to 45 have fallen for all Italy from 248 to 212, and also for every province with the doubtful exception of Sicily. It would therefore seem that the utmost which can be claimed for these measures is that, if they had not been taken, the Italian birth-rate would have fallen still more rapidly.

Measures to stimulate marriage and the birth-rate were not taken in Germany until after the National Socialist party had come into power. Since that time efforts have been made in many directions; of these one is important and the others much less so. To illustrate the latter, mention may be made of modifications in the law of inheritance in favour of large families, preference to heads of large families when men are selected for employment, a system of sponsoring third and subsequent children which has been adopted by several large towns, and minor matters such as privileges in railway trains for expectant mothers and mothers with young children. Attention, however, may be confined to the Act for the provision of marriage loans which came into force in August 1933. The aim of the Act is not only to encourage marriage, but also to withdraw women from the labour market. It is therefore laid down that the loans are payable only to couples where the woman concerned has been employed for at least nine months during the two preceding years. There is no income limit; but those who want loans must show that they could not otherwise afford to furnish a home. Loans may be of any amount up to 1,000 marks, and the average loan has been just over 600 marks. The loans take the form of the provision of coupons which may be exchanged for household goods. They bear no interest but are repayable at the rate of 1 per cent. per month; a quarter of the original loan is remitted on the birth of each child. To finance the scheme a sum of 150 million marks is set aside each year.

The scheme has been put into force with vigour; in 1933 141,559 loans were granted and the percentage of couples receiving loans was 22·4, while in 1934 the corresponding figures were 224,619 and 30·7. What has been the effect? Let us examine the data given in Fig. 47. They show some dramatic changes; marriages have jumped up and so has the birth-rate. But care must be exercised before we conclude that these changes are wholly due to the system of loans, and that the figures support all that we may be inclined to infer at first sight. To begin with marriages, we notice that they increased substantially in the second quarter of 1933, that is before marriage loans became available. We know that in several other countries marriages, which were postponed at the onset of the depression, were contracted later, causing an increase in the number of marriages, and it is clear that the rise in the second quarter of 1933 came about in this way. It is further certain that a proportion of the increase in marriages during the remaining quarter of 1933 and during 1934 would have occurred in any case. Evidence in favour of this view is provided by some figures from Württemberg, quoted by Mr. Glass, which show that the rise in marriage was exhibited by members of all economic classes and not only by those which benefited from the loans; indeed, the rise was greater among those employed on their own account, and therefore not eligible for loans, than among wage earners. On the other hand, there is no reason to doubt that in the absence of loans the increase would not have been as great as it has been; the loans are substantial and provide precisely the help and stimulus which are needed. But we can make no kind of estimate of the number of marriages which have been made possible by them.

FIGURE 47

Marriages and Births in Germany: 1932 to 1934

	No of marriages	Marriage-rates per 1,000 total population	Index (same quarter of previous year = 100)	No of live births	Live birth-rates per 1,000 total population	Index (same quarter of previous year = 100)
1933						
1st quarter .	94,686	5·8	93·5	246,915	15·2	95
2nd ,, .	157,906	9·7	116·9	243,425	14·9	97
3rd ,, .	157,715	9·7	131·1	237,720	14·6	100
4th ,, .	220,519	13·5	142·2	228,855	14·0	99·3
Average for year	630,826	9·7	122·8	956,915	14·7	97·3
1934						
1st quarter .	138,438	8·5	146·6	281,024	17·2	113·3
2nd ,,	196,129	12·0	123·7	295,819	18·1	121·5
3rd ,, .	178,638	10·9	112·4	299,667	18·3	125·4
4th ,, .	213,223	13·3	98·5	304,669	18·6	132·8
Average for year	731,431	11·1	114·4	1,181,179	18·0	122·4
Year 1932 .	509,591	7·9	..	978,161	15·1	..

The object of the German scheme, however, is to stimulate births; if it raises marriages but not births, it will be a failure. When we turn to the figures for births we find that they have risen immensely; there were 978,210 births in 1932, 956,915 in 1933, and 1,181,179 in 1934. The rise in births is reflected in the birth-rate which increased from 14·7 per 1,000 in 1933 to 18·0 in 1934. It will be

noticed that an increase in the number of births is first
shown in the first quarter of 1934; it is therefore probable
that the increase is mainly due, not to the enlargement of
families already in existence before marriage loans were
granted, but to the appearance of the first children of the
marriages contracted since the second quarter of 1933. As
already noticed, we can be sure that there would have been
some increase in marriages if there had been no loans, and
therefore we can also be sure that some increase in births
would have taken place without them. But we can form
no idea what the increase in births would have been under
these circumstances. Between August 1933 and April
1935, for example, 182,355 children were born to parents
who had received loans, but there is no justification for
crediting all these children to the scheme. On the other
hand, it is quite certain that there would not have been
such a large increase in the number of births if the scheme
had not been in operation. It is noteworthy that the
number of abortions has greatly decreased. In Chapter VI
figures were quoted to show that in Berlin in 1929 the
proportion of abortions to live births was 103·4 to 100;
in April 1935 it was 14·3 to 100. This gives an indication
of what has apparently happened. There has been an
increase in the number of recently married couples, and
many of them, who under former conditions would have
postponed the arrival of the first child, have not taken steps
to do so. In other words, there has been an increase in the
proportion of the recently married who have had a child
within a year or so of marriage; that is to say, that the
effect has not only been to stimulate marriage and with it
what was formerly the normal proportion of first births
per 100 marriages in a year, but also to raise the proportion
of first births within a year or so of marriage.

It would not be reasonable to expect a greater result
from the scheme in so short a time. But it is very necessary
to understand that what has so far happened may not
ultimately in the least affect the trend of population in

Germany. For the trend of population depends upon fertility, and apparently all that has so far happened is that an unusually large number of first births has been crowded into a year. The question is whether the families now being founded will be larger than the families founded earlier. If they do not prove to be so, then the trend will remain as before. We might perhaps infer that the decline in abortion, which indicates a willingness to have the first child sooner than was formerly the case, also indicates a frame of mind which will willingly contemplate a larger family than was formerly the rule. But it would be rash to base predictions on this argument. We can only wait and see what figures for 1935 and later years show. Figures for 1935 are only available at present for the fifty-five largest cities in Germany; they are given in Fig. 48 and appear to indicate that the effect of German legislation will only be temporary.

FIGURE 48

Marriages and Births in the fifty-five largest cities of Germany: 1934 and 1935

| | 1935 | | | | 1934 | | | |
| | Marriages | | Births | | Marriages | | Births | |
	Numbers	Rate per 1,000 total population	Numbers	Rate per 1,000 total population	Numbers	Rate per 1,000 total population	Numbers	Rate per 1,000 total population
Jan. .	11,425	6·7	27,403	16·0	12,760	7·5	21,720	12·7
Feb. .	13,498	8·7	25,539	16·5	14,896	9·6	20,756	13·4
Mar. .	18,605	10·9	27,744	16·2	22,102	13·0	24,492	14·4
Apr. .	22,744	13·7	26,874	16·2	19,825	12·1	23,796	14·4
May .	19,525	11·4	27,822	16·3	24,273	14·2	24,965	14·6
June .	21,566	13·0	26,712	16·1	20,270	12·3	24,598	14·9
July .	16,925	9·9	25,829	15·1	19,861	11·7	25,499	15·0
Aug. .	19,177	11·2	25,409	14·9	20,278	11·9	24,851	14·6
Sept. .	18,106	10·9	24,887	15·0	25,352	15·4	25,035	15·2
Oct. .	20,804	12·2	24,485	14·3	28,936	17·0	24,864	14·6
Nov. .	16,518	10·0	23,526	14·2	20,650	12·5	24,915	15·1
Dec. .	18,410	10·7	24,702	14·4	23,660	13·8	25,840	15·1

We come next to a consideration of family allowance schemes and may take the position in France first, since it was there that they were originally put into force. Family allowances may be defined as payments in cash, apart from and in addition to wages, to employees in proportion to the number of their dependent children. They are advocated a measure of social justice; the argument in their favour is that, since wages have no relation to family responsibilities, the man with dependent children is penalized; moreover it is not only the man who is penalized but also in many cases the children, since the family income, however judiciously spent, may not be sufficient to buy the requisite food and clothing. But, as we shall see, support for family allowances is now largely based upon the belief that they may tend to check the declining birth-rate.

Family allowances were introduced by an engineering firm at Grenoble during the War; they were soon extended to central and local government employees. Prices were rising, and employers, instead of, or in addition to, raising wages, began to pay allowances to men with dependent children. In France the allowances have always been paid in this way out of the employer's pocket without any contributions from the employees or the State; but since until recently the spread of the system has taken place while prices were rising, it is possible that no extra burden has been placed upon employers. The extension of the system was continuous; it was taken up by an increasing number of employers who were encouraged to fall into line when, under the laws of 1922 and 1923, local authorities were empowered to require that firms contracting with them should pay allowances. In order that there might be no reason for discriminating against married men seeking employment, the employers set up equalization pools into which they paid their contributions and out of which the allowances were allocated. Since the contributions of an employer are in proportion to the number of his employees and bear no relation to the number of dependants of these employees, there is no incentive for him to engage childless workers.

The system grew until it covered a considerable pro-

portion of all wage earners in France. Then in 1932 a law
was passed which made the payment of allowances compulsory to all employees, wage earning or salaried; the
provisions were to come into force by stages, and the
first administrative order was promulgated in October
1933. But the system has not as yet been applied to all
industries; agriculture, though it will be brought within
its scope, at present remains outside. Under this law
allowances are payable to all children under the age of
14, and to those over 14 and under 16 who remain at
school. The contributions of employers amount to about
2 per cent. of the wages bill. There is a minimum allowance which must be paid which varies in each Department.
The allowances increase for the later children in the
family; thus the minimum in the department with the
lowest rates is 15 francs per month for one child, 30 francs
for two children, 45 for three, 65 for four, and so on. If,
after the payment of the minimum allowances, a surplus
remains in the pool, it can be used either to augment the
cash allowances or to provide services in kind such as
medical attention. It is not easy to generalize concerning
the extent to which the allowances cover the cost of
caring for children. But, according to the calculations
made by Mr. Glass, it would seem that, even when the
allowances are highest, they do not cover more than fifty
per cent. of the cost of maintaining a child, and that on
the average they do not amount to more than 25 per cent.
of the cost.

The reason originally advanced for initiating allowances was, as stated above, that they helped to remove the
injustice of the wage system which took no account of
family responsibilities. No doubt employers were also
induced to adopt them in the hope that they would reduce
industrial friction. But long before the War the declining
birth-rate was the subject of public discussion and the
cause of much anxiety in France; the Alliance Nationale
pour l'Accroisement de la Population, for instance, was

founded in 1896. When those who wanted something
done in order to check the fall, but had not been able to
propose any remedy, became aware of the family allowance system, they soon saw that it might provide the
mechanism which they sought. We find, in fact, that the
population aspect of the allowance system was being discussed as early as 1919; and the powerful sentiment in
favour of a higher birth-rate was soon enlisted in support
of the extension of allowances. We can see the influence
of the population motive in that characteristic of the
system which has already been mentioned—namely that
allowances become larger with successive children. Thus
in the case mentioned, where 15 francs are payable for
the first child, we saw that the rate rises to 20 francs for
each child from the third onwards. In some schemes, in
that prevailing in the Haut-Rhin department, for example,
the grading is more marked; the allowances are 25 francs
for the first child, 37·5 francs for the second, 50 francs for
the third and fourth, 62·5 francs for the fifth, 75 francs
for the sixth—a total of 300 francs per month for six
children. If the object was merely to provide for the cost
of maintaining a child, in part or in whole, there could
be no sense in such a grading of allowances; evidently the
intention is also to encourage large families. Indeed, large
families are encouraged in France as in Italy by prizes,
presentations, and acclamation in the press.

It is therefore appropriate to inquire whether it is
possible to detect in French vital statistics any influence
of the family allowance system. But, before we do so,
some description may be given of the system as it has
developed and now exists in Belgium; for an analysis can
also be made of Belgian experience, and it is convenient
to undertake the analysis of French and Belgian experiences at the same time. The family allowance system
began later, but has developed more rapidly, in Belgium
than in France. The first equalization fund was established at Verviers in 1921; as in France, prices were rising,

and it seemed that the payment of allowances was preferable to a general rise in wages. An additional motive was
provided by the fact that the payment of allowances in
France was attracting Belgian workers across the frontier.
The system spread rapidly; the central government and
local authorities began to require that firms, with which
they made contracts, should pay allowances. Proposals
that the system should be made compulsory were advanced
as early as 1924, and in 1930 an Act was passed which
laid down that allowances were to be paid to all workers,
whatever their income, in respect of dependent children.
As in France allowances are graded and rise for later born
children; thus the minimum scale is 9 francs per month
for one child and 308 francs per month for six children.
As regards details there are many differences between the
Belgian and the French system. Under the former, employers pay a fixed contribution to the equalization fund
for each employee, whereas under the latter the contribution is calculated as a percentage of the wage bill and
adjusted from time to time so as to produce the amount
required to enable the allowances to be paid. The rigidity
of the Belgian system has caused some difficulties. Again,
in Belgium there is a super-equalization fund. But in one
important respect the two systems are alike; the allowances represent only a fraction of the cost of maintaining
a dependent child. Indeed, in Belgium the allowances
represent a smaller fraction of this cost than in France;
this is partly due to the fact that it is permissible for the
funds, after the minimum cash allowances have been
paid, to distribute what remains in the form of social
services.

In Belgium the falling birth-rate was not a cause for
public anxiety until after the War. It then began to rouse
discussion, and in 1920 the Ligue des Familles Nombreuses
was formed which has now more than a million members.
Those concerned with this problem soon saw that the
family allowance system might be an instrument where-

with to fight the declining birth-rate and they enthusiastic-
ally supported proposals for its extension. In fact it would
seem that the desire to raise the birth-rate has played a
more prominent part in Belgium than in France in bringing into being a universal compulsory system. M. Hey-
man, the Belgian Minister of Labour, when introducing
the Bill in 1929 which became law in 1930, said: 'above
all the bill aims at encouraging births and large families.'
It is also significant that under the Act of 1930 a Family
Allowance Committee was set up which includes two
representatives of the Ligue des Familles Nombreuses.

When we ask what effect these schemes have had, it is
surprising, in view of the extent to which the desire to
raise the birth-rate has been important in bringing about
the extension and finally the compulsory generalization
of the schemes, to discover how little the results have
been analysed either in France or in Belgium. There are
certain widely quoted figures, but an examination of these
shows, as indicated below, that they prove little or nothing.
In the case of Belgium the inadequacy of official statistics
is a serious impediment to any research into the matter,
but in France, where official data are more adequate,

FIGURE 49

Birth-rates in Belgium and France: 1921 to 1931

Year	Births per 1,000 total population	
	Belgium	France
1921	21·8	20·7
1922	20·4	19·3
1923	20·4	19·1
1924	19·9	18·7
1925	19·8	19·0
1926	19·0	18·8
1927	18·3	18·2
1928	18·4	18·3
1929	18·1	17·7
1930	18·7	18·0
1931	18·2	17·5

little useful work has been done with them. Let us, however, briefly survey the situation.

We may begin by taking note of the course of the birth-rate since the War. No obvious influence of the allowance system can be detected; the rates trend downwards to the present day. But it must be remembered that the Acts generalizing the system over all workers are of very recent date, and that they have not even yet been put fully into operation; it would therefore be fair to object that, so far as the rate for the whole of each country is concerned, it is too early to judge, or at least too early to see more than part of what will be the ultimate effect. Again, as we have often had occasion to observe, crude birth-rates may be misleading; we might hope to overcome this difficulty by the use of more refined data. In Belgium such data are not available, but for France we have official figures for standardized fertility of women aged 15 to 49, figures, that is to say, in which changes due to altered age composition are eliminated. They are given in Fig. 50 up to 1931, the last year for which they are available. It will be seen that they show a check to the fall in fertility between 1929 and 1931; but since the number of births in France has fallen considerably since 1931, it may be taken as certain that the standardized fertility has not been stabilized at the level of 1931 but has fallen farther.

Since the proportion of all French and Belgian workers,

FIGURE 50

Standardized Fertility Rates in France: 1926 to 1931

Year	Number of births per 10,000 females aged 15 to 49 years in a standard population
1926	735
1928	716
1929	678
1930	696
1931	679

who have up to the present received allowances, is not yet more than a third of the total, the most hopeful method of testing the effect of the system might seem to be to compare the birth-rate among those receiving allowances with the general birth-rate. Certain comparisons of this kind, purporting to show a larger birth-rate among those in receipt of allowances, have received much publicity. Colonel Guillermin, for example, presents every year, on behalf of the Comité Central des Allocations Familiales, figures showing the birth-rate per 10,000 persons aged 15 to 60 in France as a whole and also per 10,000 employees with allowances. The latter rate is markedly higher than the former. But this proves nothing for two reasons. The composition of the two populations, to which the births are respectively referred, are not alike; it is true that Colonel Guillermin makes certain corrections to get over this objection, but they are of an arbitrary nature. Secondly, since up to the present the system is only partially applied, it may well be that workers with large families seek employment in industries where allowances are paid. Therefore, even if the birth-rate is larger among employees receiving allowances, the reason may be that parents expecting additions to their families migrate to an industry within the system. Another series of figures which have frequently been quoted are contained in a pamphlet published by the Michelin Company at Clermont Ferrand. The Company has paid unusually high allowances for some years, and their figures show that the birth-rate per 10,000 Michelin families is much higher than the rate for the rest of the population of Clermont Ferrand, and further that it is rising whereas that for Clermont Ferrand is sinking. But no details are given. We do not know the age composition of the Michelin families or of the rest of the population, for instance, and it is very unlikely that they are at all similar. In all probability the Michelin population contains a much larger proportion of persons of child-bearing age than the general population, and this would account at least for part of the difference; whether it accounts for the whole difference no one can say.

There is, however, one comparison of this kind which has greater claim to attention. It is due to Professor Fisher whose figures have been continued to a later date by Mr. Glass. Professor Fisher examined the relation between the number of employees belonging to the equalization fund of the Haut-Rhin department and the number of dependent children. He suggested that an increase in fertility might be reflected in an increase over a period of years in the proportion of children aged 0 to 2 compared with the proportion aged 13 to 14; for any increase in fertility should result in an increase in the proportion of the former at later dates. The figures do show such an increase, and there may be evidence here of the stimulating effect of the system on the birth-rate; but the evidence is far from conclusive.

The most that can be said about the results of the attempts to raise the birth-rate in France, Belgium, and Italy up to date is that the rate may have fallen less fast than it would otherwise have done. In Germany the rate has been raised, but it remains to be seen whether this has been achieved by raising fertility or merely by stimulating the appearance of a large number of first-born children in a short period of time.

One other feature of the campaigns to raise the birthrate deserves attention. They have usually been accompanied by attempts to suppress birth-control. In Germany alone, among the countries which we have discussed, is this not so; but it is understood that action is contemplated. Under a law passed in Italy in 1926 propaganda in favour of birth-control is punishable by imprisonment for a year, while a woman may be imprisoned for four years for abortion; in 1932 it was made illegal to stock or list contraceptive appliances. It is not clear how rigorously these laws are enforced. In France under a law of 1920 abortion is punishable by imprisonment, while action in favour of

R

birth-control is subject to a similar penalty. But the sale of contraceptive appliances is apparently not held to come under the head of the latter, and so far as contraception is concerned the only effect seems to have been to interfere with open propaganda. A Belgian law of 1923 punishes birth-control propaganda, the sale of abortifacients, and the exhibition of contraceptive appliances; but apparently the sale of the latter is not forbidden.

In one sense the matters discussed in this chapter look back; for they assist to fill out the sketch of the situation in Europe which was given in Chapter XI; in another sense they look forward, for the inference to be drawn from the discussion is that the problem of the small family, which is the subject of the next chapter, is likely to prove stubborn.

CHAPTER XVII

THE SMALL FAMILY PROBLEM

WHERE fertility is so low that the population is not replacing itself, the problem of the small family exists. Where, as in this and some other countries, the continuance of the present low fertility means that the population will be reduced to half its present size in a century from now, the problem is urgent. The inference to be drawn from the attempts, which were described in the last chapter, to raise fertility is that the problem presents difficulty. The difficulty and urgency of the problem are, however, much greater than has yet been made to appear; for there are aspects of the situation which have not yet been examined.

The present situation is novel in human experience. It is true that a small family system prevailed in early times; the family was then small because married couples were under the compulsion of limiting the number of their children. Limitation was achieved by abortion which involved physical suffering, or by infanticide which was wounding to parental feelings or by abstention from intercourse which involved psychological tension. The primitive small family system, enjoined by convention, enforced by social pressure and involving suffering, has long passed away in Europe. But, though families were large in Europe during the Middle Ages and the succeeding centuries, they were not as large as they might have been; for the dependent section of the population was under the compulsion to delay marriage somewhat. This compulsion, though not involving methods as crude and painful as those which kept the primitive family small, was irksome; during the eighteenth century it ceased to exist, and men became free to marry as early as they liked and to have as many children as they wished. But men and women, as we remarked in Chapter IX, have never wanted as many children as 'nature' sends; up to that time, however, they did not know of any effective method of limiting the family which involved neither suffering nor offence to moral sentiments. Then they became aware of the possibility of practising contraception. For a time they hesitated to employ this method because it was repugnant to prevailing sentiment. Sentiment gradually changed; it is clear that to most people to-day contraception is not inherently repulsive. Hence came the modern small family system. It is novel because it is voluntary; all previous restrictions upon the size of the family were forced upon the parents. Parents had to be compelled because the only means by which limitation could then be achieved were all, in one way or another, painful or repulsive. But a painless, acceptable, and fairly effective method of family limitation now lies ready for use.

The result is of extraordinary significance. Since in former times the family was kept small by unwelcome means, there was always resistance to the use of those means. There was therefore no likelihood that the size of family would sink below the level needed for the replenishment of the community. The danger, which perpetually threatened, was that resistance would become too strong, and that in consequence the growth of population would be excessive. There is no resistance now. Therefore, if for any reason, however remote, trivial, selfish, or unsubstantial, parents do not want a child, the child does not come. Consequently there is no assurance whatever that children will come in numbers sufficient to prevent a decline of population and ultimate extinction.

This novel situation demands further inquiry. It will be remembered that we first became aware of it when we were attempting to account for the fall of the birth-rate. We found that this fall was not due to any general decline in the amount of marriage or to any widespread rise in the age of marriage within the sphere of European civilization. This means that there is no possibility of restoring the former birth-rate by returning to former habits in the matter of contracting marriage. But this does not imply that the marriage situation to-day is of no importance in relation to the birth-rate. The attitude towards marriage, on the part of those who contemplate it, has no little to do with the fertility of the marriages which they make. To this matter we shall return at the end of this chapter. It is also relevant to recall the result of the examination by Mr. Kuczynski of the effect which would be produced if all those who now remain celibate were to marry; he found that, except in the case of countries such as Ireland where there is relatively very little marriage, the result upon the birth-rate would not be large. The same is true of the consequences which would follow if every one married earlier. The relevance of this is that, if it should be desired to raise the birth-rate, there is not much to be anticipated from more and earlier marriage. Nevertheless more and earlier marriage would achieve something, and is moreover also desirable on other grounds.

Fertility of marriage governs the birth-rate and the trend of population, and our inquiry must be directed to discovering how the new situation affects the size of family. It must be remembered that this new situation is only in the making. It will come into its own when all children are wanted children. This term is ambiguous. A child may not be wanted before it is conceived, but it may become wanted as soon as it is conceived, or as soon as it is born. Many children, who are conceived in spite of attempts to bring the family to an end, become wanted as much as those whose advent was desired before conception. It is in the first sense that the term is used here; for it is the children, who are unwanted before conception, whose arrival would be stopped if the methods of limiting the family were better known and more effective. It is far from being the case that all children are wanted in this sense to-day. Many parents in every country are still unaware how to limit their families; there are more who, for financial or other reasons, are unable to use, or are unsuccessful in their attempts to use, the available methods. Moreover the methods at present available are not certain in their operation. It is more than likely that a cheap and effective method, which is easy to employ, will soon be at the disposal of all. We shall then have the voluntary small family system in full development. Therefore our inquiry is not directed to discovering why families in general are of their present size, since in many cases size is still determined by 'nature'; what we wish to know is why parents want to limit the size of their families, whether or not their attempts are successful.

There are certain urges which lead people to desire children. They are deep seated, ineradicable, and incapable of complete satisfaction through any form of substitution. For the sake of convenience we may say that they constitute the parental instinct. Because the parental instinct will continue to exist, men and women will continue to desire children. It is clear that the satisfaction of the instinct does not require that the physiologically possible number of children shall be born; the family was large in former times, not because all the births were desired, but because births could not be avoided. Now that they can be avoided the size of family is determined by two contrary forces: on the one hand there is the parental instinct, on the other hand there are all those considerations which make a child or an additional child unwanted. These considerations may be classified under four heads, medical, psychological, economic, and social, though it is true that many elements in the situation could be placed in more than one of these classes.

Under the first head come the fear of maternal mortality, the prospect of difficult labour, the presence of morbid or pathological conditions, and many other considerations. Taken together they probably account for the decision of many women not to have a second or a third child or perhaps not to have a child at all. If our resources for medical research were concentrated upon these matters, and if measures were taken to make the results of research available to all, the cogency of these considerations could no doubt be greatly lessened within a decade. Relatively to other medical problems they have been neglected. This is to be explained by the survival of the traditional attitude towards the dangers and difficulties of child-birth. Formerly women could not escape pregnancies, and all the attendant circumstances were regarded as part of the unalterable scheme of nature. The expression of this attitude can be observed in its most extraordinary development in relation to the ordinary pains of labour. It is not uncommon to meet people who are roused almost to fury at the suggestion that the effective, and in every respect unobjectionable, new methods of anaesthesia should be made available for all in child-birth. Under these circumstances it is no wonder that little progress has been made in the discovery of methods of mitigating these troubles and difficulties, and less progress still in making available what methods there are.

The fear of the normal pains of labour ought perhaps to be classed among the psychological conditions together with the dislike of pregnancy. In any case there is no sharp dividing line between these categories. In this class of consideration come fears and apprehensions of all kinds, of things near or remote, real or imaginary, relevant or irrelevant. Fears are probably more prevalent and important than they were. People are more sensitive and hear of more unpleasant possibilities than formerly. Enthusiastic supporters of causes, pacifists and eugenists for instance, work upon the instinct of fear. Not a few conscientious people nowadays hesitate before bringing a child into the world for fear that some hidden defect may be lurking in their strain which they may pass to their children. Popular scientific literature has made men aware of such conditions as mongoloid idiocy which may apparently arise in perfectly sound stocks. It is difficult to form any opinion as to the importance of considerations which fall under this head; but they are probably less important than those which come under any of the other three heads. Nevertheless they are not negligible, and there are aspects of the present situation, and especially of the international situation, which suggest that their importance may increase.

Under the head of economic considerations we may put in the forefront the fact that earnings are in no way related to family responsibilities. Wages and salaries are related to jobs; the man who has to support half a dozen dependent children gets no more than the man without dependants who works at a similar task. The advent of each additional child therefore reduces the average amount available for each member of the family. Since the cost of maintaining a child is on the average at least half that of maintaining an adult, a married couple with two dependent children have taken upon themselves an obligation equivalent to the support of an unemployed adult; moreover an unemployed adult might be useful in the house, whereas young children require continual supervision. To this may be added the fact that a wage earner usually reaches his maximum rate of wages before the age of 25; the consequence is that, when wages are low, the presence of three or more dependent children may depress the standard of living of the family down to or even below the poverty line. Family allowances, defined as grants of money separate from and additional to wages, are advocated in order to equalize the position as between those with and those without dependent children. Benefits derived from some social services tend in the same direction; thus, if education is free, an additional child involves no additional expense on education. But unless social services are extended to the provision of the extra accommodation, food, and clothes required by additional children, a couple with a large family, in the absence of a family allowance in cash, will remain at a financial disadvantage compared with a couple with a small family.

There weighs upon parents, not only the duty of providing for children, but also the problem of finding employment for them when they leave school. The dread of unemployment is a factor of importance; it has been much increased in late years by industrial fluctuations and also by the immense publicity given to the matter. It is important, not only because the possible lack of employment for children makes parents apprehensive on their account, but also because parents fear that their dependent children may suffer if they themselves become unemployed. There are other elements in the situation which magnify the fear of unemployment. The social and industrial structure is undergoing very rapid changes; certain kinds of employment are contracting, and parents, trained for these employments and knowing little or nothing of new openings, may under-estimate the scope of new opportunities. To a fearful generation, longing for security, these puzzling transformations are a source of anxiety, whereas, properly understood, they may be a source of hope. Then again, middle-class parents are finding it increasingly difficult to place their children in what they regard as suitable occupations. Competition for these occupations has increased; to this fact we may attribute in no small part the belief that the country is overpopulated which is so prominent among the middle classes. But the diagnosis is wrong. The increase in competition is due to the opening of careers to talents, and the children of middle-class parents have now to compete, not only among themselves, but also with the children of wage earners for the more eligible and better-paid occupations.

As a motive for keeping the size of family small the fear of unemployment is probably far less important than the ambitions of parents for their children. Those well placed want their children to find openings in their own level of society, and those less well placed want their children to have a chance to reach a higher level than they themselves occupy. To achieve these ends it is necessary to maintain children while they are acquiring further education and often to pay for that education; also it is often necessary to pay premiums and entrance fees and to support children until they can establish themselves. There is here a powerful incentive to limit the size of family in the interests of the children. Indeed it is sometimes said that these motives are inherent in the present form of society, and that the final condemnation of capitalism is that under it people are induced to keep their families so small that they no longer replace themselves.

There are two facts which cause difficulty. The first is competition. It may be observed that competition is not peculiar to the present form of society; for even if no positions were more eligible than others on account of higher pay, some positions would be more desired than others because they carried greater power. Competition could only be avoided in so far as the structure of society became segmentary, that is divided into hereditary castes; and it is away from, and not towards, social structure of this kind that those who attack 'capitalism' wish to move. Competition is not indissociably correlated with infertility; in order to destroy the correlation it is necessary to ensure that the member of the three or four child family is not handicapped in the race on account of lack of equipment, as compared with the member of the one or two child family. In other words it comes down to a matter of extending social services and allowances. The second fact which causes difficulty is class structure. We have the well-known situation that, even when the family income is five or ten times that of the income of the working-class family, the number of children is small. In part this is due to considerations, which fall under the fourth group, since they are social rather than economic. In part the low fertility of the higher-income classes is due to the possibility of what amounts to the purchase of positions

for children; for the fewer the children the more money
there is for expenditure in this direction. Positions in
business can be bought. There are not only barriers to
the professions which exclude those who are not specially
trained; there are also barriers, such as high entrance
fees, which exclude the poor. More important is the fact
that there are expensive forms of education which give
a training hardly superior to the less expensive kinds, but
which confer prestige and open doors to many desirable
occupations. In order, therefore, that size of family
shall cease to be a consideration when thinking of the
future of the children, two things must be brought about.
Those children with capacity to profit from higher education must not be impeded from obtaining it by reason of
the poverty of their parents. Though this requires large
expenditure of public money it involves no revolution;
for it merely means an extension of existing services.
Secondly, those barriers to the more desirable occupations
must be abolished which can only be surmounted by the
expenditure of money, but which do not discriminate
between those who are and those who are not intellectually
and otherwise qualified. This does demand a more revolu-
tionary change; for it involves the pursuit of a coherent
policy carefully designed to diminish the direct and indirect power of money. This conclusion, it may be
observed, is the exact opposite of that reached by many,
and especially by eugenists, who are troubled by the low
fertility of the middle classes; for these people find the
root of the trouble in high taxation and other burdens
which press upon these classes. But observation shows
that, as incomes increase from class and class, so do opportunities of spending money upon what is in effect buying
openings for children; therefore relief from taxation will
result in the long run, not in making money available for
more children, but in the expenditure of more money
upon the placing of each child. The middle classes are
indeed threatened by extinction; for their reproduction

rate is some 50 per cent. below replacement rate. But it is not taxation which constitutes the threat.

There remain those reasons for limiting the size of the family that we may call social. Expectant mothers, nursing mothers, and mothers with dependent children all require services and facilities of very specialized kinds, pre- and post-natal clinics, maternity homes, home helps, day nurseries, play centres, and a whole host of other forms of assistance in their expert task of preparing themselves for, and attending to, young children. A beginning has been made with the provision of such facilities, but it serves at present chiefly to demonstrate the magnitude of the need. The need for the provision of special facilities is more obvious than that of modifying general social institutions and mechanisms with the requirements of children in view; but it is very necessary to adapt housing, town planning, transport, leisure and recreational facilities and so on with these needs in mind, if young children and those who have to care for them are not to remain penalized. At present exactly the opposite tends to take place; for it is those without young children who have the money to spend. Therefore the ingenuity and enterprise of inventors and of entrepreneurs are exerted in the interests of the unmarried and the childless; it is the needs of the unencumbered adult that every one tries to satisfy. Housing exhibitions show us model flats upon which every care has been lavished and in which no child could ever find a home. In the last fifteen years two million houses have been built, and there is now an Act which gives a definition of overcrowding and makes it a statutory offence. It is possible that, taking the sizes of these houses and the definition of overcrowding together, the result will be to produce a situation in which the population of these houses cannot replace themselves. For there will always be a certain percentage of childless couples and of couples with one or two children only; therefore, since there must be approximately three children in the average family for replacement purposes, a proportion of four and five child families is necessary if the population is not to die out. But few or no arrangements have been made in these schemes for these larger families; their existence in the new houses, of which housing reformers are so proud, is an offence in the eyes of the law. One of the most prominent of them has recently said that 'the constant improvement in housing standards has now reached its goal'. Apparently it has not occurred to him that the situation, which he finds so satisfactory, may be incompatible with the continued existence of the community.

Finally under the head of social reasons we may place the very important fact that children are encumbrances. No matter how adequate the house and how sufficient all these facilities to which we have alluded, children are ties; in varying degrees their presence makes it difficult or impossible for parents to engage in other activities. These activities may be of the most unselfish kind, or they may take the shape of innocuous amusements and relaxations, theatres, cinemas, parties, holidays, and so on, or they may be of a less desirable type. But the pursuit of any of them is made difficult so long as there are children who require care at home. The parental instinct may be strong enough to bring one or two children into the world; but even in the case of those parents, for whom the economic considerations mentioned above create no difficulty, the desire for freedom to engage in these activities overbears the parental instinct when that number has been reached. Though the proportion of parents, for whom the economic factors are of little account, is small, the fact that size of family is a problem among them is of very great significance; for it shows that the problem of the small family cannot be solved by economic remedies alone.

This discussion is intended to be no more than illustrative of the position. An exhaustive discussion of the considerations which weigh with parents when fixing the size of their families would demand a volume to itself, and would incidentally disclose the fact that our knowledge is very limited at many important points. It is enough for our purpose to establish the fact that there is hardly anything in the whole social situation which does not have some relation to the problem which faces parents when deciding upon the size of their families.

Let us now review the position. We may say perhaps that in part the reason for the small size of family is that parents have gone on strike in protest against the neglect of their special problems. Parenthood has always involved trials and burdens; formerly, however, they were inescapable, and therefore parents were unable to force the attention of society upon them. Parents were enslaved, and slaves cannot withdraw their labour. Parents are now becoming free, and they take advantage of this freedom to bring the strike weapon into play. But the effectiveness of a strike depends upon the inconvenience which the community is made to suffer. In this case the community has not been in any way incommoded as yet. In fact the action taken by parents was welcomed; therefore the grievances of parents obtained, and still receive, little or no attention. Here the analogy fails, because the parents were not driven to return to work; they found themselves better off if they remained on strike.

It would be entirely mistaken, however, to suppose that these considerations represent more than a partial and subsidiary explanation of the present situation. If the special difficulties of parents were removed, more children would no doubt be wanted. But apart from these special difficulties incidental to parenthood which encourage limitation, there are numerous other considerations, worthy and unworthy, relevant and irrelevant, which lead in the same direction; the importance of these other considerations is evident when it is remembered that parents, who by reason of their favourable economic position suffer little from the difficulties incidental to parenthood, drastically limit their families. It follows that the major part of the explanation lies in the fact that the parental instinct is now satisfied when the average size of the family is not sufficient for the purpose of replacement.

If the parental instinct was a force of unvarying intensity and if the opposing considerations always exercised the same attraction, the position would be hopeless since extinction would be inevitable. But the parental instinct is a vague term which is used here merely to imply desire for children, and it is possible that the intensity of the desire for children may increase. The attraction exercised by the opposing considerations depends upon the scale of values, and the scale of values may also change. People may therefore come to desire the long run satisfactions of a moderate-sized family more than the short run satisfactions which are made possible when the family is small and the parents relatively free from parental cares.

There are reasons for supposing that under certain circumstances the parental instinct and the scale of values would undergo considerable changes. At present people are quite unaware of the implications of the new freedom. Hitherto throughout the whole history of the human race replacement has been automatic; indeed the danger has usually been in the direction of excessive reproduction. Replacement is no longer automatic, but of this fact there is no understanding. The most essential thing at the present time is to implant in the members of a modern community a firm grasp of the fact that they are responsible for its future in the sense that, if they do not replace themselves, the community will be extinguished. To achieve this end simple statistical demonstrations of the mode of recruitment of population in general and of the position of recruitment of the population in question from time to time should be made familiar to all. It will then become apparent that replacement is a social duty, a fact which at present is entirely unfamiliar to people at large. It will also become apparent that in many western

communities the average size of family is now such that
the duty is not being performed.

It was said earlier that, although changes in amount of
and age at marriage are of no great importance, quite the
contrary is true of attitude to marriage. For upon attitude
to marriage depends the end to which it is directed. No
institution has been so degraded and vulgarized as marriage; it would almost seem as though all the artifices
known to a sensational press and to a commercialized
literature have been employed to emphasize every aspect
of marriage except the duties which it imposes and the
opportunities of self discipline which it offers. What sort
of guidance have young people to-day when they approach
the age of marriage? It is as certain as anything can be
that, where families are voluntary, a community, in which
marriage is regarded as it is to-day in western civilization,
will die out. For it is held up to be no more than a mode of
self gratification. Those who are concerned about the
small family problem should address themselves earnestly
to a reform of the outlook upon marriage. If this outlook
is changed, the parental instinct may grow stronger and
the power of attraction, exercised by superficial and short
run satisfactions, may grow less.

This is fundamental. It would be a mistake of the first
magnitude to suppose that no more is needed than to
smooth the path to parenthood by removing the disabilities
under which parents suffer. For, if married couples are
to have children, they must desire them; they cannot be
bribed into parenthood. But given a new attitude to
marriage and parenthood, based upon the new and revolu-
tionary idea that recruitment must henceforth be a conscious process, the smoothing of the path to parenthood
has a large part to play. But it is no simple matter to
remove these disabilities. It is in the medical sphere that
results could be most rapidly and easily reached; as we
have noticed, a relatively small expenditure of money upon
research ought to achieve within a decade marked results

in reducing maternal mortality and in alleviating the difficulties, dangers, and sufferings of pregnancy and child-birth. It is a much more troublesome and expensive matter to devise and provide the special services required by parents and young children in the shape of a great extension of existing social services and of the setting up of new services. It is a still larger matter to attempt to remove those financial and other handicaps under which parents suffer when they are bringing up children and endeavouring to give them an entry into appropriate occupations. But these changes are as nothing compared with the transformation of the whole scheme of life which will gradually have to be accomplished if the inconveni-ences attaching to parenthood are to be removed, and the special problems attaching to parenthood are to receive due consideration. Taken together nothing less than a social revolution is necessary. But it is a very different kind of social revolution from that which figures in the battle-cries of politicians. For the aim is to place the family where it ought on all grounds to be, in the centre of the social field, and to bring all other institutions into appro-priate relations to it. It may be that the mere logic of the population situation will gradually divert interest from those creeds which loom so large to-day, and will lead to changes in social structure far more fundamental, but much more realistic and beneficial, than those which these creeds envisage.

In the light of this discussion it should not be difficult to understand the failure of the attempts to raise the birth-rate described in the last chapter. All that has been done by those attempts is to deal with a single aspect of a very involved problem and then only in a very inadequate manner. That family allowances, as given in France and Belgium, have been ineffective is no proof that family allowances have no part to play in the reconstruction that must take place. But there is another and very important reason for the failure of these schemes. They have been

S

accompanied by attempts to make birth-control illegal. This is bad tactics. If anything is certain it is that people will resist being driven back under the tyranny of the unlimited family; therefore all measures are suspect which are associated with an anti-birth-control movement. But it is much more than bad tactics. It implies a complete misunderstanding of the only possible solution of the small family problem. The solution must begin by welcoming the voluntary small family system, and that means welcoming birth-control. For birth-control is not merely a practice which must be tolerated; it has positive functions of great importance to perform, such as, for example, making possible the proper spacing of the family. Let it be said clearly that the escape from the unlimited family makes a very great step forward in human history. The problem is to adjust outlook to the responsibility involved by the transition to the voluntary family system.

It should now also be possible to understand why the small family problem is so much more urgent and difficult than is generally realized. At the moment in this country the reproduction rate is about 25 per cent. below replacement rate. If all children born were wanted (that is wanted before conception), the former rate would probably be 50 per cent. below the latter. But the day when all children will be wanted children is certainly coming; for contraceptive methods are undergoing continual improvement. The perfect contraceptive, cheap, easy to use, and infallible, may be invented any day. Therefore, if things remain as they are, the reproduction rate will fall, and the prospect will be a reduction of the population to less than a quarter of its present size a century from now. But the coming of this catastrophic decline will be masked for a time by the fact that in any case the fall will not be large during the next two decades. The population will decline at the most by three or four millions in the next twenty years. This fall will be welcome to the many who believe that unemployment is due to over-population. Meanwhile people will come to think that they are rendering positive service by keeping their families small. All the habits connected with the small family system will harden into customs. Any suggestion that more births are desirable will meet with the impassioned opposition of birth-control enthusiasts. The prospect of so catastrophic a fall makes it urgent that steps should be taken at once, and the difficulties, which will be encountered in undertaking the social reconstruction that is necessary, are so formidable that the urgency is much enhanced.

CHAPTER XVIII

JAPAN AND INDIA

WE parted company with non-European peoples in Chapter VII. The first six chapters were devoted to a study of the growth of world population including non-Europeans, and to an analysis of the immediate causes of this expansion. In Chapter VI our attention was arrested by the decline in the birth-rate of European peoples, and we followed this clue up to the last chapter, which was devoted to the small family problem. It is time to return to the study of non-Europeans. Although the space devoted to them is relatively small, they constitute two-thirds of the population of the world. There are two reasons for treating them so briefly. First, and most important, is the sparsity of evidence; secondly, they do not exhibit the important and intricate phenomena arising from the declining birth-rate.

Among non-European peoples are to be found communities of very diverse structure and accomplishment. At one end of the scale are the primitive peoples, as we may call them, who are characterized from the point of view of this study by the fact that they declined more or less seriously in population after they had come into contact with Europeans. This group will be considered in Chapter XX. At the other end of the scale are peoples, many of whom are of high culture and ancient civilization. They are distinguished from the former group by the fact that they did not suffer any serious decline in population, if indeed they decreased at all, as a result of contact with the European world. It is with the latter group that we shall be concerned in this and the following chapters. There are two countries belonging to this group, Japan and India, of which we know more than the others, and it will be convenient to deal with them first.

It will be remembered that there is evidence of a rapid

growth of the population of Japan between 1650 and 1720 which we attributed to a decline in the death-rate consequent upon the restoration and maintenance of internal order. Between 1720 and 1848 population was stable, and this stability was apparently attained by the extensive practice of abortion and infanticide. There is a gap in our knowledge of Japanese population history between 1848 and 1873. From the latter date onwards we begin to get figures again, but it is not until the most recent times that the census totals have approached the accuracy of a European enumeration. Taking the data as they are, they indicate that the population began to increase before 1870; during the last sixty years growth has been continuous but not extraordinarily rapid. The population was 31·1 millions in 1873, 43·8 millions in 1898, and 64·5 millions in 1930, and the average annual rate of increase was 1·1 per cent. between 1873 and 1898, and 1·2 per cent. between 1898 and 1930. This rate was little more than half that shown by the United States and the British Dominions during the same period.

From 1878 onwards we have birth- and death-rates; but the earlier figures can be no more than approximations, and even to-day their accuracy is open to doubt. They are given in the form of a graph in Fig. 51. The death-rate would seem to have risen for two decades, to have remained steady for a decade, to have risen once more, and then to have declined from 1923 to the present time. It is very uncertain what significance, if any, attaches to the reported increases. The only definite conclusion which we are entitled to draw is that the death-rate did not decline between 1878 and 1923. At the latter date a marked decline set in. Of the reality of this improvement there is no doubt; infant mortality, for instance, is known to have decreased. From this we may infer that some thirteen years ago medical and sanitary reforms began to play a part in Japanese population history.

The earlier birth-rate figures show a marked rise up to

1921, since which date the rate has declined. The earlier figures are low; if they are not to be explained by incomplete counting, if, that is to say, there was a real increase, it may be that we have to account for it by the gradual abandonment of the practices of abortion and infanticide.

FIGURE 51

Birth-rates and Death-rates in Japan, 1884–1933

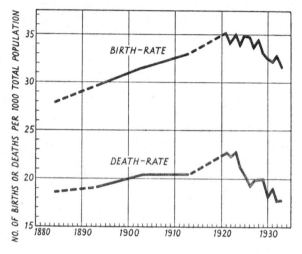

In any case, since there is no reason to suppose that the death-rate declined until very recent years, the growth of population, which began before 1873, must have been due to a rise in the birth-rate, and the most reasonable explanation of this rise is the abandonment of practices known to have been in use at least up to 1850. It is not likely that they were abandoned rapidly, but how long they lingered is uncertain.

Whatever doubt there may be about the movement of the Japanese birth-rate and its explanation until recently, it is certain that it has declined during the last ten years. Can we find the explanation of this? The annual number of births in Japan rose steadily up to 1920, when it exceeded 2 millions for the first time. Since that date a

most significant change has taken place. The annual
number of births has fluctuated; it was 2,121,000 in 1933
and this was less than in 1928. Stabilization of the annual
number of births is clearly approaching. Since the birth-
rate is obtained by referring the births which take place in
a year to the population for that year, and since the number of the former has recently changed little, while the
population has grown by nearly a million a year, the result

FIGURE 52

Annual Number of Live Births in Japan: 1920 to 1933

Year	Number of live births	Year	Number of live births
1920	2,025,564	1927	2,060,737
1921	1,990,876	1928	2,135,852
1922	1,969,314	1929	2,077,026
1923	2,043,297	1930	2,085,101
1924	1,998,520	1931	2,102,784
1925	2,086,091	1932	2,182,742
1926	2,104,405	1933	2,121,123

has been a decline in the birth-rate. Why are births ceas-
ing to increase in proportion to population? It would
seem that there are various reasons. There is a change in
marriage habits. There would seem to be less marriage;
in 1922 516,000 women got married, in 1931 only 496,000.
There is a rise in the age at marriage; in 1922 25·3 per cent.
of the women who got married were between the ages of
15 and 19, while in 1931 the percentage was only 19·3.
The fertility of women has decreased. There were 169
births per 1,000 women aged 15 to 44 in 1920 and 157 in
1930. When we consider births per 1,000 women aged
15 to 29, the drop is more striking; there were 294 such
births in 1920 and 262 in 1930.

The change in the fertility of women as a whole is
greater than can be attributed to changes in age at, and
amount of, marriage. We cannot obtain specific fertility
rates for married women, but if we could we should no

doubt find that specific fertility had declined. In fact, birth-control must have been at work. There is abundant evidence that contraception is well known in Japan, and it is reasonable to assume that it is widely practised. According to Penrose all the chief contraceptives are made and sold in Japan. There are no specific restrictions upon their manufacture or sale; but it would seem that the sale of contraceptives and of books about contraception can be brought within the provisions of the Peace Preservation Act, and that occasionally the Japanese police have initiated prosecutions. This has given rise to an erroneous idea that the sale of contraceptives is forbidden. Requien says that contraceptives are freely advertised in the papers, and that birth-control clinics have been opened at Tokio and Osaka for the poorer classes. The attitude of the government has changed from time to time, but opposition to birth-control has gradually weakened. In 1931 a minister declared that it was a personal matter and that the government would neither oppose nor encourage it.

So far as the population position in general is concerned, it is evident that Japan is to be classed with those countries in eastern Europe where the birth-rate has recently begun to decline and where medical and sanitary progress is now reducing the death-rate. What are the prospects for the future? There are certain factors which will make for an increase of population. The death-rate is declining and will continue to do so, but it is not very high since it is less than 18 per 1,000, while the infant mortality rate is about 120 per 1,000, which was the average in Italy during the period 1926–30. Therefore there is no opportunity for a prolonged or dramatic fall in the death-rate. It is also the case that the pre-reproductive age group is unusually large; this means that the women of reproductive age will be relatively numerous for some time to come, a situation which favours a high birth-rate. On the other hand, women are marrying later and, more important still, are limiting their families when they marry. There is little doubt that the latter factors will prove more important than the former. As we have observed, the annual number of births now tends to stabilize at about 2 millions. Uyeda has used this fact as a basis upon which to make a forecast of the growth of population in Japan. He estimates that the population, which was 67·5 millions in 1933, will be 78 millions in 1950. About the latter date the reproductive group will cease to increase relatively to other age groups, whereas fertility will probably continue to decline. Under these circumstances the annual number of births will fall well below 2 millions, and the population will cease to grow before it reaches 100 millions and may perhaps never approach this figure.

The population of Japan has doubled in the last sixty years. During that time the people have become better off; it has been calculated that the average real income per head has also been doubled. Thus population and standard of living have gone up together. But this does not mean that the present position is free from difficulty, and still less that the anticipated increase is not a matter for apprehension. Japan proper (that is excluding Korea, Formosa, and Sakhalin) is a small country; the total area is less than that of California. There are 439 persons per square mile. But the density is much more remarkable than these figures show. The northern island of Hokkaido is relatively infertile and inhospitable, and has a density of only 83 per square mile. This implies a higher density on the remaining islands; in Honshiu it is 559 per square mile. It reaches 1,024 per square mile in the province of Kagawa in the north of Shikoku, a province which has no industries. Much more important is the fact that, owing to the mountainous nature of the country, less than one-fifth can be cultivated; therefore the density of population on the cultivated area is very high indeed.

About half the population is engaged in agriculture and fishing. The average size of farm cultivated per family is just over 2½ acres, and the large majority of farms are less

than this in size. About three-fifths of the cultivated area
is devoted to rice, and the yield of rice per acre, nearly 34
quintals in 1932-3, is far higher than anywhere else in the
world. Nevertheless, the Japanese cannot produce enough
food to feed themselves, and over 10 per cent. of the rice
required is imported. The supply of resources necessary
for heavy industry is very limited; Japan is poor in coal
and oil and poorer still in iron. Water-power, on the other
hand, is fairly abundant. In consequence Japan has had
to exert herself in order to produce commodities for
export. She has developed a large trade in silk, an agricultural product; but the market for silk has flagged
recently, and she has had to develop artificial silk and
various light industries. The enterprise, skill, and adapta-
bility displayed have been extraordinary. But it is a precarious mode of life. While it cannot be decisively proved
by figures that Japan is over-populated, there are various
facts relating to the labour expended on the land and to
the yields received which strongly suggest that this is so.
It is not possible in fact to resist the conclusion that there
is congestion of numbers in Japan, and that the further
increase, which is to be anticipated, though less than
sometimes supposed, is a formidable menace.

This is evidently the opinion of the Japanese themselves.
They have turned their attention to finding outlets for
population, and the first possible area for colonization
which attracted attention was Hokkaido, that is within
Japan proper. The island is larger than Scotland. Until
1900 it was left to the Ainu; since then persistent attempts
have been made to attract settlers, and success has attended
these efforts to the extent that the population now numbers
2,800,000. But the climate is harsh; snow lies on the
ground for five months in the year. It is impossible to
cultivate the land intensively as in Japan, and it cannot
be anticipated that Hokkaido will take more than a few
thousands a year at the most.

Attention was next turned to the empire. Emigration

Italy	Portugal	United States (white population only)	Australia	New Zealand	Period
					1871–80
					1881–4
					1885–90
					1891–4
					1895
					1896–7
					1898–9
					1900
					1901
					1902–3
					1904–5
					1906–7
					1908–10
..	..	..	..	} 1·357	1911–12
..	..	..	..		1913
..	..	..	..		1914–15
					1916–19
..	..	1·14	} 1·319		1920
..	..	..	..	} 1·291	1921
..	..	..	..		1922
					1923
					1924
					1925
					1926
					1927
					1928
					1929
..	} 1·334	1·08			1930
1·209					1931
..	..	..	} 0·976		1932
1·18	1·29	..		0·978	1933
					1934

has been encouraged to Sakhalin (Karafuto) by free passages, grants of land, and loans for stocking farms. But
the climatic conditions are very severe, far worse than in
Hokkaido, and it is unlikely that there will be any substantial accession to the 284,000 colonists now established
there. Indeed, the annual number of immigrants has
declined heavily ever since 1924 in spite of the efforts to
stimulate immigration. Korea (Chosen) and Formosa
(Taiwan) are favoured lands; but they have dense indigenous populations, 247 to the square mile in the former
and 331 in the latter. Also the rate of increase of population in Korea and Formosa has been higher in recent years
than in Japan proper; the average annual rate of increase
in Formosa from 1920 to 1930 was 2·3 per cent.; in Japan
it was 1·3 per cent. between 1920 and 1925 and 1·5 per
cent. between 1925 and 1930. The government has made
efforts to encourage settlement in Korea; but at the present
time there are only half a million Japanese living there,
and they are mostly merchants, shopkeepers, and officials
residing in the towns. In Formosa there are about 230,000
Japanese. So far as the movement of wage earners is concerned, it has been larger from Korea to Japan than vice
versa; between 1917 and 1927 there was a net inward
movement of nearly 200,000 Koreans into Japan through
the port of Fusan alone. In spite of these efforts, which
have been pursued persistently for thirty years, there are
only about a million Japanese living in the empire outside
Japan proper. It is very much the same story in regard to
Manchuria; grandiose plans were made for the settlement
of Japanese; but there are now only a little more than
200,000 Japanese who live in that country.

It is not surprising that the Japanese government, whatever its views about the population situation may be,
should attempt to encourage settlement in the empire and
in Manchuria. It is far more significant that it has adopted
a policy of encouraging, and even of assisting financially,
emigration to foreign countries. In 1917 the government

compelled the various private emigration agencies, which were in existence, to combine, and granted to the corporation then formed a monopoly of recruitment. From 1921 the corporation received a government subvention to make known the facilities for emigration and to popularize the idea. In 1927 a comprehensive Act was passed with the intention of safeguarding the emigrant against exploitation abroad. Reduced fares or free tickets on the railways are granted to emigrants, and in some cases reduced or free passages to the port of destination. Very little success has attended these efforts; the largest number of emigrants leaving in any year between 1925 and 1930 was in 1929 when 25,700 went to foreign countries, of whom 15,500 went to Brazil. Further, in five out of the ten years between 1921 and 1930 returning emigrants exceeded departing emigrants. Therefore, on the balance there has been recently little movement between Japan and foreign countries.

There are only about half a million Japanese not living in Japan proper, the Japanese empire, or Manchuria; and about half of them are in the United States and Hawaii. How are we to interpret this? The government favours emigration. Are the people unwilling to go? The Japanese are undoubtedly home-loving people; their culture is very distinct, and they are deeply attached to their peculiar mode of life. Nevertheless, the facts show that they are willing to go far afield under certain circumstances. It has been said that they are unable to live under hard climatic conditions; but there is no evidence for this, and such knowledge as we have about the adaptation of peoples to different environments lends no support to the idea. The fact seems to be that the Japanese will go, though perhaps with more reluctance than some other peoples at leaving their homes, to any country where they have not got to compete with others whose standard of living is lower than their own. They went freely enough to Hawaii and western America; the western sea-board of the latter continent would now be the home of millions of Japanese if they had not been prevented from settling. The difficulty which faces the Japanese is that the countries to which they would willingly go are shut against them.

Let us now turn to India. We have some information about the course of population in India during the last six decades. A census was taken in 1872 and has been repeated on five occasions. To make an enumeration in an area which includes a sixth of the total world population is a great administrative achievement, especially when it is remembered that even now only 18 per cent. of the population of India is literate. It is claimed that the figures are accurate to within a small margin of error; whether this is so or not, it remains true that reasonably accurate knowledge of the population history of India is available over a longer period than is the case for any other large area outside the sphere of European civilization with the exception of Japan. The census returns are summarized in Fig. 53.

FIGURE 53

Growth of Population in India: 1872 to 1930

(millions)

Period or year	Population at beginning of period	Total increase of population	Increase due to Inclusion of new areas	Increase due to Improvement of method	Real increase of population	Average annual rate of real increase
1872–81	206·2	47·7	33·0	12·0	2·7	0·137
1881–91	253·9	33·4	5·7	3·5	24·2	0·903
1891–1901	287·3	7·1	2·7	0·2	4·2	0·145
1901–11	294·4	20·8	1·8	..	19·0	0·627
1911–21	315·2	3·7	0·1	..	3·6	0·114
1921–31	318·9	33·9	0·0	..	33·9	1·015
1931	352·8	..	..	..	..	..
1872–1931	..	146·6	43·3	15·7	87·6	..

In this figure an attempt has been made to show how much of the increase recorded in each decade was due to the inclusion of new areas and how much to improvement of census methods; the balance gives the absolute real increase. The last column shows the average annual rate of real increase, that is, of the increase which is not accounted for by an enlargement of the territory surveyed or by better ascertainment. We are at once impressed by certain remarkable facts. The average annual rate of increase over the whole period has been low; it is less than half that shown by Japan during the same period, and the Japanese rate of increase, it will be remembered, has been low compared with that of European countries overseas. But the variations in the rate of increase from decade to decade are even more remarkable. Decades with a low rate of increase alternate with decades having a moderate rate. This is the first time that we have met with a country the population history of which shows this peculiar feature.

In order to throw light on the situation we may examine the vital statistics which are available from 1885. These records are very defective; even at the present day they are officially admitted to be at least 20 per cent. below the probable figures. But we may assume that, although they give an erroneous impression of the absolute rates by understating the true figures, they give a fair picture of the trend of the rates. Let us take the birth-rate first; it shows considerable fluctuations but no definite trend either up or down. There is no sign whatever of a decline in the rate during recent years as in Japan. When we bring the death-rate into the picture, we can detect signs of an inverse correlation between the two rates. During periods such as 1910 to 1917 and 1922 to 1930 the birth-rate was higher and the death-rate lower than usual; this inverse relationship is fairly well marked for particular years or shorter periods, 1892, 1897, 1900–1, and 1918–19 for example. As to the death-rate itself, the fluctuations are much more marked than in the case of the birth-rate, but there is no sign whatever of any trend upwards or downwards. It is true that some improvement has recently been reported in the infant mortality rate. On the other hand, we read in the Census Report for 1931 that 'the constant figure for mean age at this census as compared with previous ones and in conjunction with the consistency

FIGURE 54

Birth-rates and Death-rates in India: 1885 to 1930

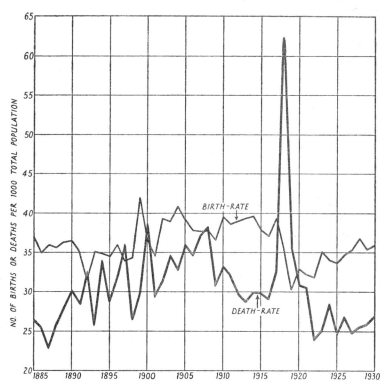

of the decennial age groups suggests that the expectation of life has not much altered since 1891'. We may take it, therefore that secular improvements in mortality rates, if any, are very small.

How are these facts to be interpreted? Mortality rates show no trend and are very high as is evident from the fact that the mean expectation of life at birth for male infants was only 26·7 years in 1931. Here, then, is a population the members of which are so thinned by disease and other death-dealing agencies in early life that relatively few reach middle, and fewer still old age. This thinning process is not of constant intensity; in three out of the six last decades it was so vigorous that the surplus of births was small. Indeed, in five separate years since 1885 deaths have exceeded births. These periods of high mortality are marked by crop failures and consequential food shortage, amounting sometimes to famine and accompanied by epidemics. While deaths directly due to famine are less numerous than formerly, it is probable that this does not indicate an improvement in the total food supply so much as improvement in transport and organization which enables food to be brought to the stricken districts. In any case, the high mortality in the bad periods has always been mostly due to epidemics which are enabled to spread on account of the enfeebled condition of the population consequent upon lack of sufficient food. As we have noticed, these bad periods are marked by a birth-rate lower than the average; in this phenomenon we may perhaps have to recognize the debilitating effects of disease and food shortage upon the physiological capacity to bear children, though other factors may be at work at the same time.

If a population, which did not control births, had increased to the point where there was only just enough food to keep the members alive, it would show high birth- and death-rates running parallel. For, even if death from disease was controlled, deaths would take place from lack of food. But such a situation could hardly arise, or in any case could not endure for any length of time, because the amount of food raised varies owing to climatic and other fluctuations. Therefore under such conditions there would be periods when owing to a temporary increase in the food supply the death-rate would fall below the birth-rate and the population would increase, and periods when the opposite would take place, though the final result would be the same, namely, a population which trended neither up nor down. This is not the case with India; but India does not fulfil all the conditions implied in the above hypothetical case. For in India large areas have been brought under cultivation and still larger areas have been improved by means of irrigation, while industry has been expanded; in other words the total food supply has been continuously increased. Under these circumstances what shape would the vital statistics of a country be expected to assume which was pressing upon the means of subsistence? It is probable that they would look very much like those exhibited by India. In other words, Indian statistics are compatible with, and may be said to suggest, pressure upon the means of subsistence, and that is the situation which Malthus assumed to be more or less universal in time and space.

Let us glance at the available evidence, which may throw some further light upon the situation and may enable us to judge whether there is serious pressure of this kind. It may be of assistance to take into consideration the period before figures can be given. The Census Report of 1921 quotes Edye as follows:

'The population of India at the death of Akbar (1606) is roughly estimated by Mr. Moreland to have been about 100 millions, of which the share of what is now the United Provinces would not exceed 20 millions. The common people of Northern India were then undoubtedly almost naked. Blankets were unknown to them; shoes were seldom worn and little furniture was used save a few earthen vessels. The population of the United Provinces is now 46 millions, and the people have long been more or less substantially clothed and shod; there are few who do not possess blankets, and brass pots are in almost universal use. The amusement which the peasantry gets out of attendance at the law courts and railway travelling—these two diversions are to the Indian what the picture palace is to the European proletariat—is entirely new since Akbar's day. In recent times the standard of living has not risen in such an obvious way, but even during the last fifteen years (i.e. pre-war period) there has been observable an increasing addiction to the

T

use of small comforts and conveniences, such as tea, cigarettes, matches, lanterns, buttons, pocket knives, looking glasses—even gramophones—and of countless similar trifles. It seems unquestionable that up to the present time the number of the people and the standard of living have been rising together.'

In the last sentences the author was referring to conditions at the beginning of the present century. Regarding changes during the last twenty years opinions differ; it is held by some that things have improved somewhat, and by others that they have deteriorated. It is significant that there are no clear signs of progress.

When looking at the position to-day it must be remembered that India is almost a continent in itself, and that it contains an abundance of cultures, creeds, and traditions. Generalization is therefore dangerous, but there is no room here for detailed observation. Taking the country as a whole the density of population is 195 persons per square mile, whereas in Europe (excluding Russia) the density is only 184 per square mile. This in itself is a noteworthy fact. But the population of India is very unevenly distributed; there are only 6·5 persons to the square mile in Baluchistan, whereas in the Dacca division of Bengal 13,800,000 persons live at a density of 935 to the square mile. When we remember that in England and Wales there are only 695 persons per square mile, it is evident that an almost wholly agricultural population living at this density must be overcrowded. For in India only about 10 per cent. of the population is engaged in industry; furthermore, the proportion of the population so engaged declined from 10·7 per cent. in 1921 to 9·8 per cent. in 1931. This means that in 1931, as compared with 1921, a slightly larger proportion of a population, absolutely larger by 33 millions, had to be supported from the land. It would appear from the Report of the Royal Commission on Agriculture that 72 per cent. of the holdings are uneconomic in the sense that they cannot support a family of average size at the very frugal traditional standard

of living. To this it may be added that the average acreage
per head of population supported by agriculture is declining; it was 1·24 in 1911 and 1·20 in 1931. It is also of
interest to note that the acreage under food crops per head
of total population was 0·82 in 1911 and 0·79 in 1931.

Taken together, this evidence points strongly to the
conclusion that India, or in any case large areas of it, is
over-populated; and there are facts which indicate that
the position is not improving and may be deteriorating.
Therefore the inference suggested by a study of the vital
statistics is almost certainly correct. India is not a country
where the whole population lives at the margin of subsistence; perhaps there never has been a country in that
position, at least not for any considerable length of time.
But the margin is narrow, much narrower than it need be,
having in view the natural resources and the existing
methods of food production. The position in India is
therefore in sharp contrast to that which we have found
to prevail in the countries so far studied, including Japan.
In these countries the population has been raised above
the immediate impact of natural forces, and the vital
statistics, even in those cases where there is evidence of
congestion of population, are not affected by the vagaries
of climate and the yield of harvests.

This being so, it is not possible to forecast the future
population of India on lines similar to those employed
when dealing with other countries; for there is no question
of projecting into the future present birth- and death-rate
trends with appropriate modifications. The future population of India will be governed by such expansion of opportunities for subsistence as may take place. Irrigation and
land reclamation may increase these opportunities, and so
may industrial development. But it would seem that the
likelihood of expansion of the former kind is limited, and,
as we have seen, industrial employment suffered a relative
decline during the last decade. The prospect is therefore
that growth of population will be slow and fluctuating.

There are some additional features of the present situation in India to which attention may be called. Taken together, they make a tragic picture. There is little occasion to emphasize the urgent need for better health services, and to point out that progress might tend merely to increase malnutrition and the danger of starvation. It is less obvious that there are urgent social reforms which would, however, increase the birth-rate. In India the average number of children born to a woman is not large. The census of 1931 gives the results of a special inquiry into 900,000 families scattered among all classes and over all parts of India. The conclusion derived from an analysis of the returns is that 'the average married woman in India has four children born alive and that 2·9 in every four, 70 per cent. that is, survive'. The relatively small number of children is not due to birth-control, of which there is no sign, or to postponement of marriage, since all women marry early. The explanation is in part that many women die before they reach the end of the reproductive period. To an unknown but not inconsiderable extent premature death of married women is caused, or hastened, by the practice of child marriage. Child marriage occurs among Muslims as well as among Hindus; in India as a whole in 1931 no less than 181 out of each 1,000 married women were under 15 years of age. Though pre-puberty consummation of marriage appears to be uncommon, consummation follows very soon after puberty, and intercourse at this age is inimical both to health and fecundity. Child marriage is a pernicious practice, not only on grounds of health but also as a social institution; nevertheless, its abolition would increase the birth-rate. The same is true of the prohibition upon widow remarriage which prevails almost universally among Hindus, though not among Muslims, and which is another agency tending to keep the fertility of women low. In 1931 there were no less than 26 million widows in India, of whom 19 millions were Hindus; relatively to other countries widows are very numerous (15 per 1,000 of total female population in India, as compared with 7 per 1,000 in Europe), and the reason is child marriage. Prohibition upon the remarriage of widows withdraws large numbers of young women from child bearing, and its abolition would raise the birth-rate. But on social grounds its abolition is very much to be desired; a widow is a despised and unprotected drudge whose position is pitiable. There could scarcely be a more tragic situation; three of the most urgent social reforms would only magnify another pressing evil.

Family limitation is the only way of escape. It is commonly said that the practice is so contrary to the religious and social traditions of the country that it can only spread slowly. But we read in the Census Report of 1931 that

'a definite movement towards artificial birth-control appears to be taking place and is perhaps less hampered by misplaced prudery than in some countries which claim to be more civilized; thus not only is artificial control publicly advocated by a number of medical writers but Madras can boast a Neo-Malthusian League with two Maharajas, three High Court judges and four or five men very prominent in public life as its sponsors'.

Further, in 1930 the Government of Mysore sanctioned the establishment of birth-control clinics in the four principal hospitals of the State.

It remains to say something about Indian emigration. When slavery was abolished in the empire a demand grew up for labour in the tropical dependencies, and this led to the emigration of Indians under indenture. Indians have played a large and little-recognized part in the development of the colonies; they have also made some contribution to the French colonial empire. The government of India has imposed a series of restrictions upon movement of this kind in the interests of the emigrants, and in 1915 finally prohibited emigration under indenture. Since many labourers chose to remain after their period of indenture was over, the movement has resulted in the presence of Indians scattered all over the tropical dependencies,

269,000 in Mauritius, 139,000 in Trinidad, 131,000 in British Guiana, 75,000 in Fiji, and smaller numbers in other places. But they receive no accessions through free movement. Movement into the Dominions was small except to Natal; there are now about 165,000 Indians in South Africa. The Dominions, moreover, have closed their doors to Indians, and the government of South Africa even offers financial assistance to Indians who wish to return home. The position therefore has come to be that the colonies alone are open to Indians; but, since not only is indentured emigration prohibited, but also, under powers taken by the government of India in 1922, emigration of unskilled labourers whose position is likely to be unsatisfactory, the only countries to which Indians have recently gone in large numbers are Ceylon and Malaya. In 1931 there were 778,000 in the former and 624,000 in the latter country; at that date there were in all about $2\frac{1}{4}$ million Indians living outside India, nearly all of them in the empire. The net result, therefore, of Indian emigration is that the number of Indians abroad is equal to little more than two-thirds of the average annual increase of the population of India between 1921 and 1931. Though Indian emigration has great political significance, it is numerically negligible in relation to the population problem.

CHAPTER XIX

OTHER NON-EUROPEAN PEOPLES

FOR reasons which will appear at the end of this chapter there are a number of non-European peoples whom we may group with Japan and India from the point of view of their population history and their present population position. We may select some half-dozen from among these countries for special mention, since there are statistics relating to them. In Fig. 55 are shown the population at various dates, the rate of growth of population, and the present density per square mile for Java, Ceylon, Egypt, Algeria, Formosa, and the Philippines. In Fig. 56 are given graphs for the vital statistics for some of these countries. China also belongs to this group of countries, but no figures are available for the country as a whole. Since, however, it is likely that one-fifth of the human race is to be found in China, some mention must be made of the Chinese situation so far as it is illuminated by partial figures and general impressions. We may first glance at each of these countries in turn, and then we can attempt to review the position so far as this group of countries is concerned.

Java is of no great size; the area (including Madura) is under 51,000 square miles. In 1930 the population was 41,720,000; of this number about 40,890,000 were natives, and the remainder mostly Chinese and Europeans. The census of 1930 took the form of a simultaneous count, and is said to have yielded trustworthy results. It is worthy of note that the total considerably exceeded the official estimate. Estimates are available at irregular intervals from 1815 onwards. It is difficult to know what confidence to place in them; judging from the experience of 1930 it is probable on the whole that the tendency at earlier dates was towards under-estimation. It is supposed that in 1815 there were about $4\frac{1}{2}$ million inhabitants, and that this figure had more than doubled by 1850. If we take the native population only, the average annual rates of increase for the periods between the years for which estimates are available work out as is shown in Fig. 57. It is doubtful

FIGURE 55

Growth of Population in Java, Ceylon, Egypt, Algeria, Formosa, and the Philippines

Country	Date	Population Amount (thousands)	Average annual rate of increase per cent. Period	Rate	Present density of population per square mile
Java	1850	9,700	1850–1900	2·2	817
	1900	28,747	1900–30	1·3	
	1930	41,720			
Ceylon	1850	1,576	1850–1900	1·6	210
	1900	3,566	1900–30	1·4	
	1930	5,313			
Egypt	1880	6,817	1880–1907	1·9	1,126 (inhabited area only)
	1907	11,287	1907–34	1·1	
	1934	15,281			
Algeria	1850	2,496	1850–1901	1·3	8
	1901	4,739	1901–31	1·1	
	1931	6,554			
Formosa	1908	3,037	1908–20	1·6	331
	1920	3,655	1920–30	2·3	
	1930	4,594			
Philippines	1877	5,568	1877–1903	1·2	112
	1903	7,653	1903–34	1·7	
	1934	12,850			

how much importance should be attributed to the apparent variations in the average annual rates; it may be that the population was more under-estimated at certain dates than others. The average rate has in any case been high for well over a century. But it is not the magnitude of the rate which is especially remarkable; that has been equalled or approached in some of the countries shown in Fig. 55 for short periods. The striking fact is the length of time over which a high rate has prevailed, resulting in a tenfold increase in 120 years. In fact the population history of Java since 1815 resembles that of the European countries

FIGURE 56

Birth-rates and Death-rates in Egypt, Ceylon, and Formosa. The rates for Ceylon before 1921 are doubtful

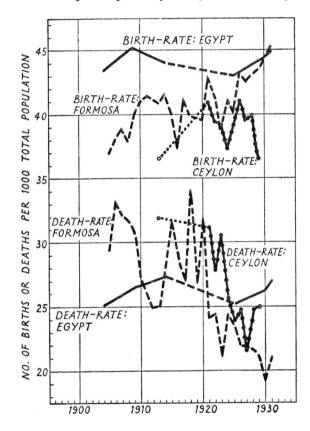

overseas, and Java stands at the top of the list when countries of ancient settlement are arranged in order according to their expansion in population during the last century.

Unfortunately the published vital statistics do not enable us to probe much farther into this extraordinary story. They relate to deaths only. The record of births is so incomplete that no figures are published. The record of deaths is also admittedly incomplete; it would seem to show a steady death-rate of about 20 per 1,000. It is generally believed that the true rate is at least 23 per 1,000. If this is so, the birth-rate must be about 38 per 1,000, since the natural increase must stand near 15 per 1,000. There is no evidence of any marked fluctuations in the rates; so

FIGURE 57

Rate of Growth of Population in Java: 1815 to 1930

Period	Average annual rate of increase per cent.
1815–45	2·45
1845–58	1·76
1858–80	2·34
1880–90	1·91
1890–1900	1·85
1900–5	1·06
1905–20	0·94
1920–30	1·73

far as we know, they run evenly with a wide gap between them.

There are clear signs that the real income of the people has increased during the last hundred years, and it follows that increase in population and increase in prosperity have so far gone hand in hand. This does not mean, of course, that the people would not have been better off if they had increased less fast, but only that the increase has not been such as to counteract material improvement due to technical and other progress. But the position cannot be regarded as otherwise than menacing; and this is now the view of the Dutch authorities. Java is extraordinarily fertile; the volcanic rocks rapidly disintegrate, and thus the soil is continually replenished with many of the necessary constituents of plant food. Rainfall is sufficient and dependable; there is little fear of drought or flood. The population is almost wholly rural; there are only four

towns with more than 100,000 inhabitants. The conditions are ideal for intensive agriculture by irrigation, and
so far the policy of extending this intensive use of the soil
has been successful in supporting a rapidly growing population at a standard that is certainly not lower than before.
But further extension is becoming impossible; there are
no new areas to be brought under this kind of cultivation,
and the attempt to urge more out of the soil must presently
be accompanied by a smaller return to the same amount
of labour. When that happens there will be a check to
the improvement of the material condition of the people.
The government has attempted to stimulate emigration to
the neighbouring Dutch islands, which are very sparsely
inhabited by primitive peoples. The results are utterly
insignificant; so far some 15,000 Javanese have emigrated
to Sumatra, and this is the total result of such efforts last-
ing over two decades.

If by Egypt we mean the cultivated area of that country,
there is some resemblance between it and Java. The soil
is very rich and its fertility is regularly renewed, though in
this case, not by the disintegration of volcanic rocks, but
by the silt of the flood waters of the Nile. Again the climate
is both very favourable for agriculture and very dependable, and there is little danger of destruction from natural
occurrences. The population history, so far as we know it,
is not dissimilar. An estimate made at the time of Napoleon's expedition gave a total of about 2½ millions. Another
estimate in 1846 gave a figure of 4,716,000. Between these
two dates there was considerable immigration, but it is
evident that the population grew by natural increase with
considerable rapidity. For 1882 there are the results of
a census which was unsatisfactory for several reasons, but
from 1897 onwards there are decennial censuses which
may be regarded as fairly trustworthy. The earlier estimates are for the total population including the nomadic
Arabs. If we include an estimate for the latter in the
figures for 1897, we can calculate the average annual rate

of increase for three periods between 1800 and that date. They are shown in Fig. 58. This figure also shows the average annual rates of increase from 1897 to 1927 during each decade for the population exclusive of the nomadic Arabs.

FIGURE 58

Rate of Growth of Population in Egypt: 1800 to 1927

Period	Average annual rate of increase per cent.
1800–46	1·29 (including nomadic Arabs)
1846–82	1·05 ,, ,,
1882–97	2·41 ,, ,,
1897–1907	1·52 (excluding nomadic Arabs)
1907–17	1·24 ,, ,,
1917–27	1·11 ,, ,,

It is probable that the population was under-estimated in 1882; if this was so, the rate of increase has been fairly steady. As in the case of Java, increase has been in progress for over a century; but the average rate of increase has been lower in Egypt than in Java. In one respect Egypt is a very remarkable country; there is the sharpest possible division between the desert and the sown. It is possible to stand, straddling a ditch, with one foot on irrigated land teeming with fertility, and the other on sterile desert. If the cultivated area alone is considered, the density of population is immense; it is now no less than 1,126 persons per square mile. This method of calculating density somewhat misrepresents the condition of things in Egypt for comparative purposes, because it includes no land that is not highly fertile, whereas all other countries include considerable areas of poor fertility. Nevertheless, it would be still more misleading to include for these purposes the tens of thousands of square miles of absolute desert which fall within the frontiers of Egypt.

It would appear that the possibilities of enlarging the cultivated area are not great, and that the engineering and other operations involved would be very expensive. Since there is little expectation of industrial expansion, the population situation and prospects, though not as menacing as in the case of Java, constitute a threat. That the threat is serious seems to follow from an inspection of such vital statistics as we possess. Registration of births and deaths dates from 1904 and was made compulsory in 1912. The rates are shown in Fig. 56. The birth-rate is very high and steady; there is no sign whatever of any decline in fertility. The death-rate is high relatively to other countries where it is known; again there is no sign whatever of any downward trend. But it is to be supposed that medical and sanitary progress will soon begin to bring the death-rate down; if that happens before the birth-rate begins to fall, the rate of increase, already high, will be further increased.

For the Philippines we have an estimate for 1877, which can only be regarded as a very rough approximation, together with figures at irregular intervals since that date. So far as these statistics can be trusted they show an average annual rate of increase during the last sixty years which is at least as large as that observed in Egypt; the rate will be found in Fig. 55. Vital statistics for the Philippines are available since 1921, and they exhibit a steady birth-rate ranging between 31·5 and 35·5 per 1,000, and a steady death-rate ranging between 17 and 19 per 1,000. We have a figure for Formosa for 1908, and the rate of growth since that date has been very rapid and comparable with that prevailing in Java; the same is apparently true of Korea during the last fifteen years. Vital statistics are available for Formosa since 1905 and are shown in Fig. 56. They exhibit a rise in the birth-rate, but this may be due to more complete registration. They also show a fall in the death-rate, of which there are no signs in Egypt, Java, and the Philippines. Fig. 56 also gives data for Ceylon. The birth-rate for Ceylon has fluctuated, but it cannot be said to show any trend. The death-rate in Ceylon, however, has apparently fallen, much as in Formosa, since

1920. Concerning the growth of population in Ceylon we have a rough estimate for 1850, and it would appear that the rate of increase since that date has been steady and rapid. There remains only Algeria for which figures can be given. The growth of population during the present century has been similar to that in Egypt. From 1901 we have vital statistics for the Algerian natives. Both the birth- and the death-rate exhibit fluctuations from 1901 to 1921, and there is some evidence of a downward trend in both rates during that period. Since 1921 the downward trend of the death-rate has become definite, but the birth-rate has risen.

The points of chief importance which emerge from an examination of such figures as exist for these countries relate to the rate of growth and to the trend of the birth- and death-rates. In every case the rate of growth has been high and in some cases very high. There is some evidence from Algeria, Formosa, and Ceylon of a fall in the death-rate during the last decade or so; in that respect these three countries resemble Japan. But in none of them is there any evidence of a fall in the birth-rate such as comes from Japan. Before commenting upon the significance of these facts we may make some reference to the position in China.

In addition to China proper there are the dependencies of Mongolia, Sinkiang, and Tibet and the former dependency of Manchuria. The inner region of Mongolia is being organized in provinces, and is now generally held to form part of China proper. If the usual estimate of the population of China proper is accepted, the density of population is high, having in mind the facts that agricultural operations, while in one sense highly skilled, are performed almost without mechanical aids, and that industry is very little developed. The density is about 250 per square mile, while it is 184 in Europe, excluding Russia. The population is very unevenly distributed. There are six areas of high concentration, the central portion of the great plain of north China, comprising portions of Shantung, Honan, Chili, and Anhwei, the Yangtze delta from Hong Kong to the sea, the Canton delta, the Red Basin of Szechwan, the coastal fringe between the Yangtze and Canton deltas, and the basin of Hupeh. It has been estimated that six-sevenths of the total population are to be found in one-third of the area. In this area the density is very high, over 600 per square mile in Shantung and Chekiang and about 900 in Kiangsu. In the plain of Chengtu the density is thought to reach 1,700 per square mile.

Some good authorities put the proportion of the population engaged in agriculture at 80 per cent. According to returns made some years ago by the Department of Agriculture and Commerce over a third of all farms were under an acre and a half in size, while a quarter were between 1·5 and 4·3 acres. The average holding was 3·6 acres. The figures in this return are only to be accepted as an indication of the condition of things; but there is no doubt that the mass of the people are supporting themselves by labour on the land and that these holdings often resemble our idea of an allotment rather than of a farm. Moreover, whole families support themselves from these 'farms', and the Chinese family is generally larger than the western family, not only because there are more children, but because it includes grandparents and other relatives. There are no comprehensive figures for the incomes of farmers as there are for the size of their holdings, but we have the result of some sample inquiries. One inquiry covering some 7,000 families, which was conducted in 1922, showed that 17·6 per cent. of the families in the eastern region and 62·2 per cent. in the northern region had incomes of less than $50 a year ($1 equals 1s. 3d.). In two villages near Peiping 34 per cent. of the families had incomes of less than $100. Investigations into the poverty line suggest that $150 are required to support a family at the minimum standard.

These figures illustrate what all observers report, namely, excessive congestion in those highly populated districts in which the greater part of the population is to be found. At the best the people scrape a living by incredible labour and the patient expenditure of traditional skill; but they can never accumulate reserves. Hence, they are liable to be plunged into utter destitution by the commotions of nature and the turbulence of men. The figures given for deaths caused by famine are, of course, guesses; but there is reason to suppose that the 13 million deaths attributed to the famine of 1849, and the 10 million to the famine of 1878, represent the scale on which these catastrophes operate.

'Whole provinces, as large as European states', writes Mr. Tawney, 'may properly be described as congested districts. The struggle of a swarm of human beings for a bare physical existence is an ever-present reality. All the phenomena of rural distress— minute holdings, tiny incomes, female infanticide, starvation—are the unavoidable result of it. The catastrophes which shock the West are merely the sensational revelations of a process of readjustments which is continuous and inevitable. They are the occasions, so to say, on which nature shows her hand. Famine is the economic, civil war the political, expression of the pressure of population on the means of subsistence.'

The opinion is widely held that, though numbers fluctuated, there was no increase in the population of China during the last half of the nineteenth century. It is thought by some observers that there has been a growth of population during the present century, while others hold that the population continues to fluctuate round the same level. There seems to be no doubt that there has lately been an increase of population in some districts, but it is doubtful whether this is true of the country as a whole. Whatever the truth may be, it is clear that the recent history of population in China is very different from that in the other countries mentioned in this and the last chapters. Of these countries India shows the slowest rate of increase;

but the population of India has grown by at least 40 per cent. during the last sixty years, and it is certain that nothing of this kind has happened in China. In the remaining countries the population has been increasing, and is still increasing, rapidly. How are we to account for this? In China marriage is early and universal, and the size of family is unlimited. Since the practice of child marriage and the prohibition upon widow remarriage do not obtain in China as in India, the birth-rate is probably higher in the former than in the latter country. The explanation must lie in a very high death-rate, as high, taking one year with another, as the birth-rate.

In the last chapter it was pointed out that, though India and Japan may be classed together as belonging to a distinct group of countries where the basis of classification is population history and situation, there was a marked difference between them. In Japan the birth- and death-rates do not fluctuate but show steady trends as in Europe. In India, on the contrary, they exhibit marked fluctuations; nevertheless, the death-rate keeps generally below the birth-rate, and in consequence the population increases though the increase is spasmodic rather than steady. It would seem that in China, since the population is probably fluctuating, but not increasing, the birth- and death-rates must each be fluctuating round the same level, with the consequence that, since the fluctuations of the two rates do not always coincide, at one time the birth-rate exceeds the death-rate and the population grows, and at another time the death-rate exceeds the birth-rate and the population declines. When discussing India we pointed out that the facts are compatible with the explanation that the people are living near subsistence level, and that numbers are in consequence under the immediate influence of natural conditions; we explained the growth of population as due to the filling up of the new spaces created by land reclamation, irrigation, and so on. In China there has been little or no creation of new spaces. In consequence the

U

pressure of natural conditions is more severe, and the death-rate higher. It is possible, if not likely, that the population of China is at or near the Malthusian limit.

If this is so, and if we range these countries according to their approach to European conditions, we must place China at the bottom of the list with India next and Japan at the top. Japan takes this position because both birth- and death-rates are now declining for the same reasons that they are declining in Europe, namely birth-control and sanitary improvement. Between them come the other countries. Since it would seem that in Ceylon, Formosa, and Algeria the death-rate is declining, we may place these countries above the remainder which continue to show steady birth- and death-rates.

In order to appreciate more fully the past history and future prospects of numbers among these peoples, it may be of assistance if we give the reasons for including them together in one group. In Chapter IX it was mentioned that there is abundant evidence of the prevalence of a small family system in earlier times. This system, under which families were kept small by the pressure of social customs, broke down with the rise of the early civilizations. But it lingered later in the east than in the west; we have seen, for instance, that it prevailed in Japan in the eighteenth century. But it has now disappeared, and among the peoples under discussion we have the unlimited family. It was at this point in their population history that European influence began to make itself felt. Intimate contact with Europe was developed; large areas such as India, Java, and Ceylon came under European control, and such countries as maintained their independence were more or less deeply influenced by Europe. But however deep the influence, the social structure and the religious and cultural traditions of these countries were sufficiently highly developed to resist disintegration as the result of contact with Europe. The social system, the complex of beliefs, and the way of life were only slowly modified, if modified at all. Therefore the unlimited family remained, and that is to say that the birth-rate continued at a high level.

Contact with Europe, however, was not without its influence upon the death-rate. But this was not because Europeans brought with them diseases which were unknown to these peoples. On the contrary, in so far as there was any spread of disease, as a result of contact, to areas where it was unknown before, it was a spread from east to west, from Asia to Europe, of cholera from the Ganges valley to Europe for instance. Nor was contact with Europe accompanied by fighting or slave raiding on a scale that involved any considerable increase in deaths; the result of contact with Europe was not to increase but, on the contrary, to diminish them. This was the consequence of the establishment of order and security, of the development of communications, and of the end of feuds and local wars. These changes were either directly brought about by Europeans who assumed control of India, Java, and other countries, or were accomplished by native rulers as in Japan and Egypt. But in China neither foreign conquerors nor native rulers have succeeded in reducing the country to order since the eighteenth-century régime broke down; as a result the death-rate remains high. But elsewhere among these countries the death-rate has come to run at a lower level than the birth-rate, and the population has grown and is still growing rapidly.

As to the future there is no doubt that, however strong nationalism may be and however distinct cultures may remain, European sanitation and medicine will spread in these countries, and will tend further to reduce the death-rate; indeed, this is now happening in Japan and elsewhere. As this goes on the rate of growth of population will tend to increase. But it is scarcely likely that the adoption of European methods of decreasing the death-rate will be unaccompanied by the adoption of methods for limiting the family. Indeed, European marriage habits and the European voluntary small family system are now spreading in Japan. It is frequently said that the religious beliefs, and especially the desire for male progeny, are inimical to birth-control. But, while there is truth in this, the strength of the opposition is apparently over-estimated. Some remarks from the recent census of India were quoted in the last chapter, and were to the effect that the attitude of Indians to this matter may be more realistic than is generally supposed. If birth-control is likely to spread in India, the auguries are promising for its spread in China and Java where, according to the reports of recent observers, there is less prejudice than in India to be overcome.

However rapidly birth-control spreads in these countries, it must be a long time before the birth-rate will be much reduced. But this does not mean that it will necessarily be a long time before the gap between the birth- and death-rates is narrowed. For a fall in the birth-rate is not the only agency which can close the gap; it can also be narrowed by a rise in the death-rate. It is not implied that any one would advocate measures with the latter object in view; indeed, one of the most urgent social needs is the improvement of sanitary and medical services which would tend the other way. But congestion may reach a point at which deaths will be increased. The death-rate is very high in India and probably higher still in China, and if the population of the remaining countries under discussion continues to grow, their death-rates may rise to the Indian level in spite of medical and sanitary progress. For, even if owing to medical progress diseases due to infection are reduced or eliminated, in the absence of sufficient food men will die of deficiency diseases and finally of starvation. It is impossible to say how near such a country as Java is to the point where any further increase in numbers will mean a serious reduction in real income and in time increased mortality. But, even if this point is still some way ahead, the future is menacing. In Japan alone among these countries can an end to increase through control of births be foreseen, and even there the problem of accommodating the extra numbers that are still to come is a matter of very great anxiety. In the other countries it is an open question whether increase will cease on account of a rising death-rate or on account of a falling birth-rate. This means that a very serious threat hangs over these countries, since a rising death-rate would imply not only much suffering but also the possibility of social retrogression. The danger is a relapse into Chinese conditions.

Whatever the precise course of events, there can be no doubt that the contrast, which already exists between these countries and those of Europe or of European origin, will be sharpened in the near future. Europe and its oversea derivatives will be engaged in a struggle for population; these countries will be entangled in the difficulties which arise from excessive numbers. This will bring up the question of the half-developed and under-developed countries which are mostly under European control. Discussion of this matter may be postponed until we have examined the position in the under-developed countries which will be the subject of the next chapter. Meanwhile, a reference to some aspects of the migration problem is not out of place.

We are dealing now with peoples who between them account for more than half the total world population. The numbers that would have to emigrate annually in order to remove even a substantial fraction of the natural increase are so enormous that the task of transporting them would be quite impossible, to say nothing of the other difficulties involved. The annual surplus of births over deaths in India alone was more than 3 millions during the decade 1920–30. Further, there is reason to think that the relief so given would be only temporary. Where families are unlimited, there is a gap-filling mechanism at work; any gap caused by war or famine is filled by those who would otherwise have died, and the same is true of gaps caused by emigration. The fact that emigration is no solution, and perhaps not even a palliative except in the case of a country such as Japan where births are coming under control, does not rule it out as an important question. For there are problems of international justice involved, and it may also be that opportunities for emigration would have important psychological results.

Finally, it may be observed that there is and can be no organized pressure to secure opportunities for emigration from these countries except in the case of Japan. They are too weak, and their weakness, it may be noted, is not unconnected with excessive density of population. China, as the experience of Manchuria shows, is like a saturated sponge. It is easy enough to place such a sponge in a water-tight container and to prevent the escape of liquid. It has no force to expand and burst its bonds; but, if the barriers are removed on one side, liquid oozes out. Since the prohibition upon the entry of Chinese into Manchuria was removed, millions of Chinese have passed over the frontier, and the population of Manchuria, now estimated at over 30 millions, has doubled in a relatively short period of time. It is, however, apparently impossible to affirm that congestion of population in northern China has been diminished by this movement.

CHAPTER XX

PRIMITIVE PEOPLES

THE non-European peoples, which have been discussed in the last two chapters, suffered little or no diminution in numbers following upon the establishment of contact with Europe. The remaining peoples, whom we may class as primitive peoples, experienced a decline in population subsequent to the coming of Europeans. In some cases the decline has not been arrested, and in one case at least, that of the Tasmanians, a people has perished. In other cases the decline has ceased, and in others again population is on the increase once more. These peoples include the American Indians, the Africans south of the Sahara, the Pacific Islanders, and other scattered communities. Much as they differ from one another in culture and in technical accomplishment, it may be said of all of them that they can be distinguished from the peoples just discussed by the possession of the following circumstances when they came into relations with Europe. In the first place, in consequence of the primitive nature of their technique and social organization, they were unable to maintain their culture intact in the face of European influence; their whole scheme of life tended to break down and to disintegrate. Secondly, the primitive small family system had not disappeared as among the Indians and other Asiatic peoples; by means of customs, such as prolonged abstention from intercourse which was prevalent among the Africans, or abortion and infanticide which was practised in the Pacific region, the average size of the family was kept small. Lastly, they had had no experience of many diseases which were common elsewhere.

Owing to lack of space there is room for no more than a brief reference to these peoples, and we may confine our remarks to the peoples of the Pacific Islands and to the Africans. The former provide examples of peoples who have suffered, and in some cases are still suffering, from serious diminution of numbers; the latter mostly provide cases where the decline was less serious and has now been arrested. In 1927 Professor S. H. Roberts made a careful inquiry into the past history of population in the Pacific region. He found reason to conclude that there had been some decline in numbers before the Europeans appeared on the scene. It is impossible to suggest the extent of this decline since the evidence, though it clearly points in this direction, is vague. After contact was made with Europeans the decline was accelerated. Until we come to recent times, and then only for certain places, figures are no more than guesses. A few examples may be given. About the middle of the last century the native population of Fiji was estimated at 150,000. It was then decreasing. It is believed to have fallen by over 9,000 in each decade between 1881 and 1911, and by 2,600 between 1911 and 1921; it was (excluding Indians who now number 79,000) at one time as low as 90,000. Since 1921 it has increased by over 6,000. The population of the Marquesas was estimated at over 20,000 in the earlier part of the last century; it has declined steadily, and is said to be now about 1,000. The estimate for the Maori population of New Zealand was in excess of 100,000 in 1850. By 1870 it had declined to 37,000, but it has risen since that date, and is now over 71,000. In the Gilbert group the loss, which was serious for some decades, has been less recently; between 1911 and 1929 the population was declining in eight of the islands and increasing in four, giving a net loss of 1,786 (from 25,336 to 23,550) during this period. During the same period a gain was shown by all nine islands of the Ellis group, though at one time loss was experienced. Summing up the situation in 1927 Professor Roberts concluded that, of the total estimated population of the Pacific Islands, 35·04 per cent. was increasing, 39·31 per cent. was stationary, 25·48 per cent. was decreasing, though at a diminishing rate in most cases, while 0·16 per cent. was faced with annihilation. Since that date the situation has improved somewhat; some populations which were declining have become stationary, and others which were stationary show signs of increase.

The causes of these changes are much debated. With regard to the decline in population before the advent of the whites it has to be remembered that the facts are very uncertain. But there seems to be evidence that some depopulation took place. In explanation of this decline attention has been directed to signs of a degeneration which is supposed to have set in after the migrations had come to an end; it appears to be the case that lassitude had replaced adventurousness. This may have caused an increase in mortality, especially among infants, owing to poor food and lack of parental care. Again, it would appear that abortion and infanticide were very extensively practised; in Tahiti, for example, it is said that two-thirds of all children born alive were killed. However that may be, it is certain that in most of the Pacific Islands there was a serious and rapid decrease of population after the arrival of Europeans. Much attention has been given to this phenomenon, but it cannot be said that there is yet any general agreement concerning the explanation.

It is admitted on all hands that in many places the arrival of Europeans was accompanied by attacks upon natives, by kidnappings, and other outrages which resulted in many deaths. Further, the natives obtained fire-arms and were enabled to make their own tribal warfare more murderous than before. But this stage did not last very long, and the greater part of the depopulation has taken place at a time when these conditions were not operative. All those who have investigated the problem lay great stress upon the effect of the introduction of diseases which, up to the time when Europeans arrived, these people had never experienced. Among such diseases are tuberculosis, malaria, measles, whooping-cough, chicken-pox, dysentery, venereal and pulmonary affections. Owing to lack of previous experience they were very deadly to the natives; it is said that in Fiji in 1874 measles carried off 40,000 persons. As time goes on resistance to many diseases is acquired, and a recent epidemic of measles in Fiji did not have very serious consequences; but, though tuberculosis may not be as fatal to natives as it was once, it still takes a far more acute form and rapid course among them than among Europeans. Other diseases such as scurvy, rickets, beri-beri, and pellagra are also prevalent, and indicate inadequate and improper diet. Observation shows that the natives have largely abandoned their traditional diet and have taken to more easily acquired and less wholesome forms of food. There seem to be two reasons for this. Owing to the lassitude and despondency which the prevalence of disease brings, the natives no longer exert themselves as formerly; secondly, owing to the breakdown of tribal organization and the disappearance of ancestral habits, they are no longer disposed, even if they are not under the depressing influences of ill-health, to follow the old and healthy routine.

The depopulation is due, not only to an increase in the death-rate, but also to a decrease in the birth-rate. At least, this is a fair conclusion from the facts. There are no trustworthy figures for birth-rates, but there is evidence that families are small, in some cases so small that the population could barely maintain itself even if the death-rate was normal. There is also some evidence that families were larger in former times. The small size of the family to-day has been attributed to the abolition, or the attempted abolition, of polygamy, and to the temporary removal of young men to labour on plantations. Though these factors may account in some small degree for what has happened, the major part of the explanation must be sought elsewhere. It seems clear that miscarriages are frequent, and we may attribute this fact to ill health and poor nutrition. But there is also evidence that abortion is very common. As we have pointed out, abortion is an ancient custom, and was employed before the arrival of Europeans to keep the size of the family small; that is to say, after the family had reached a certain size, no more living children were brought into the world, or in other cases such additional children as appeared were killed soon after birth. But it seems that it is now more extensively practised than in the past. Two reasons are given for this. On the one hand, the disintegration of tribal organization has removed many of the things which seemed to make life worth living; on the other hand, the prevalence of disease makes it seem not worth while to bring children into a world where they are likely soon to perish.

Thus it would appear that disease is the most important cause of depopulation in the Pacific Islands. For it not only raises mortality rates but also makes children unwanted. The recent tendency towards recovery may be attributed partly to the acquirement of a higher resistance to diseases after some decades of experience of exposure to them, and partly to better medical and sanitary organization. The chief cause of disagreement between those who have discussed this problem is the place of psychological factors. There are those who consider that the apathy and listlessness arise from the breakdown of tribal organization and who attribute most of what has happened to an outlook which sees no hope. There are others, now apparently in a majority, who attribute most importance to disease, first, as a direct cause of the high death-rate and, secondly, as a cause of the apathetic attitude which leads to a repugnance to bear children.

The total population of the Pacific Islands is little more than a million, and therefore from the purely numerical point of view they hardly deserve mention in a short book on world population. But an examination of the population situation among the primitive peoples which inhabit them is a useful approach to the study of other primitive peoples; for the peculiar features of the population situation among all primitive peoples reach their fullest development in the Pacific Islands. The other primitive peoples number over 100 millions and are therefore of considerable numerical importance. Let us take the American Indians as an instance. Generalization is almost impossible because among them are some tribes even as yet hardly touched by European influence, while there are also detribalized remnants gathered into reserves who have lost all traces of their former culture. Nevertheless, it may be said that, as in the case of the Pacific Islanders, they suffered at first heavy depletion in numbers from the attacks of Europeans, and subsequently from the ravages of disease. America seems to have been entirely free from the most serious diseases before the visit of Columbus, and there is ample evidence that introduced diseases, especially tuberculosis, have wrought untold havoc among the American Indians. Nevertheless, in spite of the fact that they were driven from their homes by force in a manner that was not paralleled in Oceania, they do not seem to have fallen a prey to that lassitude, or at least not to the same extent, which left the Pacific Islanders with little desire to have progeny. In any case, it seems certain that there are now more American Indians of pure blood in the world than in 1492; therefore they have more than recovered from the very heavy losses which they sustained, whereas the most that can be said of the Pacific Islanders is that in many cases recovery has begun. From the point of view of the international situation the future of numbers among the American Indians is not a matter of great importance, since they do not lay any claim to the exclusive occupation of territories which are coveted by others. Therefore we may turn to consider the Africans who are far more numerous and whose huge territories are a source of envy to many.

Some reference was made to the history of numbers in Africa in the third chapter. It will be remembered that there is no material upon which to found any estimate until we come to very recent times. We can only suppose that the population had remained for many centuries at approximately the density which obtained when European influence began to penetrate. There can be little doubt that slave raiding caused extensive depopulation in many districts, and that the direct effect of European contact was more serious than in the Pacific Islands. On the other hand, the indirect effect was not of the same magnitude because, since the Africans had not been entirely cut off from the infiltration of outside influences, their experience of disease was not so limited as in the case of the American Indians or of the Pacific Islanders. But there can be no doubt that, during the last two centuries, certain lethal diseases have found their way into Africa which were not known there before. Among them are apparently dengue fever, small-pox, plague, cholera, typhus, and syphilis. While there has been no increased mortality through disease on anything approaching the scale in the Pacific Islands or perhaps even in America, there can be no doubt that the death-rate was raised. The inference, which is supported by some evidence, is that the Africans, in any case in some large areas, declined in number during the eighteenth and nineteenth centuries.

When we come to recent times we begin to get the results of so-called censuses. Thus there are figures for Gambia and Lagos from 1881, for Basutoland and Bechuanaland from 1891, for Nyassaland from 1911, and for Kenya from 1921. The value of these figures differs for different areas, but they are nowhere claimed to be more than approximate. A report from the Government of Kenya in 1930 states that 'the official figures of population are arrived at largely as a result of the enumeration of huts as a necessary part of the collection of hut tax', and goes on to give an illustration of the misleading nature of the figures, prefacing it with the following introduction: 'As showing how incorrect for the purpose of statistical calculation are the present figures. . . .' We may take the warning. If we examine the results of enumerations in those areas where estimates have been made at different dates, we find that in almost all cases an increase of population is shown. Should this be taken as proving that population has increased? As is apparent from the above quotation, official opinion is aware of the large margin of error which attaches even to the latest figures. But the official view is that, when allowance is made for inaccuracy, the native population in most parts of Africa is increasing. The report from Kenya, which has already been quoted, says, for example, that 'apart from the figures all the indications are that, taken as a whole, the native population of Kenya has increased in numbers, at any rate of late years, but what the rate of increase is it is impossible to specify'. This judgement deserves respect, but it is permissible to doubt whether it is well founded for two reasons. In the first place, whenever for some purpose or another an accurate count is made of a small district, it is more often found that the population is above than below the figure which was given for that district in the so-called census for the whole area to which the district belongs. Thus the population of the Digo Reserve in Kenya was estimated in the census at under 50,000, but in the course of a treatment campaign more than 2,000 persons in excess of the census figure were treated. Therefore, as enumeration becomes more complete, the returns tend to become larger rather than smaller. Secondly, certain diseases are still spreading in Africa and are probably causing an increase in mortality. In so far as the mortality is that of adults, this would tend to decrease the population if the number of children in a family is limited.

This brings us to the question of birth- and death-rates in Africa. The recorded rates are admittedly even less accurate than the enumerations. They show relatively low birth-rates, except where, as will be mentioned later, tribal organization has been disrupted, and death-rates which are not far below the birth-rates. The relatively low birth-rate is due to the maintenance of an ancient custom which keeps the family small—the custom of abstaining from intercourse until the child has been weaned, and weaning may be postponed for a long time. The length of time differs from tribe to tribe, but the practice does effectively keep the successive children spaced out and makes large families of living children impossible. Increased child mortality might up to a point be compensated for by an increased birth-rate; for intercourse would be resumed on the death of a child. On the other hand, increased adult mortality would probably not affect the birth-rate, and would therefore tend to decrease the population.

It seems that judgement must be suspended about the present course of population in Africa south of the Sahara. It is probably not decreasing; it may very likely be about stationary: it is not impossible that it may be increasing, but if so the rate of increase is certainly slow.

So far we have spoken of conditions where tribal organization and ancient customs remain more or less intact. But there are places where they have vanished or are becoming obsolescent. This is the case in some parts of the Union of South Africa. The situation under these conditions is of interest because it may throw some light upon the future in other parts of Africa. We possess census figures for the non-European population of the Union for 1904, 1911, and 1921; the census of 1931 only included Europeans. The figures show an average annual rate of increase for the Bantus of 2·03 per cent. between 1904 and 1911, and of 1·57 per cent. between 1911 and 1921. But it is impossible to say how much of this increase was due to immigration. The registration of births and deaths is compulsory for all races in urban areas, but is optional for non-Europeans in rural areas of the Union. An official publication states that

'the registration of non-European vital events in the towns, though probably complete so far as the actual number of events is concerned, is an entirely misleading index of the birth- and death-

rates of the non-European community of the towns. Possible
exceptions are the municipalities of Capetown, Port Elizabeth, and
Kimberley which have a large mixed non-European population of
a stationary type, who live in the towns in a similar manner to
Europeans.'

Elsewhere the native population fluctuates, and therefore
there is no settled population to which to refer the recorded
births and deaths; women may leave the towns for con-
finements and both men and women may go home when
ill. When we examine the figures for the towns which are
stated to provide trustworthy records, we find very high
birth-rates, over 50 per 1,000 in Capetown and Port Elizabeth, and moderate death-rates in the region of 20 per
1,000. This would appear to indicate that, when native
customs vanish, the family becomes unlimited. This being
so, and in view of the fact that medical and sanitary progress is probably reducing the death-rate, it might be
supposed that the stage was set for a rapid increase in the
native population of Africa. But this may be doubted.
Some observers are of opinion that the native women, who
have no religious motives for desiring a large family and
are of a realistic turn of mind, will rapidly adopt the practice of family limitation. Indeed, an observer in Nigeria
says that some native women are now limiting their families
by means of abortion, and are doing so, not because they
are following an ancient custom, but for the same sort of
reasons that lead to family limitation in Europe. It may
therefore be that the Africans are not fated to pass through
a prolonged period characterized by the unlimited family
which has brought a threatening situation into being
among many Asiatic peoples.

The density of population in Africa, south of the Sahara,
is about 12 per square mile. It varies much from area to
area; in Nigeria it is over 50 and in Kenya about 13 per
square mile. The view is sometimes expressed, for instance
by settlers in Kenya, that there are large areas of bushland
which are unused by the natives. But this bushland is

essential to the natives because it provides pasture for sheep and goats. There can be little doubt that, given the existing native methods of finding a living and the native mode of life, the areas which they occupy are fairly fully used. In any case, there are no large territories which can be appropriated by immigrants without upsetting native economy; and the disturbance caused in this way tends, unless counteracting factors come into play, to produce congestion among the native population. There are, indeed, some congested districts, such as Kano in Nigeria. Another illustration may be taken from the report from Kenya, from which quotations have already been made; it says that

'in certain areas the density of population is such that further con-siderable increase cannot possibly take place therein under existing conditions. As examples of congested districts may be quoted, certain parts of the Kiambu District of the Kikyu Native Reserve with a population of over 500 to the square mile, and Bangore, in North Kavirondo, with over 900 to the square mile.'

While this is so, it is also true that certain areas could apparently carry a somewhat heavier native population with advantage to all; and it is probable on the whole that, on the basis of the present native practices and mode of life, there are more districts which could take a larger population with benefit than districts which are already overfull. This judgement is compatible with what we have found to be the probable history of numbers in Africa. Primitive peoples do not seem easily to become over-populated because they control the size of family. We may assume therefore that in general Africa was not over-populated three hundred years ago. The native population has certainly suffered from an increase in mortality owing to new diseases, and in certain places underwent heavy decline owing to slave raiding. While the decline may have been arrested, there is no reason to suppose that there has been an increase of population sufficient to make up all the losses.

x

Africa is an under-developed continent; it is not under-populated having regard to the resources of the native inhabitants, though it might accommodate without inconvenience a slightly more dense population in certain areas. Therefore the view that, as things are, Africa could be used as an outlet for the surplus population of other continents has no foundation. If Africa is to support a much larger population, the whole scheme of African life must be transformed.

CHAPTER XXI

NON-EUROPEANS AND MIGRATION

IT emerged from the last chapter that there are some under-developed non-European countries which are often regarded as offering scope for immigration, while the non-European countries, whose position was discussed in chapters XVIII and XIX, appear to be too densely peopled. A reference to the experience of Palestine in recent years, that is of a non-European country into which heavy immigration is taking place, is a useful introduction to the problems of migration as they affect non-Europeans. But that does not exhaust the interest of recent events in Palestine, for they also illustrate in a striking fashion some of the matters to which attention was paid in earlier chapters.

FIGURE 59

The Growth of Population in Palestine: 1919 to 1934

(thousands)

Year	Moslems		Jews		Others		Total
	Number	*Per cent.*	*Number*	*Per cent.*	*Number*	*Per cent.*	*Total*
1919	568	81·1	58	8·3	74	10·6	700
1922	591	78·1	84	11·1	82	10·8	757
1931	760	73·3	174	16·9	99	9·8	1,033
1934	807	68·9	254	21·7	110	9·4	1,171

Fig. 59 shows the growth of the population of Palestine since 1919; the totals for 1922 and 1931 are from the censuses of those years while those for 1919 and 1934 are merely estimates. Increase of population has been very rapid; the average annual rate of increase was about 4·5 per cent. during the whole period, but was higher for the later than for the earlier years of the period. Immigration has accounted in large part for the increase of the Jewish section of the population, though the Arabs have also received some reinforcement from this source. Both Jews and Arabs, however, exhibit a large surplus of births over deaths as is evident from Fig. 60.

The natural increase of both Jews and Arabs is in the neighbourhood of 20 per 1,000. The Jews have a birth-rate which is high compared with European birth-rates,

FIGURE 60

Birth-rates and Death-rates in Palestine: 1927 to 1934

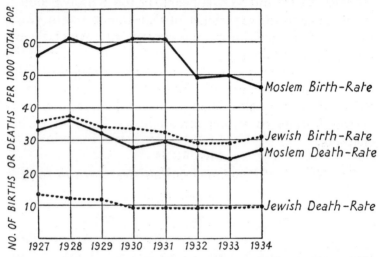

and a markedly low death-rate. To a considerable extent this is due to the peculiar age composition of the Jewish population. Persons of child-bearing age form a very high proportion among the Palestinian Jews, while old people are scarce, as is always the case among recent immigrants. In most countries the Jewish birth-rate is related to the birth-rate of the people among whom they are living; it is, generally speaking, high in eastern Europe and low in western Europe. But it is an almost invariable rule that the Jewish birth-rate is lower than the surrounding birth-rate. Ruppin has collected statistics for sixteen different countries and five large cities; in every case, with the exception of New York, the birth-rate of the Jews is lower, and in most cases much lower, than that of the non-Jews. Thus Ruppin gives the birth-rate for Jews in Poland in 1929 as 20·0 per 1,000, and for non-Jews as 31·1 per 1,000. Since we have found that the small size of the family constitutes a very serious problem in many European countries, it is clear the size of the family is a matter of the utmost gravity for the Jews; for it is hardly too much to say that, if Ruppin's figures are correct, the extinction of the Jews is in sight.

Other important conclusions are suggested by a study of the Jewish birth-rate. In the first place, it tends to confirm the conclusion, at which we arrived in Chapter VII, that the fall in the birth-rate was due to birth-control. We know that orthodox Jews are permitted to employ contraceptive methods after two children have been born, and that many Jews are no longer orthodox and therefore are not under the obligation to raise even this small number of children. We also know that Jews have stronger motives than non-Jews for limiting their families. There is persecution and the fear of persecution; in addition, Jews are more careful about their children and in general more calculating and far-sighted than others. Since it is easier to do well for one or two children than for three or four, and easier to assure the future of one child than of many, the explanation of the peculiarities of the Jewish birth-rate as due to birth-control offers no difficulties, whereas it seems quite impossible to explain the facts in any other way. In the second place, although the high Jewish birth-rate in Palestine is largely due to the favourable age composition of the population, it is almost certain that Jewish fertility in Palestine is higher than Jewish fertility in the countries whence the immigrants came. To prove this, we should have to calculate specific fertility rates for Jews in Poland and for Polish Jews in Palestine and similarly for other groups of Jews; but there are no materials for making the calculation. If it is true, as seems likely, that Jewish fertility in Palestine is higher than Jewish fertility elsewhere, it must be because Palestinian Jews limit their families less than other Jews. This may well be so, since in Palestine they are co-operating in an endeavour which gives them hope and confidence; moreover, their aim is to repeople their former home. Those who are concerned about the fall of the birth-rate in this and certain other countries may perhaps discern a lesson in this fact and conclude that, if the reproduction rate is to become a replacement rate, people must be brought deliberately to found families as a contribution to a society in whose future they have confidence and in whose ideals they find inspiration.

The vital statistics of the Palestinian Arabs also illustrate problems which were discussed in earlier chapters. We have no statistics for Palestine when it was under Turkish rule, but it is plain that, while the population may have fluctuated, the fluctuations cancelled out; for there is no evidence that the population increased or diminished during the last two centuries. Then under European supervision a dramatic change took place, and a wide gap was established between the birth- and death-rates. It is another example of the result of substituting order and security for misrule or lack of rule. While this is clear, it is not easy to discover the mechanism whereby the gap between the rates came into existence. Has the birth-rate risen since the Turks departed? Some observers believe this to have been the case and point to the former conscription for the army of young men who were drafted to remote parts of the Turkish empire. But the effect of a system of this kind upon vital statistics is commonly much over-estimated; while its abolition may have been followed by some rise, it cannot have occasioned a large rise, in the birth-rate. It is far more likely that the death-rate has fallen. Medical and sanitary progress, so far as it affects the personal habits and customs, has made little headway among the Palestinian Arabs as yet, and cannot account for any considerable fall in the death-rate. But general administrative measures, in the region of quarantine for example, have been designed in the light of modern knowledge and have been adequately carried out. Measures of this kind can be enforced almost overnight, whereas those which require changes in social organization and habits can only come about slowly. Therefore we can find in these administrative changes, brought about by the British occupation of Palestine, what is in any case a tenable explanation of the natural increase of population among the Arabs.

Recent events in Palestine, however, have been introduced in this chapter, not because they illustrate matters already discussed, but on account of the light which they throw upon a matter which awaits discussion, namely, the opportunities which an under-developed, but not an under-populated, country offers to immigrants. For this description was true of Palestine; under the system of agriculture, as practised by the Arabs, the country was patently under-developed, but was not, so far as we can tell, under-populated. That is to say, there is no reason to suppose that, so long as their mode of life remained unchanged, the Arabs would have been better off if the country had been more densely peopled. In 1919 the density was about 78 per square mile. It is now over 130 per square mile, and there are about a quarter of a million more Arabs and 200,000 more Jews than in 1919. Is this to be taken as showing that under-developed countries, such as Palestine, can be made to accommodate within a few years much larger numbers with benefit both to the original inhabitants and to the new-comers?

When attempting to answer this question it must be remembered that there is much uncertainty about many matters concerning which information is required. Wholly contradictory statements are made and maintained in the course of the chronic Jewish-Arab controversy, and the accuracy of almost every official figure is challenged by one or other side. The more important facts appear to be as follows. Palestine (that is Palestine under the mandate and not biblical Palestine) is a small country; it covers about 10,000 square miles and is therefore smaller than Wales. Between 1,250,000 and 1,500,000 acres are said to be cultivated; of the cultivated area 335,000 acres are owned by Jews. About 50,000 Jews, that is approximately 20 per cent. of the Jewish population, are engaged in agriculture. The PICA (the Palestine Jewish Colonization Association) owns about 125,000 acres and the J.N.F. (Jewish National Fund) owns about 80,000 acres. The J.N.F. never sells land and only leases it to Jews who undertake to cultivate it with their own hands. Therefore some of the Jewish-owned land is entirely withdrawn from the Arabs, but on the remainder Arabs may find some employment. Though the cultivated area has been extended since 1919, there is now an Arab population, larger by 250,000, with less cultivated land than before 1919 at its disposal. There are undoubtedly a number of landless Arabs, who have been rendered landless by the change in ownership; but their number is a subject of acute controversy.

It is often alleged that, owing to the changes in land ownership, the Arabs have suffered. It is difficult to discover the truth because at the present time there is abundant prosperity on account of the import of capital and its expenditure on constructional works in connexion with which considerable employment is created for Arabs. The problem is whether, when this abnormal period has passed, the Arabs will be better or worse off than before, whether, that is to say, an under-developed country can be exploited swiftly enough to give a rapidly increasing population at least as good a living as under previous conditions. It must be remembered that this experiment is being conducted under most exceptionally favourable circumstances. First, though less than a million and a half acres are now cultivated, no authority puts the cultivable area at less than 3 million acres, and some authorities put it much higher. These areas were left uncultivated by the

Arabs because they did not possess the financial and technical resources which are necessary either to irrigate the waterless but potentially very fertile areas in the Beersheba region or to drain the marshes and swamps such as are found in the valley of Huleh. Secondly, given sufficient capital, there are large possibilities, partly in process of realization, of developing hydro-electric power and with it chemical and light industries. In other words, given enough capital, technical ability, and enterprise, there are unusual opportunities for creating new employment on the land and in industry. Thirdly, the immigrants, though culturally very distinct from the Arabs, are apparently not dissimilar genetically; in any case, the two peoples are not separated by easily observable physical differences.

Nevertheless, in spite of these exceptionally favourable circumstances, the success of the experiment is in doubt. The Arabs, hitherto a purely agricultural and pastoral people, are increasing rapidly and have lost land. In order to maintain their standard of living they must either make their use of land more intensive or find employment in Jewish enterprises. The extent to which Jewish enterprise will be able to afford employment for Arabs must remain uncertain for some time to come. There is ample scope for more intensive use of land by the Arabs, and, as any visitor to Palestine can see, Arabs whose farms adjoin Jewish farms are beginning to copy the intensive methods employed on the latter. But in view of the conservatism of farmers everywhere, and especially in the East, intensification of cultivation must be a slow process. As to the Jews, it is doubtful whether, if heavy immigration continues, 20 per cent. of them can continue as at present on the land; for to find land for 20 per cent. of a rapidly growing figure means a continual enlargement of land in Jewish ownership. The processes of land reclamation and irrigation can be continued for a very long time, but they take time and it will be difficult to continue to accommodate

20 per cent. of the Jewish population in agriculture. This means that 80 per cent. of the Jews at least must always find occupations otherwise than in farming, and no one can say with any degree of confidence that so large an amount of non-agricultural employment can be created. The other favourable feature of the Palestinian experiment is the absence of obvious physical differences between Arabs and Jews. There are religious and cultural differences, but they are not accompanied and enhanced by differences in pigmentation and other physical features. Nevertheless, tension between the two peoples is acute, and there have already been serious conflicts. There is as yet no sign whatever of any growth of understanding one of the other, and there remains the possibility of further conflict which might make it impossible to continue with those industrial and agricultural projects which alone can make the experiment a success. In short, although this experiment is being conducted under very favourable circumstances, it is not yet clear that Palestine can accommodate such rapidly growing numbers with benefit to all concerned.

Let us consider what light events in Palestine throw upon the opportunities which other under-developed but not under-populated countries offer to immigrants. The matter is sometimes discussed on the assumption that the countries which remain under-developed offer similar opportunities to those which were presented by North America in 1500 and by Australia in 1800. But this is a complete misapprehension. In 1500 there were apparently not more than a million Indians in North America, that is one person to each six square miles. In Australia the density of population was even less. In Africa the density of population south of the Sahara is at least fifty times greater than in North America in 1500, and in those parts of Africa which are most usually spoken of in relation to immigration, about a hundred times greater. North America, Australia, and the southern part of South

America were therefore virtually empty lands when European immigration began. There are no similarly empty lands to-day, and there is no possibility of repeating in the under-developed countries of to-day the story of the colonization of North America and of Australia. The situation in the under-developed countries is in one respect like that in Palestine. If room is to be found for immigrants, it can only be provided by reclaiming land, by taking it from its present owners, or by creating new forms of employment. As to reclaiming land, it is very unusual to find any large proportion of land, as in Palestine, which is now quite unused and capable of being rendered fertile; moreover, the cost of irrigation, drainage, clearance, or whatever may be required is very high. Opportunities of this kind are therefore limited, and can only be taken when an ample supply of capital is available. As a rule, therefore, the only practicable method is to take land now in use from its present owners with or without compensation. Unless expropriation, however accomplished, goes very slowly, the natives will certainly suffer, because it will take a long time for them to learn how to use their remaining land more intensively. But, however land may be acquired for immigrants, it will give little employment for them unless they do the work of the fields themselves. If they merely employ the dispossessed natives, the number of immigrants occupied in supervision will be negligible. But it is impossible to imagine that immigrants will permanently subject themselves to a self-denying ordinance and refuse to employ native labour. Indigenous native labour was not employed in Australia and North America because the natives could not or would not enter the European economic system, and it is noteworthy that the immigrants imported native labour from elsewhere in consequence. There has only been one case where immigrants have undertaken the work of the fields themselves when there were no natives to do it for them. That case is Palestine; but the Jewish immigrants think of themselves as reoccupying their ancient home, and undertake the task in the fulfilment of an ideal. A parallel situation is not likely to arise elsewhere.

So far as the creation of opportunities for the employment of immigrants, otherwise than upon the land, is concerned, the situation varies greatly from one country to another. But it would appear that few of the underdeveloped countries offer as much scope in this direction as Palestine. Moreover, the same question arises in connexion with work in the factories as in connexion with work in the fields. It is certain that, except under the very unusual circumstances which obtain in Palestine and are never likely to arise elsewhere, native labour will be employed in the factories, leaving very little scope for the employment of immigrants. In short, the possibilities of creating employment for immigrants in the countries which are now under-developed are very limited. It may be objected that we have discussed the matter on the assumption that the native inhabitants will be treated with more consideration than a realistic policy of expansion would permit. But even if a return was made to the ruthless methods which prevailed three hundred years ago, it is hardly likely that a larger result would ultimately be achieved than under the milder methods which have been contemplated. For, wherever the native population was fairly dense, in Central America for example, natives still constitute a very large proportion of the population in spite of the methods employed against them. Further, even supposing that a territory, a portion of Abyssinia perhaps, is cleared of its native population, a reservoir of native labour will remain in adjacent territories, and it is certain that the immigrants who occupy the cleared land will sooner or later draw upon this reservoir for manual labour occupations and so leave for themselves only those relatively few positions which are of a supervisory nature. It has also to be remembered that, in almost every case in which immigration into an under-developed country is discussed, it is a question of Europeans or Asiatics settling among peoples from whom they are physically differentiated. In Palestine there is at least the possibility of the development of a harmonious community because there are no permanent outward marks serving to remind the two sections of the population of their different origins. But, where there are such marks, grievances will not die out, and the stability of the new order of things will always be threatened by a recrudescence of ancient animosities.

In connexion with this discussion it is of some interest to note that between the years 1923 and 1929 there was a net outward balance of migration from Great Britain and Northern Ireland to the British Empire, excluding the Dominions, of 1,848 persons only. It must be remembered that during these years the people of this country had free access to the Dominions and the advantage of a large American quota, and that in many parts of the colonial empire settlement on the land is impossible. But the colonial empire includes Kenya, Rhodesia, and other places where European settlement is possible and even encouraged, and it is a remarkable fact that the outward movement only averaged 264 persons a year. It does not seem, therefore, that the possession of under-developed countries by a European people offers much scope for emigration.

The question is sometimes asked whether the inhabitants of under-developed countries have a right to the exclusive possession of territories of which they do not make full use. If there were to-day areas in the former condition of North America, that is to say areas of great potential population-carrying capacity and very thinly inhabited by peoples showing no indication to abandon their primitive mode of life, the question would be relevant. The answer would probably be that, so long as reasonable provision could be made for the million natives of North America in some part of the area, the remainder of the country should be developed by those able and willing to exploit it. But there are no such areas, and the question is of no practical importance. For the reasons given, existing under-developed countries offer very little scope for settlers from the densely peopled European and Asiatic regions. Even if we grant that the inhabitants of these countries should not be allowed to continue indefinitely to fail to exploit their possessions, the practical question is whether they should be taught to exploit them under the mandate system or under the plantation system. For there are only three choices; to leave the under-developed countries alone, to put the inhabitants to school but to leave them their possessions, or to take the land and employ the former owners as servants. There can be little doubt that in the interests of the inhabitants the second system is preferable.

If the position of the under-developed countries has been correctly stated, it follows that the only possible areas to which emigrants from the densely populated non-European countries can go are those which constitute Europe overseas. The present situation in these countries has been described, and the problems which arise have been discussed. A summary of what has been said will suffice. If we admit the validity of the view that the resources of all countries ought to be fully exploited, it follows the population of the European countries overseas should continue to grow for several decades at about the same speed as has obtained during the last half century. If these countries were willing to take part of the natural increase of south and east Europe, where there is congestion and where an unwanted surplus of births over deaths will continue for some time to come, this speed could be maintained for some decades. But in view of the decline in fertility throughout the sphere of European civilization, it is doubtful whether these countries would be adequately peopled before the sources of migration dried up.

When discussing restriction of immigration we concluded that every country has a right and even a duty to act so as to attempt to ensure that the foundations of a harmonious community will be laid. When attempting to apply this principle we said that in the light of existing knowledge and experience it was wise not to attempt to build up a community by mixing the major groups of mankind. On these lines it is possible to make a case for the exclusion of Asiatics from the European oversea countries. But if these countries do not become adequately peopled by Europeans, the choice will be between leaving them only partially exploited or experimenting with a mixture of peoples.

If the position is put in this way it will no doubt appear to non-Europeans to do less than justice to their case. For the argument proceeds on the assumption that the mere chance, which led a handful of Europeans to settle in these vast areas before Asiatics appeared on the scene, should be allowed to govern the whole future history of these places. That is the essential weakness of the European case. In further support of that case it may be said that, so long as the family remains unlimited among non-Europeans, emigration will not help to ease the difficulties which arise from over-population. There is much substance in this point; for it cannot be said that the policy of peopling the United States and the British Dominions exclusively from Europe increases the difficulties from which non-European countries suffer on account of congestion of population. The only exception at present to this statement is Japan where births are coming under control. But if and when births become controlled in other Asiatic countries this consideration will no longer apply, and the case for excluding non-Europeans will rest entirely on the argument that in a country where the population is being recruited both from Europeans and non-Europeans, no harmonious society can arise.

CHAPTER XXII
CONCLUSION

AT various times the population situation has been a matter of interest to peoples or at least to governments, and attempts have been made to influence the trend of population. The Greeks were anxious to keep numbers stationary, the Romans were concerned about the infertility of the older families, and the governments of the national states, which arose in Europe as medieval conditions passed away, wanted the number of citizens to be as large as possible. The methods employed to increase population were intended to stimulate the birth-rate; so far as we know they achieved nothing. It does not seem that those who desired an increase of population ever turned their attention to the more promising method of decreasing the death-rate. From time to time, and especially during the seventeenth and eighteenth centuries, encouragement was given to groups and communities, such as the Huguenots, to immigrate and settle, and if such actions are included among the efforts to influence the course of population, something was occasionally accomplished. During the last century public policy was seldom directed to population. The reason is that increase of population was considered beneficial, and that, since numbers were growing, all seemed to be well.

The population situation to-day is therefore not the result of policy adopted with the direct intention of influencing numbers. It is the consequence of the whole story of social evolution. We may, however, pick out two strands in the story which are closely woven round the development of world population. The first is the abandonment by all, except the primitive races, of the ancient small family system. Among non-European peoples, other than those who have retained their primitive culture, the family became unlimited, and still remains unlimited.

But European peoples in recent times, after a lengthy experience of the unlimited family, have adopted the voluntary small family system. The second is the overflow during the last three centuries of Europeans to countries overseas, where, since these countries were virtually empty, they have established themselves.

The importance to each country of the composition and size of its population needs no elaboration. But it may be of interest to attempt briefly to summarize the manner in which the population situation in a country may affect its attitude to other countries and may lead to making claims from them. We have in mind what are often called expansionist sentiments which give rise to expansionist policies. It is possible for such sentiments to arise when the population situation is not in view. Thus colonies may be wanted merely because of the prestige which they confer or because of the access to raw materials which they provide. But as a rule population considerations play a part in the origin of these sentiments, and rapid growth of population is especially likely to generate them. Growth of population may or may not lead to over-population. Nevertheless, it is generally believed, in countries in which the population is increasing rapidly, that over-population, if not present, is threatened; therefore growth of population is important whatever it may imply regarding the real condition of the country concerned. On the other hand, from the point of view of the countries upon whom claims are made, it is very important to ascertain the true condition of the country which claims the right to expand. For these countries may take one view of a claim if there is over-population and another if there is not.

A reference to the recent histories of France, Germany, and Italy may serve to illustrate the bearing of the population situation upon expansionist sentiment and expansionist policy. Between 1880 and 1900 France pursued a more deliberate and more vigorous expansionist policy than has been followed by any other country in the last hundred

Y

years. In West Africa, the Nile Valley, and the Far East she sought colonies, and successive French ministries continued to encourage the making of claims by explorers and officials on behalf of France. French policy may be traced primarily to the desire for rehabilitation after the Franco-German war. But the population situation was not without its influence. The French were acutely aware of the fact that, while the population of Germany was increasing rapidly, the population of France was almost stationary, and on this account they were rendered more anxious than they would otherwise have been to enhance their position in the world.

During the period preceding that in which Germany became industrialized, the population of the country was growing slowly; nevertheless, there were signs of over-population, for there was congestion in the rural areas and heavy emigration. But of expansionist sentiment there was no trace. As industrialization became rapid the rate of population growth increased; signs of congestion vanished, and Germany became a country of immigration. Expansionist sentiment, however, made its appearance and became very prominent; it would be possible to give numerous quotations from German authors in the earlier years of the century who were demanding outlets for Germany's growing millions and who implied, if they did not say, that Germany was over-populated. Since the War, and especially in recent years, opinion in Germany has become seriously perturbed about the prospect of a decline in the population of the country, and the German government is now taking energetic measures to avert the decline by stimulating the birth-rate. Though Germans fear depopulation and not over-population, they are again making expansionist claims and are demanding colonies; the present position of Germany is similar to that of France sixty years ago.

Italy was already showing signs of congestion in rural areas in 1900. But the doors through which emigrants could pass into other countries were wide open, and the rate of increase was kept down to a low figure by loss of emigrants. Italy was not satisfied with the relief thus afforded, and attempts were made to secure colonies in which Italians could settle under the Italian flag. After the War signs of congestion became more evident. There was a rapid growth in expansionist sentiment. The closure of the channels by oversea countries through which the Italian emigrant stream had hitherto flowed provoked no resentment; indeed the Italians took steps to block these channels at their own end. The explanation is that the only policy which could satisfy the powerful Italian expansionist sentiment was the settlement of Italians in a greater Italy overseas. At the same time, in spite of the continuing increase of population, the Italian government took steps intended to arrest the fall in the birth-rate.

The most obvious conclusion to be drawn from these stories is that considerations other than those relating to population are often of great importance in the generation of expansionist sentiments. So far as population comes into view, the element in the population situation which is most likely to generate expansionist sentiment is a rapid rate of growth, and especially a more rapid rate of growth than that manifested by surrounding countries. A people conscious of rapid growth thinks of itself as unusually vigorous, and believes that it is destined, if not to inherit the earth, at least to inherit the territory of its less dynamic neighbours. Colonies confer prestige; to obtain colonies gives the same kind of satisfaction in the international scene as the grant of a peerage in this country; and countries with growing populations desire that their increasing wealth and importance should be recognized in this fashion. In most cases, since it is believed that increase of population implies over-population, or at least the prospect of over-population, the possession of colonies is also desired as a means of relief. But colonies may be demanded even if there is no anxiety about over-population, present or future, as the examples of France in the last century and of Germany at the present time show; the German demand for colonies may be in part due to a desire for access to raw materials, but it is mainly due to a desire that her size, importance, and accomplishments, relative to those of other countries, should be recognized.

It also emerges from a study of these stories that, so far as over-population is concerned, it is the belief that it exists or is threatened, and not its presence and consequences, which is important in the generation of expansionist sentiment. Italy may have been somewhat over-populated, but Germany was not, when expansionist sentiment attained its great height, though in each country there was much talk about over-population. Indeed, a serious degree of over-population is hardly compatible with expansionist sentiment, for it implies internal weakness in the presence of which a people can scarcely picture itself as destined to extend its frontiers. In relation to the growth of expansionist sentiment, so far as it is prompted by the population sentiment, it is difficult to lay too much emphasis upon the importance of relative rates of growth; a study of the changing sentiments of the more important countries of the world towards one another and towards less prominent countries during the last century will provide ample confirmation of this statement. But, when we pass to consider the justice of the claims for expansion which are put forward, the question whether or not the country making such a claim is over-populated assumes importance. We may remember in this connexion that those countries which are over-populated cannot be held to be blameworthy, since the present population situation is not the result of policies directly designed to influence the course of population.

If we confine the discussion to changes which are possible in the near future, we must assume that the countries of North and South America and the British Dominions will continue to retain their independence, and, however much the composition of their populations may alter, will not pass under the flag of some other country. It follows that the only possible territorial changes are those which concern areas which are now administered as colonies or under mandates. If the argument put forward in the last chapter is valid, these areas, which alone can be transferred to another flag, offer very limited opportunities for settlement, so limited in fact that migration to them from an over-populated country of any size could not be on a scale which would afford any appreciable relief. This does not dispose of the case for considering such changes, because it may be that certain countries deserve to shoulder the responsibilities and to obtain the prestige which the possession of colonies gives, and also that only in this fashion can access to raw materials be justly apportioned. But these latter questions fall outside the scope of this book. Nevertheless, it may be urged here that, whatever may be the case for transfer on the grounds of prestige and raw materials, there is an additional argument for transfer of this kind. Many expanding countries, though they are mistaken, think themselves to be over-populated, and therefore a failure to find room for settlement in such colonies as they might obtain would do no harm, whereas the mere possession of colonies would provide a cure for the psychological troubles which do arise from the population situation.

It follows that only migration to the United States, the British Dominions, and South America can provide opportunity for the movement of substantial numbers. If a country suffering from over-population has opportunities for emigration to these countries and refuses to take them, no effective remedy for the trouble can be suggested. Italy, however, is the only country in this position which is unwilling to avail itself of this avenue of escape from its difficulties. Other countries, Poland for instance, show no such disinclination, and Japan has encouraged and even given financial assistance to emigration to South America. We must therefore ask under what circumstances, if any, permission to enter these developing countries can rightly be refused. When discussing under-developed countries we suggested that world opinion will probably not admit the right of the inhabitants of any of these countries to continue indefinitely to fail fully to exploit them. The same principle must be applied to those countries which are only partially developed. There is clear evidence that these partially developed countries will not become adequately peopled by surplus of births over deaths. Therefore it will probably be generally held that complete prohibition upon entry into these countries for the purpose of settlement cannot be justified. On the other hand, it is admitted that restriction and even exclusion may be practised under certain circumstances which have already been discussed. It remains to ask whether there are any other circumstances relating to the countries claiming the right of admittance which are relevant to the questions of exclusion and restriction. It has been pointed out that a country, where births are unrestricted, will not experience any relief from emigration. Following up this line of thought it is sometimes said that the claim of an over-populated country for consideration is only valid when it is making efforts to control numbers. If by this it is meant that the government should conduct propaganda in favour of birth-control, it is surely too much to ask. The evidence is that, once the small family system has gained a hold, it continues to spread. Evidence of a definite fall in fertility is enough to show that numbers are coming under control. All that it is legitimate to demand is that the government of an over-populated country should not hinder the spread of birth-control and attempt to arrest the fall in fertility. But this is precisely what the government of one over-populated country, namely Italy, is attempting to do. The claim of Italy is obviously weakened on this account.

It will probably be held that Italian population policy

not only puts her out of court when she presents her claim but is foolish on other grounds; for it would appear that she is attempting to magnify or at least to prolong the evils from which she is suffering. But there is perhaps something to be said for the Italian policy of attempting to stimulate the birth-rate which does not appear at first sight. In Chapter XVII the problem of the voluntary small family was examined. We found reason to believe that, once the voluntary small family habit has gained a foothold, the size of family is likely, if not certain, in time to become so small that the reproduction rate will fall below replacement rate, and that, when this has happened, the restoration of a replacement rate proves to be an exceedingly difficult and obstinate problem. It would appear that this has not escaped the observation of Signor Mussolini.

'My conviction is that,' he is reported to have said, 'even if the laws [i.e. Italian population measures] were shown to be of no avail, it is necessary to try them, just as all sorts of medicines are tried when, and more especially when, the case is a desperate one. ... But I think that our population measures, negative and positive, may prevent or retard the decline, provided the social organism to which they are applied is still capable of reaction.'

The Italian case might be put as follows. Italy is not in the position of an Asiatic country with an unlimited birth-rate. Family limitation has come, and come to stay. Experience shows that the difficulty is to prevent excessive limitation. Unless something is done the Italian reproduction rate will fall below replacement rate. This is very undesirable, and it is not too early to apply measures which are most unlikely to be so successful as to raise the birth-rate, but which may prevent its rapid decline to a very low level. If there is truth in the conclusions reached in Chapter XVII, there is something to be said in justification of Italian population policy stated in this way. Nevertheless, it is scarcely likely that Italian claims for expansion will be heard with much sympathy so long as the government appears to be engaged in a campaign to increase the difficulties which it asks that other nations should assist to solve.

The upshot of this discussion is to suggest the following conclusions. When expansionist sentiment takes its origin in rapid population growth which is not accompanied by over-population, though popular opinion may hold that over-population is present or is threatened, the difficulty may be eased by territorial readjustment of under-developed countries. For the basis of the trouble is psychological. But when there is over-population the only possibility of easing the situation is to permit migration to the developing countries, though, since there are likely to be psychological troubles as well, colonial readjustment may have a part to play. It may be said that it is impossible to contemplate continual juggling with colonial possessions. That is obviously true, but it is beyond the scope of this discussion to inquire whether all under-developed countries could be held under mandates and if so how far this would solve the problem.

It remains only to say that, though the present population situation is not the result of population policies, attempts will soon everywhere be made to control the trend of population. Since the population policies of Germany and Italy have attracted much attention, it is sometimes thought that action of this kind is especially associated with authoritarian régimes. But there are two other countries with population policies, France and Belgium, and they are democracies. Swedish opinion is also profoundly disturbed by the trend of fertility; measures are under discussion, and the adoption of a definite policy is only a matter of time.

The Chancellor of the Exchequer, when introducing the Budget last year, used the following words:

'I must say that I look upon the continual diminution of the birth-rate in this country with considerable apprehension. At the present time it may seem that we have here a larger population than we are able to support in England. At the same time we know the difficulty which the Dominions find in accommodating a larger population when they themselves are troubled with unemployment. But I have a feeling that the time will not be far distant when that position will be reversed, when the countries of the British Empire will be crying out for more citizens of the right breed and when we in this country will not be able to supply the demand. I think that if to-day we can give even a little help to those who are carrying on the race, the money will not be wasted.'

The Chancellor accompanied these remarks with the announcement that he proposed to modify both the personal allowance of a married tax-payer and the children's allowances. There is little doubt that in time to come these measures will be regarded as marking the beginning of the formulation of a population policy for Great Britain. But in order to construct a policy the relevant facts must be assembled and analysed, and this book has been written in the hope that it will be of some use for this purpose.

NOTE ON OVER-POPULATION

THE discussion of over-population in the text is in very general terms. It was thought that it would be confusing to enter upon a technical discussion of the meaning of the word, to examine in detail the tests which have been proposed in order to discover the existence of over-population, and then to say that these tests are in most cases inconclusive. But a very brief summary in more exact terms may be made in order to indicate what lies behind the remarks in the text.

1. The statement that, with reference to any given area, the optimum population is that population which produces maximum economic welfare is unexceptionable. Maximum economic welfare is not necessarily the same as maximum real income per head; but for practical purposes they may be taken as equivalent. Over-population exists when numbers exceed the optimum, and under-population when they fall below it: in either case real income per head is less than it would be if the optimum prevailed.

2. The agencies which govern the optimum may be grouped under three heads: (*a*) the natural resources of the area, (*b*) the constitution, natural endowment, and acquired skill, knowledge, and habits of the inhabitants, and (*c*) the opportunities, internal and external, for economic activity. But a given kind of change, e.g. increase in skill, does not always shift the optimum in the same direction.

3. Of the various tests for the existence of over-population which have been proposed one only deserves careful consideration, namely movements in real income. Supposing that we have figures for population ($= P$) and for real income ($= I$) over a period, but that we do not know in what direction the optimum ($= O$) is moving, we can infer nothing with certainty. Take the case of P rising and of I rising, the case of many industrial countries in the

last century. P may equal O throughout; if O is rising fast, under-population may be increasing; if O is falling fast, under-population may be decreasing. There are other possibilities.

4. In certain cases we can discern with some confidence in what direction O is moving. Thus, in many industrial countries in the last century, of the three agencies governing O mentioned above, while (a) was stable, (b) and (c) were tending on the balance to push O up. This cuts out certain otherwise possible interpretations of the case when P and I are both rising. But in the present century, and especially since the War, it is by no means clear in which direction O has moved. For, while (a) has been stable and (b) has risen, (c) has undergone violent and mostly deleterious changes. Thus, even if we possess figures for I in industrial countries in recent years, their interpretation is very doubtful. But we can at any rate say that, if serious maladjustment has occurred in industrial countries since the War, it has come about through shifts in O and not through movements of P.

5. In other cases, those of self-supporting agricultural countries, we can infer that O has moved little, even in recent times. For, of the agencies governing O, none have changed much. This fact cuts out certain otherwise possible interpretations of recorded changes in P and I. The trouble is that we have seldom any trustworthy figures for I in such countries, and can only base guesses at its recent movements on general observations.

6. Lastly, while it is possible to infer from comparisons between two countries that P is farther from O in one than in the other, it is impossible on this basis to say whether P, in the country in which it is less maladjusted, is on a level with or some way from O.

INDEX

Abortion, in Berlin, 98, 232; frequency of, 98.
Adaptation to climate, 170.
Africa, 27, 34, 44.
Africans, 300–6.
Algeria, 9, 27, 35, 279, 285.
Aliens, in France, 154; in French industries, 157; in French agriculture, 158.
America, Central and South, 8, 27, 33–4, 44, 56, 160, 180, 220. See also separate countries.
America, North, see United States and Canada.
American Indians, 300.
Angola, 18.
Arabs in Palestine, 307–16.
Argentina, 8, 27, 49, 55, 56, 177.
Asia, 36, 44.
Assimilation of immigrants, 211–25.
Australia, 8, 13, 24, 25, 66, 71, 124, 160–81, 185–202.
Austria, 12, 74, 124, 129, 151, 196, 198.

Baptisms, record of, 10, 60.
Basutoland, 301.
Bechuanaland, 301.
Belgium, 12, 131, 140, 142, 146, 156, 196, 198, 221.
Beloch, J., 31.
Berlin, 98.
Birth-control, origin of term, 96; propaganda for, 99; and Catholics, 104; among Jews, 104, 309; in European civilization, 105; laws against, in Italy, 241, in France, 241, in Belgium, 242; in Japan, 264; in India, 277; in non-European countries, 292; among Africans, 304.
Birth-rate, defined, 59; in England, Sweden, and Norway, 61; in Europe, 63; in Ireland and France, 64; in United States, Australia, and New Zealand, 66; in Quebec, 67; among non-Europeans, 68, 284; analysed, 86; reasons for fall of in, United States, 88, France, 89, Ireland, 90, England, 92, Europe, 95; features in the decline of, 95; fall of, in United States, Australia, and New Zealand, 176, in South Africa and Argentina, 177, in Central and South America, 180; fall of in United States, 204; attempts to raise, in Italy, 227, in Germany, 229, in France, 233, in

Belgium, 236; decline of, and small family system, 244, and marriage, 245, and unwanted children, 245, and medical factors, 246, and psychological factors, 247, and economic factors, 248, and social factors, 249; in Japan, 261; in India, 270; among Africans, 302; in Palestine, 308; among Jews, 308.
Bolivia, 8.
Brazil, 8, 55, 56, 198, 211, 268.
British Columbia, 177.
British Guiana, 278.
Brownlee, J., 19.
Bulgaria, 124, 144.
Burgdörfer, F., 98, 130.

California, 183.
Canada, 6, 8, 24, 25, 26, 32, 55, 124, 160–81, 184–98.
Catholics, and birth-control, 104; and immigration into France, 159.
Census, nature of, 1–5; early attempts, 6; development of, 8–10.
Ceylon, 27, 58, 82, 160, 279–94.
Chang-Heng Chen, 37, 38, 39.
Charles, Enid, 130.
Chevalier de Pommelles, 10.
Child-bearing Period, and birth-rate, 86.
Child marriage, 276.
China, 30, 37, 38, 40, 41, 43, 57, 82, 84, 279, 286–9.
Chinese, in United States, 167, 183; in New Zealand, 169; in Australia, 169; excluded from United States, 184, Canada, 184, Australia, 185, New Zealand, 185, South Africa, 186, Central and South America, 186.
Civil registration, 12–14.
Contraception, data regarding, 98; in France, 100; in Japan, 264; among Jews, 309. See also Birth-control.
Council of Trent, 11.
Cromwell, Thomas, 11.
Czechoslovakia, 146, 151, 186.

Death-rate, defined, 59; in England, Sweden, and Norway, 60–3; in Europe, 63–6; in Europe overseas, 66–9; analysed, 70–4; true and crude in various countries, 71–4; reasons for fall of in England 75–8; reasons for fall of in Europe, 78–81; reasons for fall of in non-European